T0383143

Donald R. Self
Walter W. Wymer, Jr.
Editors

Volunteerism Marketing: New Vistas for Nonprofit and Public Sector Management

Volunteerism Marketing: New Vistas for Nonprofit and Public Sector Management has been co-published simultaneously as *Journal of Nonprofit & Public Sector Marketing,* Volume 6, Numbers 2/3 1999.

Pre-Publication
REVIEWS,
COMMENTARIES,
EVALUATIONS . . .

"**T**he first element that strikes the reader is the humanitarian aspect of this effort by Self and Wymer. In view of the fact that volunteerism has been clearly on the rise not only in the U.S. but also around the world, this work is both commendable and timely. Hopefully, it will expand the consciousness and spur the conscience of the reader. The volume represents the core of volunteerism, and, akin to icing on cake, provides summaries of salient research on volunteerism, which make it a very useful addition to any collection in the public or private domain. Finally, the use of marketing for noble causes is refreshing."

Rajan Nataraajan, PhD
Executive Editor
Psychology & Marketing

More advance
REVIEWS, COMMENTARIES, EVALUATIONS . . .

"**S**elf and Wymer have compiled an important contribution to the understanding of volunteerism and how the concept of marketing exchange is used to attract non-clients as volunteers to education. Some of the most important parent research on volunteerism is reviewed in this volume.

Based upon previous research, Wymer reviews a large volume of literature as a foundation on his current study of how to differentiate higher performing senior volunteers from lower performing senior volunteers. Implications for management of volunteer services are discussed.

A marketing oriented approach to volunteer recruitment is employed by Stearns and Wymer to increase the understanding of hospice volunteers.

Wymer further explores the notion of volunteer recruitment in his article on hospital volunteers as customers and how hospital volunteers differentiate themselves from other volunteers.

Material in this volume will be helpful to researchers in the area of volunteer management and marketing and the material will be an important reference source."

Dwight F. Burlingame, PhD
Associate Executive Director

"**E**very nonprofit organization can benefit from the assistance volunteers provide. *Volunteerism Marketing* offers the volunteer coordinator in these organizations the information needed to better understand where, and how, to effectively recruit and mobilize these increasingly important "customers"

While some chapters speak to specific volunteer opportunities, *Volunteer Marketing* is easily adaptable to any organization relying on the altruism of individuals. I have found that financial support is often easier to obtain then someone's time. For my line of work, combining the concepts of volunteer and organdonor recruitment offer an interesting insight in the world of blood-donor recruitment."

Michael J. Tullier, MPA
Branch Director
East Alabama Community Blood Bank
a LifeSouth blood center

More advance
REVIEWS, COMMENTARIES, EVALUATIONS . . .

"This is a very timely book, appearing at a crucial juncture for non-profit organizations who face an increasing challenge in identifying, enticing and managing volunteers. The first section of the book will be particularly valuable to practitioners who seek research-based advice on attracting volunteers for specific causes. Walter Wymer's articles and his with Becky Starnes offer practical implications based on sound conceptual foundations and solid research. Cossé and Weinberg's article extends the literature on human organ donation and offers an innovative solution to enhancing that form of volunteering. Marshall presents a social marketing model within the framework of exchange as a mechanism for attracting non-client volunteers. Researchers will find the second section, which contains 131 entries in an annotated bibliography of marketing to volunteers, an excellent guide to major research studies in the field."

Glen Riecken, PhD
*Professor of Marketing
and Chairman
Management and Marketing
East Tennessee State University*

"Nonprofit Organizations (NPOs), long insulated from the effects of competition, are increasingly finding that marketing is a critical component of their success. Perhaps, starting first in the area of fund raising, most NPOs now find that they need to develop effective marketing strategies for attracting, retaining, and deepening their relationships with volunteers. This book provides valuable insights into the nature of volunteers, what motivates them to agree to volunteer, and what effects their willingness to spend more time helping nonprofits. Reflecting a modern marketing approach, the book examines different segments of volunteers from demographic and lifestyle perspectives. Different types of volunteers and comparisons to non-volunteers are also presented.

A particularly useful aspect of the book is the annotated bibliography of more than 100 empirical studies on volunteerism, dating back more than twenty years.

Finally, email addresses for the chapter authors and editors are included, so the book is just a first step in learning about volunteerism."

Charles B. Weinberg, PhD
*Alumni Professor of Marketing
University of British Columbia
Vancouver, BC V6T 1Z2*

"*Volunteerism Marketing*, edited by Donald R. Self and Walter W. Wymer, Jr. is an important new research collection that will interest both marketing scholars and executives in volunteer service organizations. Marketing scholars will welcome the wide variety of new research studies in this area of marketing services, from senior volunteer behavior, to hospice and hospital volunteers, human organ donors, and non-parent volunteers in schools. Reflecting a higher level of sophistication in research methodology, each study provides significant applications of marketing research techniques. Also, marketing scholars will appreciate the extensive and well-annotated bibliography by the editors.

From the perspective of the volunteer-service organization executive, *Volunteerism* provides useful insights and knowledge of volunteer motivations and behavior. For example, the study of human organ donors by Thomas Cossé and Terry Weisenberger provides an excellent overview of the procurement and allocation system in the United States. Overall, this book is outstanding as a significant contribution to the important field of marketing in volunteer services."

Joseph Miller, PhD
Professor of Marketing
Indiana University

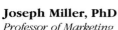

More advance
REVIEWS, COMMENTARIES, EVALUATIONS . . .

"The research collected in this volume represents a significant contribution to both practitioners who manage the recruitment and retention of volunteers and academics interested in studying volunteerism. This volume should be useful to anyone wishing to understand the nature of volunteerism with a special usefulness to those who manage organizations that rely on volunteers for their very survival. Given the strong context focus, the book should be especially pertinent to the health services industry as it struggles to adjust to its changing environment.

For practitioners, the papers by Wymer and Wymer and Starnes offer a comprehensive analysis of the determinants of volunteerism and rare examples of cross-group comparisons of different subsets of volunteers. Marketers have long recognized that the best prospective customers (or in this case, volunteers) are people who closely match the demographics and psychographic characteristics of your loyal customers. These papers will help not-for-profit managers segment the market of potential volunteers to more effectively target their limited resources.

For academics, Marshall's paper offers an application of broader marketing theory to a context that has yet to initiate significant theory development and thus represents a move toward integrating volunteerism research into the larger body of marketing research. Additionally, the annotated bibliography by Wymer and Self should prove an invaluable resource to academics interested in furthering research in this area. The bibliography offers a concise yet thorough summarization of a vast number of relevant papers from a wide variety of sources."

Ellen Garbarino, PhD
Assistant Professor
University of Miami

"**T**his authoritative volume presents a thought-provoking account and analysis of the important issues relating to volunteerism. The well-researched articles written by an array of experts in the field provide invaluable insights into such diverse topics as organ donation, volunteering for hospitals and hospices, characteristics of senior volunteers and creative ways of attracting non-volunteers to public school systems.

The theoretical and managerial perspectives presented in the book will enable practitioners to enrich their understand of their target audiences and devise focused recruitment and retention strategies. The Annotated Bibliography provides an excellent compendium of major cross-disciplinary work on the topic. It will be a must source of lasting value that current and future researchers will want to refer to again and again."

Ugur Yavas, PhD, MBA
Professor of Marketing
East Tennessee State University

"**T**his collection of articles contains interesting insights into the complex web of factors that influence the decision to volunteer. The volume provides much food for thought for volunteer administrators and for researchers alike who are concerned about the dynamics of why people volunteer in the specific ways that they do.

I think that the editors did a superb job on and performed a great service to the field in preparing the annotated bibliography. I believe this chapter will be a wonderful resource for both practitioners and researchers."

Morris Okun, PhD
Professor of Psychology
Arizona State University
Tempe

"**N**onprofit ogranizations face increasing competition for limited resources and the need to make good planning decisions for the effective use of these resources, including volunteers, who represent key human resources for most nonprofit organizations. *Volunteerism Marketing*, written and edited by reputable marketing research scholars, represents an important addition to the field of nonprofit marketing. Selected research contributions provide understanding and insight into the challenges and opportunities presented by the volunteer market subgroups of seniors, hospice and hospital volunteers, organ donors, and volunteers in the public education system. The editors, ensure the broad appeal of the book to both researchers and practitioners by including 131 abstracts derived from the editors' review and cross-disciplinary categorization of significant works on volunteerism.

Researchers of social marketing will be interested in the predictive potential of differing and interacting variables on volunteer behavior, as well as the implications for future research activities. Managers of nonprofit agencies will be interested in the practical application of the findings to their marketing tasks of attracting, recruiting, retaining, and reactivating volunteers. The selection, "Hospital Volunteers as Customers," by Walter W. Wymer, Jr., is presented within the context of a marketing-oriented approach and will provide even novice nonprofit managers with a fundamental framework for treating volunteers as customers in cultivating mutually beneficial exchange relationships between the organization and its volunteers."

Alice Widgeon, MPA
Coordinator of Children's Services
Division of Mental Retardation
Alabama Department of Mental Health
and Mental Retardation

Volunteerism Marketing: New Vistas for Nonprofit and Public Sector Management

Volunteerism Marketing: New Vistas for Nonprofit and Public Sector Management has been co-published simultaneously as *Journal of Nonprofit & Public Sector Marketing*, Volume 6, Numbers 2/3 1999.

The *Journal of Nonprofit & Public Sector Marketing* Monographic "Separates"

Below is a list of "separates," which in serials librarianship means a special issue simultaneously published as a special journal issue or double-issue and as a "separate" hardbound monograph. (This is a format which we also call a "DocuSerial.")

"Separates" are published because specialized libraries or professionals may wish to purchase a specific thematic issue by itself in a format which can be separately cataloged and shelved, as opposed to purchasing the journal on an on-going basis. Faculty members may also more easily consider a "separate" for classroom adoption.

"Separates" are carefully classified separately with the major book jobbers so that the journal tie-in can be noted on new book order slips to avoid duplicate purchasing.

You may wish to visit Haworth's website at . . .

http://www.haworthpressinc.com

. . . to search our online catalog for complete tables of contents of these separates and related publications.

You may also call 1-800-HAWORTH (outside US/Canada: 607-722-5857), or Fax 1-800-895-0582 (outside US/Canada: 607-771-0012), or e-mail at:

getinfo@haworthpressinc.com

Volunteerism Marketing: New Vistas for Nonprofit and Public Sector Management, edited by Donald R. Self, DBA, and Walter W. Wymer, Jr., DBA (Vol. 6, No. 2/3, 1999). *Focuses on characteristics of volunteers which can help organizations attract, train and retain them.*

Marketing University Outreach Programs, edited by Ralph S. Foster, Jr., BS, William I. Sauser, Jr., PhD, and Donald R. Self, DBA (Vol. 2, No. 2/3, 1995). *"Should be required reading . . . The authors not only know marketing but they also reflect a deep understanding of outreach and its place in the 21st century university." (James C. Vortruba, Vice Provost for University Outreach, Michigan State University)*

Public Mental Health Marketing: Developing a Consumer Attitude, edited by Donald R. Self, DBA (Vol. 1, No. 2/3, 1993). *"Provides a balance of theoretical and practical information on marketing local, state, and national mental health agencies." (Reference and Research Book News)*

Volunteerism Marketing: New Vistas for Nonprofit and Public Sector Management

Donald R. Self, DBA
Walter W. Wymer, Jr., DBA
Editors

Volunteerism Marketing: New Vistas for Nonprofit and Public Sector Management has been co-published simultaneously as *Journal of Nonprofit & Public Sector Marketing*, Volume 6, Numbers 2/3 1999.

The Haworth Press, Inc.
New York • London • Oxford

Volunteerism Marketing: New Vistas for Nonprofit and Public Sector Marketing has been co-published simultaneously as *Journal of Nonprofit & Public Sector Marketing,* Volume 6, Numbers 2/3 1999.

The Haworth Press, Inc., 10 Alice Street, Binghamton, NY 13904-1580 USA

Cover design by Thomas J. Mayshock Jr.

Library of Congress Cataloging-in-Publication Data

Volunteerism marketing: new vistas for nonprofit and public sector management/Donald R. Self, Walter W. Wymer, Jr., editors
     p. cm.
     "Co-published simultaneously as Journal of nonprofit & public sector marketing, volume 6, numbers 2/3 1999."
     Includes bibliographical references and index.
     ISBN 0-7890-0967-6 (alk. paper–ISBN 0-7890-0985-4 (alk. paper)
     1. Nonprofit organizations–Marketing. 2. Voluntarism–Marketing. I. Self, Donald R. II. Wymer, Walter W.
HF5415.V64 1999
658.8–dc21

                                 99-056467

INDEXING & ABSTRACTING

Contributions to this publication are selectively indexed or abstracted in print, electronic, online, or CD-ROM version(s) of the reference tools and information services listed below. This list is current as of the copyright date of this publication. See the end of this section for additional notes.

- *AURSI African Urban & Regional Science Index*
- *BUBL Information Service: An Internet-Based Information Service for the UK Higher Education Community <URL:http://bubl.ac.uk>*
- *Business & Management Practices*
- *CNPIEC Reference Guide: Chinese National Directory of Foreign Periodicals*
- *Digest of Neurology and Psychiatry*
- *Health Care Literature Information Network/HECLINET*
- *Human Resources Abstracts (HRA)*
- *IBZ International Bibliography of Periodical Literature*
- *Industrial Hygiene Digest*
- *Journal of Academic Librarianship: Guide to Professional Literature, The*
- *Journal of Marketing (abstracts section)*
- *Management & Marketing Abstracts*
- *Marketing Executive Report*
- *Mental Health Abstracts (online through DIALOG)*
- *Operations Research/Management Science*
- *OT BibSys*
- *PAIS (Public Affairs Information Service) NYC*
- *Political Science Abstracts*
- *Social Work Abstracts*
- *Sport Search*

(continued)

Special Bibliographic Notes related to special journal issues (separates) and indexing/abstracting:

- indexing/abstracting services in this list will also cover material in any "separate" that is co-published simultaneously with Haworth's special thematic journal issue or DocuSerial. Indexing/abstracting usually covers material at the article/chapter level.
- monographic co-editions are intended for either non-subscribers or libraries which intend to purchase a second copy for their circulating collections.
- monographic co-editions are reported to all jobbers/wholesalers/approval plans. The source journal is listed as the "series" to assist the prevention of duplicate purchasing in the same manner utilized for books-in-series.
- to facilitate user/access services all indexing/abstracting services are encouraged to utilize the co-indexing entry note indicated at the bottom of the first page of each article/chapter/contribution.
- this is intended to assist a library user of any reference tool (whether print, electronic, online, or CD-ROM) to locate the monographic version if the library has purchased this version but not a subscription to the source journal.
- individual articles/chapters in any Haworth publication are also available through the Haworth Document Delivery Service (HDDS).

Volunteerism Marketing: New Vistas for Nonprofit and Public Sector Management

CONTENTS

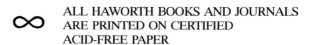

ALL HAWORTH BOOKS AND JOURNALS
ARE PRINTED ON CERTIFIED
ACID-FREE PAPER

ABOUT THE EDITORS

Donald R. Self (DBA, Louisiana Tech University, 1977) is Professor of Marketing at Auburn University Montgomery and a Principal in Paradox Marketing Consultants. He is Editor of the *Journal of Nonprofit & Public Sector Marketing* and serves on the Editorial Boards of several other journals including *Health Marketing Quarterly* and *Journal of Consumer Marketing*. He has served as a Section Editor or Associate Editor of the *Journal of Marketing*, *Journal of Direct Marketing*, and *Journal of Personal Selling and Sales Management*. Active in professional societies Don has also served as President and/or Program Chair of the Atlantic Marketing Association, The Georgia Association of Marketing Educators, and the MidSouth Marketing Educators. Dr. Self has also authored numerous journal articles and conference papers, and has edited collected works on Alcoholism Treatment Marketing, Public Mental Health Marketing, Wellness, and University Outreach Programs. he currently is the Academic Host for the *Very Important Professor (VIP)* program for the Promotional Products Association International.

Walter W. Wymer, Jr. (DBA, Indiana University, 1996) is Assistant Professor of Marketing at Christopher Newport University. His areas of interest are marketing management of nonprofit organizations, volunteer segmentation and psychology, church marketing, professional services marketing, and service marketing performance. Walter's work has been published in several academic journals and presented at academic conferences. Dr. Wymer currently serves on the Editorial Board of the *Journal of Nonprofit and Public Sector Marketing*.

Foreword

Periodically, a "strategic window of opportunity" opens for those of us involved in research and marketing management. The concept of the strategic window implies a time period during which the need and supply for a product or service (such as research) are at a high level. Such is the case with this volume. First, volunteerism in the USA is at a maturation level. Second, during the last year or so, I've had the opportunity to review the work of several researchers, each of whom has something significant to add to the field. As an added bonus, each of the contributors to this work is a special colleague, with whom I've had the opportunity to work on other projects.

Overall, the current level of volunteer efforts is roughly equivalent to that of 1987 (Independent Sector 1996a) although there have been several one-year increases and decreases in the level. The value of current volume of volunteerism in 1988 (Payton 1988) was estimated to exceed $200 billion per year and would be considerably higher ten year later. In 1995, almost half of Americans (48.8%) of the US households reported giving slightly over four hours per week (Independent Sector 1996b).

This volume is composed of two areas. The first is to provide insights into four aspects of Volunteerism: Volunteering by Seniors, Volunteering for Hospices, Volunteering for Hospitals, Organ Donation, and utilizing the concept of marketing exchange to attract non-clients as volunteers in public education. Each of these areas represent special challenges for those interested in the study, and more importantly, the attraction and implementation of volunteers.

The second area is to provide summaries of much of the important research on volunteerism. Summary briefs of much of outstanding articles in the field complete this collection.

ABOUT THE CONTRIBUTORS

Walter W. Wymer, Jr. is one of the most knowledgeable researchers in the area of volunteerism. I first came into contact with Walter when he was a

[Haworth co-indexing entry note]: "Foreword." Self, Donald R. Co-published simultaneously in *Journal of Nonprofit & Public Sector Marketing* (The Haworth Press, Inc.) Vol. 6, No. 2/3, 1999, pp. xiii-xx; and: *Volunteerism Marketing: New Vistas for Nonprofit and Public Sector Management* (ed: Donald R. Self and Walter W. Wymer, Jr.) The Haworth Press, Inc., 1999, pp. xi-xviii. Single or multiple copies of this article are available for a fee from The Haworth Document Delivery Service [1-800-342-9678, 9:00 a.m. - 5:00 p.m. (EST). E-mail address: getinfo@haworthpressinc.com].

graduate student at Indiana University in the mid-1990s and a dedicated volunteer. Since then he has published much of the important research on the area. He currently is a marketing professor at Christopher Newport University, and still a volunteer.

Thomas J. Cossé and Terry M. Weisenberger both teach at the University of Richmond, and I've known them for years through their volunteer efforts in the Atlantic Marketing Association. Currently, they are in their fifth year of a longitudinal study on organ donation, truly a work of love.

Similarly, I've come to deeply respect Kimball P. Marshall (Jackson State University) through his efforts for the Atlantic Marketing Association, as well as his research into volunteerism, school marketing, and other social marketing programs.

Finally, Becky J. Starnes is one of my very favorite students. After a distinguished career in both the Marines and the Air Force, Major Starnes earned an MBA at Auburn University Montgomery, where she is currently a PhD student in the Public Administration program. She is an Instructor at Alabama State University. I've had the opportunity to work with Becky in research on hospice programs, blood donation, and alliances in the health care field.

The addresses and a selected list of the authors' previous volunteerism publications are included immediately after this introduction. I encourage readers to contact the individuals for any further information, consultation, or collaborative research projects.

ABOUT THE WORKS INCLUDED

In "Understanding Volunteer Markets: The Case of Senior Volunteers," Walter W. Wymer, Jr. compares the lifestyle, demographic, personality, social, and core values of 114 non-volunteers, 387 senior volunteers, and 605 non-senior volunteers. Important differences in this group and managerial implications are presented.

In "Segmenting Subgroups of Volunteers for Target Marketing: Differentiating Traditional Hospice Volunteers from Other Volunteers," Walter W. Wymer, Jr. and Becky J. Starnes compare 63 hospice volunteers and 950 other volunteers in 40 nonprofit organizations in 2 mid-western cities. While most (8) of the significant predictors of hospice volunteering were values, several other differentiating variables were discovered.

Walter W. Wymer, Jr. compares 105 hospital volunteers and 908 volunteers in over 40 nonprofit organizations in 2 mid-western US cities in "Hospital Volunteers as Customers: Understanding Their Motives, How They Differ from Other Volunteers, and Correlates of Volunteer Intensity." Hospital volunteers are different in two demographic variables (age and average hours volunteered), two social lifestyle variables (the number of volunteer organizations which they serve and frequency of attendance at religious services), self-esteem, and one value (a world of beauty).

Thomas J. Cossé and Terry M. Weisenberger have conducted a longitudinal analysis of human organ donation for four years. In 1996, donations totaled only 25% of the established need for this critical act of volunteering. In "Encouraging Human Organ Donation: Altruism versus Financial Incentives," these authors use data from their tracking study to gauge public attitudes toward the use of financial incentives in increasing the supply of cadaveric donors. Of special importance to both practitioners is the excellent overview of the procurement and allocation system within the United States and current proposals to introduce financial incentives.

Understanding the attitudes of non-parents concerning public school issues and volunteering is a crucial element in improving public education. Kimball P. Marshall compared parents and non-parents in a sample of 296 adults, using the SERVQUAL and SERVPREF scales. For practitioners, this manuscript predicts willingness to volunteer for public school activities, based on perceptions of community benefits, social responsibility, and service quality. Researchers will enjoy the social marketing model presented in the context of generalized exchange.

The final component in this collection is "Major Research Studies: An Annotated Bibliography of Marketing to Volunteers," by Walter W. Wymer, Jr. and Donald R. Self. The study represents a three-year inquiry into the field and is designed to represent a cross-section of the best research into volunteerism as a part of social marketing. One hundred, thirty-one research briefs are included and categorized into six categories.

ABOUT THE REVIEWERS

The following scholars and practitioners have reviewed all or parts of this collection of studies. We are deeply grateful for their contributions.

Dr. Dwight Burlingame, Indiana University Center on Philanthropy

Rick Crandall, Editor, *Journal of Social Behavior and Personality*

Dr. Brenda Gainer, York University (Toronto)

Teri Henley, MBA, Director, Shawn M. Donnelly Center for Nonprofit Communications

Sue McInnish, MPA, Alabama Civil Justice Foundation

Dr. Joseph Miller, Indiana University

Dr. Rajan Nataraajan, Executive Editor, *Psychology & Marketing*

Dr. Morris A. Okun, Arizona State University

Dr. James Perry, SPEA, Indiana University

Steve Prince, MPA, Voices of Alabama's Children

Dr. Glen Riecken, East Tennessee State University

Dick Summers, American Heart Association

Michael J. Tullier, MPA, East Alabama Community Blood Bank

Dr. Chuck Weinberg, University of British Columbia

Alice Widgeon, MPA, Alabama Department of Mental Health/Mental Retardation

Ugur Yavas, PhD, East Tennessee State University

Dr. Dennis R. Young, Editor, *Nonprofit Management and Leadership*

CONCLUSION AND CALL FOR RESEARCH

Hopefully, this collection will provide decision-making support for practitioners in a wide variety of non-profit settings as well a road map for future meaningful research. Readers are encouraged to contact me or any of the contributors for help on future projects. A special area for future research is the reactivation of former volunteers. We were unable to find studies in re-marketing to former volunteers to include in this study.

We are especially indebted to Debby Weinberg, Secretary, and to Karen Crossen, Graduate Assistant, in the Department of Marketing, Auburn University Montgomery, for their assistance, and to Vaughan Judd, Department Head, for his indulgence.

Donald R. Self
Editor

ADDRESSES AND PREVIOUS VOLUNTEERISM RESEARCH BY MAJOR CONTRIBUTORS

Walter W. Wymer, Jr., is an Assistant Professor in the Department of Management and Marketing, College of Business and Economics, Christopher Newport University, Newport News, VA 24606 (E-mail: wwymer@ drake. cnu.edu).

Wymer, Walter W., Jr. (1999), "Youth Development Volunteers: Their Motives, How They Differ from Other Volunteers, and Correlates of Involvement Intensity," *Journal of Nonprofit and Voluntary Sector Marketing*, 3 (4), 321-366.

_____ (forthcoming), "Hospital Volunteers as Customers: Understanding Their Motives, How They Differ from Other Volunteers, and Correlates of Volunteer Intensity," *Journal of Hospital Marketing*.

_____ and Fay X. Zhu (forthcoming), "Professional Services Marketing: Does Understanding Your Customers Really Improve Sales?" *Journal of Professional Services Marketing*.

_____ (working paper), "Marketing Management in Arts and Cultural Organizations: A Customer Analysis of Arts and Culture Volunteers."

_____ (1998), "Understanding Volunteer Markets: The Case of Senior Volunteers, *Journal of Nonprofit & Public Sector Marketing*, 6(2/3), 7-29.

_____ (1998), "Becoming Marketing Oriented: Applying the Marketing Concept in Small Group Settings," *Journal of Ministry & Marketing Management*, 4 (2), forthcoming.

_____ (1998), "Strategic Marketing of Church Volunteers, *Journal of Ministry & Marketing Management*, 4 (1), 1-11.

_____ (1997), "Marketing Management in Nonprofit Organizations: A Customer Analysis of Church Volunteers," *Journal of Nonprofit & Public Sector Marketing*, 5 (4), 69-90.

_____ (1997), "A Religious Motivation to Volunteer? Exploring the Linkage between Volunteering and Religious Values," *Journal of Nonprofit & Public Sector Marketing*, 5 (3), 3-13.

_____ (1997), "Segmenting Volunteers Using Values, Self-esteem, Empathy, and Facilitation as Determinant Variables," *Journal of Nonprofit & Public Sector Marketing*, 5 (2), 3-23.

_____ (1997), "Church Volunteers: Classification, Recruitment, and Retention," *Journal of Ministry & Marketing Management*, 3 (2), 61-70.

_____, Glen Riecken, and Ugur Yavas (1996), "Determinants of Volunteerism: A Cross-disciplinary Review and Research Agenda," *Journal of Nonprofit & Public Sector Marketing*, 4 (4), 3-26.

_____ (1996), "Formal Volunteering as a Function of Values, Self-esteem, Empathy, and Facilitation," D.B.A. Dissertation, Indiana University.

_____ and Fay X. Zhu (1998), "Gap Analysis and Services Marketing: Does Understanding Your Customers Really Improve Sales?" *Proceedings of 1998 Academy of Marketing Science Conference*, Norfolk, VA, May 28-31.

_____ (1998), "Marketing Management in Arts and Cultural Organizations: A Customer Analysis of Arts and Culture Volunteers," *Proceedings from the American Marketing Association's 1998 Winter Educators' Conference*, Austin, TX, Feb. 21-24.

_____ (1997), "Formal Volunteering as a Function of Values, Self-esteem, Empathy, and Facilitation," *Proceedings from the 1997 Academy of Management Conference*, Boston, Aug. 10-13.

Olshavsky, Richard and Walter Wymer (1995), "The Desire for new Information from External Sources," *Proceedings from the 1995 Society of Consumer Psychology Conference*, San Diego, Feb. 10-11.

Wymer, Walter W., Jr. (1995), "Consumers as Volunteers: Factors that Influence Voluntary Participation," *Proceedings from the 1995 Annual Convention of the American Psychological Association: Society for Consumer Psychology (Division 23)*, New York City, Aug. 11-15.

_____ (1995), "Determinants of External Information Search: A Conceptual Model," *Proceedings from the 1995 Annual Convention of the American Psychological Association: Society for Consumer Psychology (Division 23)*, New York City, Aug. 11-15.

_____ (1995), "Determinants of Participation: A Four Factor Model," *Proceedings from the 1995 ARNOVA Annual Conference*, Cleveland, Nov. 2-4.

*   *   *

Thomas J. Cossé is a Professor in the Department of Marketing, E. C. Robins School of Business, University of Richmond, VA 23173 (E-mail: tcosse@richmond.edu).

Terry M. Weisenberger is an Associate Professor in the Department of Marketing, E. C. Robins School of Business, University of Richmond, VA 23173 (E-mail: tweisenb@richmond.edu).

Cossé, Thomas J. and Terry M. Weisenberger (forthcoming), "Words versus Actions About Organ Donation: A Four Year Tracking Study of Attitudes and Self Reported Behavior," *Journal of Business Research*. Publication date not yet set.

_____, "Words Versus Actions About Organ Donation: A Four Year Tracking Study of Attitudes and Self Reported Behavior," presented at the Society for Marketing Advances annual conference. New Orleans, LA, November 1998. Received Outstanding Research/Best Paper in Consumer and Buying-Related Research Track award. Received The Stephen J. Shaw Award for Best Paper in Conference. Summary brief published in *Marketing Advances in Theory, Practice and Education*, J.

Duncan Herrington and Ronald D. Taylor, eds., Society for Marketing Advances, 1998, pp. 104-105.

_____, G. J. Taylor, L. J. McGaw, and G. Mayes, "The Coordinator Attrition Problem in the U.S.: Myth or Reality?" *Journal of Transplant Coordination*, June 1998, pp. 88-92.

Cossé, Thomas J. and E. C. Kingston, "The Relationship Between Attitude Toward Posthumous Organ Donation and Demographic and Personal Experience Variables," in Joseph Chapman (ed.), *Proceedings of the Association of Marketing Theory and Practice 1998 Annual Meeting.* Charleston, SC: Association of Marketing Theory and Practice, 1998, pp. 169-178.

Cossé, Thomas J. and Terry M. Weisenberger, "Perspectives on the Use of Financial Incentives for Human Organ Donation," in Jerry W. Wilson (ed.), Marketing: Innovative Diversity. *Proceedings: Atlantic Marketing Association 1997 Annual Conference.* Nashville, TN: Atlantic Marketing Association, 1997, pp. 89-100.

_____ and Patrick Saxton, "A Meta Analysis of the Impact of Incentive Compensation on Human Organ Procurement," in David L. Moore (ed.), *Proceedings of the Association of Marketing Theory and Practice 1997 Annual Meeting.* Jekyll Island, SC: Association of Marketing Theory and Practice 1997, pp. 186-194.

_____ and G. J. Taylor, "Walking the Walk: Behavior Shifts to Match Attitude Toward Organ Donation-Richmond, Virginia 1994-1996," *Transplantation Proceedings,* 29, December 1997, 3248. Paper by same title presented at the 1997 Society for Organ Sharing Congress and International Transplant Congresses, Washington, D.C., July 1997; abstract published in *The Organ Shortage: Meeting the Challenge, Book of Abstracts-The Fourth International Society for Organ Sharing Congress and International Transplant Congresses,* abstract number 89, p. 103.

_____ and Gloria J. Taylor, "Public Feelings about Financial Incentives for Donation and Concern about Incurring Expenses Due to Donation in One U.S. City," *Transplantation Proceedings,* 29, December 1997, 3263. Paper originally presented at the 1997 Society for Organ Sharing and International Transplant Congresses, Washington, D.C., July 1997. Abstract published in *The Organ Shortage: Meeting the Challenge, Book of Abstracts-The Fourth International Society for Organ Sharing Congress and International Transplant Congresses,* abstract number 98, p. 107.

_____, G. J. Taylor, L. J. McGaw, and G. Mayes, "The Coordinator Attrition Problem in the U.S.: Myth or Reality?" Paper originally presented at the International Transplant Coordinators Society Meeting and International Transplant Congresses, Washington, D.C., July 1997. Abstract published in *The Organ Shortage: Meeting the Challenge, Book of Abstracts-The Fourth International Society for Organ Sharing Congress and International Transplant Congresses*, abstract number 52, p. 82.

Cossé, Thomas J., L. J. McGaw, G. J. Taylor, F. L. Chabalewski, M. C. Cossitt, E. Foltz, and D. L. Seem, "Business Schools: An Untapped Resource for U.S. Non-Profit Organizations," poster presentation at the 1997 International Transplant Coordinators Society Meeting and International Transplant Congresses, Washington, D.C., July 1997. Abstract published in *The Organ Shortage: Meeting the Challenge, Book of Abstracts-The Fourth International Society for Organ Sharing Congress and Transplant Congresses*, abstract number 56, p. 85.

* * *

Kimball P. Marshall is an Associate Professor of Marketing, Department of Management and Marketing, School of Business, Jackson State University, Jackson, MS 39217 (E-mail: kmarshal@netdoor.com).

Marshall, Kimball P. and Carolyn Craig, "Public Education as an Emerging Market for Marketers: A Study of Market Conditions and Administrators' Needs," *Journal of Professional Services Marketing*, Vol. 16, No. 1, 1998. Accepted 1996, Printed Winter 1998.

Marshall, Kimball P., "Non-Client Volunteerism as Marketing Exchange," *Southern Marketing Association Annual Meeting*, Proceedings Abstract, November 4-7, New Orleans, LA, 1998.

_____, "Relationships of Service Quality Perceptions to Public School Volunteerism Among Non-Parents: A Social Marketing Study," *Marketing Management Association* Annual Meeting, Chicago, IL, March, 1998.

* * *

Becky J. Starnes is an Instructor in the Business Administration Department, Alabama State University, Montgomery, AL 36101.

REFERENCES

"America's Independent Sector in Brief," (1996b) *The Nonprofit Almanac*, Independent Sector, Washington, D.C.

Giving and Volunteering in the United States. (1996b) Independent Sector, Washington, D.C.

Payton, Robert H., (1988). *Philanthropy: Voluntary Action for the Public Good*, Collier MacMillan, New York, NY, 1988.

Understanding Volunteer Markets:
The Case of Senior Volunteers

Walter W. Wymer, Jr.

SUMMARY. The research objective was to investigate if seniors could be meaningfully differentiated from other volunteers using selected determinant variables. Another purpose of this study was to determine if higher performing senior volunteers could be differentiated from lower performing senior volunteers. Lifestyle, demographic, personality, social, and core value measures were obtained from a sample of 114 non-volunteers, 387 senior volunteers, and 605 non-senior volunteers. The results indicate that (1) seniors can be treated as a homogenous group for target marketing; (2) males are more likely to volunteer when they are seniors; (3) senior volunteers are differentiated by higher rates of church membership, church attendance, and by their religious values; and (4) senior volunteers are more altruistic (less egoistic) than younger volunteers, but they still desire a sense of accomplishment from their service. Other findings and managerial implications are discussed. *[Article copies available for a fee from The Haworth Document Delivery Service: 1-800-342-9678. E-mail address: getinfo@haworthpressinc.com <Website: http://www.haworthpressinc.com>]*

KEYWORDS. Volunteer, motivation, segmentation, senior, recruitment

Volunteering in America is increasing. In 1993, the estimated annual labor volunteers donated to nonprofit organizations (NPOs) was 19.5 billion hours.

Walter W. Wymer, Jr., DBA, is Assistant Professor of Marketing, Christopher Newport University (E-mail: wwymer@cnu.edu).

Address correspondence to: Walter W. Wymer, Jr., Dept of Management & Marketing, Christopher Newport University, Newport News, VA 23606.

[Haworth co-indexing entry note]: "Understanding Volunteer Markets: The Case of Senior Volunteers." Wymer, Walter W., Jr. Co-published simultaneously in *Journal of Nonprofit & Public Sector Marketing* (The Haworth Press, Inc.) Vol. 6, No. 2/3, 1999, pp. 1-23; and: *Volunteerism Marketing: New Vistas for Nonprofit and Public Sector Management* (ed: Donald R. Self and Walter W. Wymer, Jr.) The Haworth Press, Inc., 1999, pp. 1-23. Single or multiple copies of this article are available for a fee from The Haworth Document Delivery Service [1-800-342-9678, 9:00 a.m. - 5:00 p.m. (EST). E-mail address: getinfo@haworthpressinc. com].

1

In 1995, this number increased to 20.3 billion hours (Independent Sector, 1996). Many NPOs are highly dependent upon donated labor from their volunteers, who are willing to forego alternative consumption activities to expend some of their time in volunteer service. NPO managers view their volunteers as customers, possibly their most important group of customers-the supply of volunteers is scarce whereas the supply of consumers needing NPO services is plentiful (Wright & Higgs, 1995). Effective marketing of volunteers, then, is an important task for NPO managers.

Senior adults (i.e., persons age 60 and older) are an important subgroup of the U.S. population. From a marketing perspective, seniors are an attractive segment of the volunteer market for targeting. The population of senior adults (seniors) is large and swelling as baby boomers grow older. Seniors are also attractive to marketers because they, typically, have fewer constraints on how their time is consumed. Seniors are much more likely to be retired or part-time employed. They are generally less encumbered by time-consuming familial responsibilities (e.g., child rearing) than younger adults in earlier life stages. Seniors are also an attractive group for target marketing because they possess important skills, developed over a lifetime of occupational and personal experiences (Cnaan & Cwikel, 1992).

In its study on senior volunteerism, the Marriott Senior Living Services (1991) reported that 41 percent (15.5 million) of 37.7 million Americans over the age of 60 performed some type of volunteer work during the previous year. It also reported that four million active senior volunteers would volunteer additional hours if asked. Among seniors not performing volunteer work, 14 million (37.4 percent) indicated they might be willing to volunteer if they were asked, suggesting a sizeable potential market of senior volunteers exists in the United States.

Another dimension of the senior population which makes it attractive is that volunteering provides seniors with an important productive activity (Moody, 1988). Volunteerism is viewed as a key in helping seniors age well (Herzog & House, 1991). Seniors not only represent a valuable untapped resource, but volunteering is a meaningful activity for them (Kouri, 1990; Okun, 1994). The reciprocity of benefits between seniors and NPOs provides a foundation for an equal-value exchange, the basis of marketing. From a social marketing perspective, encouraging seniors to volunteer is an important NPO management task. Not only does volunteering benefit a large and growing segment of the American population, senior volunteering provides prosocial benefits to American society as well. Developing a better understanding of senior volunteers as an important market segment, and how they differ from other groups, will provide useful information to managers for more effective target marketing.

Previous research on senior volunteers shows that seniors are more likely to volunteer as their education, income, and occupational status increase. Seniors who regularly attend church services are more likely to be volunteers, as are seniors who are married (Fischer & Schaffer, 1993).

In terms of their reported motivations for volunteering, seniors appear to have multiple motives (Okun & Eisenberg, 1992). In general, seniors report that they volunteer to help others, to feel more useful and productive, to fulfill a moral/civic responsibility, and for social interaction (Fischer & Schaffer, 1993; Marriott Senior Living Services, 1991; Okun, 1994).

Smith (1994), in his literature review, recommended that future research should take into account multiple factors which would more completely account for voluntary participation in NPOs. Smith stated that a weakness of prior studies was a tendency to rely on only a small number of variables contained within one or two conceptual domains. Another criticism of prior research is that the samples of volunteers tends to be limited to a single organization or organization type, limiting the generalizability of the findings (Cnaan & Goldberg-Glen, 1991; Wymer, Riecken, and Yavas, 1996).

The purpose of the study reported in this article is to extend previous research in this area by developing a more complete profile of senior volunteers. The study reported here extends previous research by (1) developing a profile of senior volunteers using a number of determinant variables from multiple conceptual domains, (2) sampling seniors across an array of volunteer organizations and volunteer roles, (3) differentiating senior volunteers from non-senior volunteers, (4) differentiating senior volunteers from non-volunteers, and (5) differentiating higher performing senior volunteers from lower performing senior volunteers.

HYPOTHESES

In general, *senior volunteers should be distinguishable from both non-senior volunteers and non-volunteers using a number of determinant variables.* There are several reasons for thinking that senior volunteers are different from these two groups. Senior volunteers and non-senior volunteers are living in different life stages. There should be demographic correlates differentiating the two groups. For example, senior volunteers would more likely be retired than non-senior volunteers. They would tend to live in smaller families (e.g., widowed or empty nesters). They would be more likely to have smaller (i.e., fixed) incomes. Seniors would be more likely to own their homes. *In this study, senior volunteers are expected to be distinguishable by demographic variables.* In addition to demographic variables, there are reasons to believe other determinant variables would be useful in developing a profile of senior volunteers.

Social and Lifestyle Variables

Wymer, Riecken, and Yavas (1996) discussed previous research showing the importance of social influences on volunteering. "Social influences provide incentives or disincentives for an individual's volunteer behavior by supporting, failing to support, or discouraging the behavior of volunteering" (p. 11). There is some prior research showing a positive relationship between church membership/attendance and volunteerism (Marriott Senior Living Services, 1991; Wymer, 1997). Church provides a means of social support for seniors. Churches require a great deal of congregational support to function, creating a need for volunteers willing to serve. It has already been noted that seniors report as a motivation for volunteering the desire to feel useful and productive. Therefore, in a church setting, seniors have the ability, motivation, and opportunity to serve as volunteers. *Church membership/attendance should differentiate senior volunteers from non-senior volunteers and non-volunteers.*

Facilitation is a variable which has been used in volunteer research to account for the degree of social support and connectedness between the volunteer and non-volunteer. Facilitation are those activities which provide a potential volunteer with information or social support (Wymer, 1997). Prior research has shown that people who are asked to volunteer (typically asked by an associate in an organization to which both belong) are about five times more likely to volunteer than people not personally asked to volunteer (Independent Sector, 1996). Church, as previously discussed, provides a social context through which facilitation occurs naturally. *In this study it is expected that senior volunteers will be differentiated from non-volunteers by higher levels of facilitation.*

While facilitation accounts for current social influences, it is reasonable to believe that parents' attitudes/behaviors concerning volunteerism might exert a lasting influence on their children. In their literature review, Wymer, Riecken, and Yavas (1996) identified two studies which supported parents' future influence on their children's future volunteer service as adults. *Therefore, it is expected that senior volunteers be differentiated from non-volunteers by reporting a higher incidence of parental volunteerism.*

Personality

Wymer, Riecken, and Yavas (1996) reviewed previous research on volunteerism and reported that most prior studies attempting to account for volunteer behavior using personality variables were largely unsuccessful. However, volunteers have been found to exhibit higher levels of emotional empathy than non-volunteers (Allen & Ruston, 1983; Fahey, 1986; Wymer, 1997). Empathy is thought to be a motivating dimension underlying an altruistic personality. People with higher levels of emotional empathy are more concerned about the welfare of others, and are more likely to provide help by voluntary assistance than people with lower levels of emotional empathy. *In this study, it is expected that senior volunteers will be differentiated from non-volunteers by higher levels of emotional empathy.*

Personal Values

While studying the motivations of volunteers, it is important to include values or beliefs in addition to other variables (Schwartz & Howard, 1984). For example, Fahey (1986) studied motivations in a sample of volunteers and non-volunteers. She found that "volunteers were guided significantly more by internalized principles and motivations than are non-volunteers who are more susceptible to peer pressure" (p. 88). Clary and Snyder (1991) wrote that volunteering "helps individuals remain true to their conception of self and allows the expression of deeply held values . . . " (p. 125).

In their literature review, Wymer, Riecken, and Yavas (1996) identified a small number of previous studies which have used values to differentiate volunteers in a particular organization from non-volunteers. A value is defined as "an enduring belief that a specific mode of conduct or end-state of existence is personally and socially preferable to alternative modes of conduct or end-states of existence" (Rokeach, 1968, p. 160). Values are useful in understanding volunteerism because: (1) there are a relatively small number of values compared to other constructs like attitudes, (2) values determine attitudes, (3) values have a motivational component, and (4) core values are enduring (p. 7). No studies could be found that examined the values of senior volunteers, and one contribution of this study is that it provides insights into this important group's core values.

Senior volunteers, compared to non-volunteers, obviously feel that volunteering is important. Non-volunteers feel that volunteering is comparatively unimportant. In comparing senior volunteers to other volunteers, seniors are at a different stage in their lives. Their priorities are different. In fact, seniors are about a generation older than their younger counterparts and are likely to have different values due to the generational gap in addition to the difference in life stages. *Therefore, values should be useful in differentiating senior volunteers from non-senior volunteers and non-volunteers.*

Intensity of Volunteer Service

For an NPO manager, a desirable volunteer performance attribute would be a relatively generous amount of time donated on a regular basis. In general, volunteers who donate a large number of hours are more valuable to the organization than volunteers who give very little of their time. There are reasons to believe that senior volunteers may be willing to donate more of their time than their younger co-volunteers. As previously discussed, senior volunteers may be seeking greater social benefits from their volunteer work than other volunteers more likely to have larger occupational and familial social networks.

Wymer, Riecken, and Yavas (1996) discuss contextual barriers, which can affect a person's desire to volunteer. "For example, an organization may require a minimum time commitment that exceeds the maximum time the recruit is willing to donate" (p. 16). They also point to prior studies which find that many people who do not volunteer report insufficient free time as a reason for not volunteering. Because senior adults are likely to have less demands on their time from employers and family duties than younger adults, *it is expected that senior volunteers will, on average, volunteer more hours than other volunteers.*

It is also important for managers to obtain a better understanding of what variables may influence the amount of time senior volunteers are willing to donate. Because no prior studies could be found to assist in predicting an association between senior volunteerism and number of hours donated on a regular basis, this relationship will be examined in an exploratory manner.

METHOD

Sample and data acquisition. Approximately 40 NPOs in two mid-western U.S. cities (one large, one small) agreed to participate in the study. The participating NPOs represented a diversity of missions (human service, religion, education, health, youth development, and arts/culture). Volunteers, serving in various roles, were mailed a survey which contained a cover letter, a questionnaire, and a business reply return envelope. No incentives were offered to respondents. Non-volunteers were comprised from a convenience sample of staff/parents associated with an elementary school as well as staff at a university. Of 3,500 surveys distributed, 1,058 were returned. There were 944 completed questionnaires from volunteers, 114 from non-volunteers. The response rate was approximately 30 percent. This response rate is similar to that reported by Gillespie and King (1985). They conducted a mail survey of Red Cross volunteers, reporting 1,346 returned questionnaires for a 26.9 response rate.

There were 389 senior volunteers and 605 non-senior volunteers. Senior volunteers ranged from 60 years of age to 93 (mean = 70). Non-senior volunteers ranged from 16 to 59 years of age (mean = 39). The mean age of non-volunteers was 38. Volunteers tended to be female (72 percent female). This gender imbalance is similar to that reported by Cnaan, Kasternakis, and Wineburg (1993). Using a mail survey, they collected data from a sample of 871 persons from over 60 NPOs in three cities. They reported that 71.2 percent of volunteers were female.

Because a sample frame for this population is not available, a non-probability sample was taken. Therefore, sample representativeness is a concern. Collecting data from a number of NPOs in two cities to comprise a relatively large sample help to reduce the likelihood that the sample will differ in some important way from the population of interest (Bryman and Cramer, 1990). Also, as a representativeness check, administrators familiar with their volunteers in 10 participating organizations were contacted after the sample was collected. They were asked to describe the demographic characteristics of their volunteers. Then the administrators were asked to describe the demographic characteristics of other NPO volunteers with which they were familiar. Finally, the administrators were given a description of the sample and asked to comment on the degree of similarity. Results of this check supported the representativeness of the sample.

Measures. Consistent with the approach of previous studies of volunteers, demographic and lifestyle variables were obtained. These included church membership, church attendance, age, gender, education, income, home ownership, marital status, employment status, parental volunteerism, family volunteerism, and family size. Empathy was measured using the Emotional Empathy Scale (Mehrabian & Epstein, 1972). Values were measured using the terminal values portion of the Rokeach Value Scale (RVS; Rokeach, 1973). (See RVS in Table 1.) Facilitation was measured using five 9-point Likert scales which assess the degree to which respondents had access to information or social support linked to an NPO (Cronbach alpha reliability coefficient = .70; Wymer, 1997). Finally, respondents reported the average monthly number of hours they volunteer.

Analysis. The statistical analysis involved a series of stepwise multiple regression procedures. First, the independent variables were regressed on a dummy dependent variable representing two groups, senior volunteers and non-volunteers. Second, the independent variables were regressed on a dummy variable representing senior volunteers and non-senior volunteers. Finally, for the group of senior volunteers, the independent variables were regressed on dependent variables representing the average monthly hours donated in primary and multiple volunteer organizations. Data set diagnostics included examining the correlation matrix, Cook's distance statistics, and variance inflation factors (VIF). One outlier was detected and removed.

FINDINGS

Senior Volunteers vs. Non-Volunteers

The regression results in Table 2a show the standardized and unstandardized parameter estimates of variables which were significant differentiators of senior volunteering from non-volunteering subgroups. As shown in the

TABLE 1. Eighteen Terminal Values from Rokeach Value Survey

A Comfortable Life (a prosperous life)	An Exciting Life (a stimulating, active life)
A Sense of Accomplishment (lasts contribution)	A World at Peace (free of war and conflict)
A World of Beauty (beauty of nature & the arts)	Equality (brotherhood, equal opport.)
Family Security (taking care of loved ones)	Freedom (independence, free choice)
Happiness (contentedness)	Inner Harmony (freedom from inner conflict)
Mature Love (sexual & spiritual intimacy)	National Security (protection from attack)
Pleasure (an enjoyable, leisurely life)	Salvation (saved, eternal life)
Self-Respect (self-esteem)	Social Recognition (respect, admiration)
True Friendship (close companionship)	Wisdom (mature understanding of life)

table, the predictors account for a substantial proportion of the variance between senior volunteers and non-volunteers ($R^2 = 54\%$).

It is worth noting that empathy and parental volunteering were predicted to be significant predictors of senior volunteering, but are not significant in this regression. Facilitation, however, is significant. Senior volunteers are more likely to have social ties to other volunteers than are people who are not active volunteers. Senior volunteers, compared to non-volunteers, are more likely to have friends, relatives, and associates who are themselves volunteers. In terms of social influences, facilitation, a significant predictor of senior volunteering, adds to previous research. As Wymer, Riecken, and Yavas (1996) reported: "Friends, family members, and others who are part of an individual's social network can exert varying degrees of influence on voluntary participation" (p. 11).

People within social networks are likely to share some values. In terms of values which distinguish the two groups in this regression, pleasure, a com-

TABLE 2a. Regression Results: Senior Volunteers and Non-Volunteers[a]

Independent Variables	b	Std. Error	Beta	T
Employment[b]	−.512	.035	−.485	−14.6***
Home ownership[c]	.239	.034	.218	7.0***
Size of household	−.083	.012	−.219	−6.7***
Pleasure	−.060	.014	−.137	−4.2***
Church attendance[d]	.009	.003	.095	3.0**
Facilitation	.027	.009	.100	3.2**
Mature love	−.042	.013	−.101	−3.2**
Gender[e]	−.082	.028	−.091	−2.9**
Comfortable life	−.032	.014	−.076	−2.3*

$R^2 = .548$

$R^2_{adj} = .540$

$N = 508$

a ☞ dep. variable = senior vol (1)/non-vol (2) dummy.
b ☞ full-time = 1, other = 0.
c ☞ rent home = 1, own home = 0.
d ☞ average monthly church service attendance.
e ☞ female = 1, male = 0.
*p < .05
**p < .01
***p < .001

fortable life, and mature love are negative predictors of senior volunteering. Senior volunteers, therefore, place significantly less importance on these values than non-volunteers. In evaluating the meaning of this set of differentiating values, on an egoism/altruism continuum it appears that senior volunteers are less concerned with themselves and their own self-regard than are non-volunteers. Senior volunteers appear to be more altruistic and less egoistic than non-volunteers. Non-volunteers place a greater importance on self-gratification as evidenced by the greater importance they assign to pleasure, achieving a comfortable life, and having a spiritually and sexually intimate interpersonal relationship.

In terms of the demographic and lifestyle variables which predict of senior volunteering, employment status, home ownership, household size, church attendance, and gender are significant in the regression. As shown in Table 2b, senior volunteers attend church more frequently than non-volunteers.

TABLE 2b. Descriptive Statistics of Senior Volunteers and Non-Volunteers

Predictor Variable		Range			Std Dev
	N	Min	Max	Mean	
Church attendance[1]	380	0	34	4.8	4.9
	(110)	(0)	(12)	(2.4)	(2.8)
Employment[2]	379	0	1	.07	.24
	(119)	(0)	(1)	(.67)	(.47)
Gender[3]	381	0	1	.65	.48
	(119)	(0)	(1)	(.72)	(.45)
Home ownership[4]	378	0	1	.88	.33
	(109)	(0)	(1)	(.57)	(.50)
Size of household	364	0	6	1.38	.91
	(113)	(0)	(7)	(2.35)	(1.52)

Note: Values in parentheses represent non-volunteers. Values not in parentheses represent senior volunteers.

1 → Ave monthly church attendance.
2 → 1 = full time, 0 = part time.
3 → 1 = female, 0 = male.
4 → 1 = rent, 0 = own.

Senior volunteers attend church an average of 4.8 times each month. Non-volunteers attend church an average of 2.4 times each month. Senior volunteers are more likely to be male. They are more likely to rent their homes than non-volunteers. Senior volunteers live in households about half as large as non-volunteers. The average household size for senior volunteers is 1.4, whereas non-volunteers' average household size is 2.4.

In terms of employment status, senior volunteers are much less likely to hold full-time employment than non-volunteers. About 87 percent of senior volunteers are retired or not employed. Because most senior volunteers are retired, it is likely that they have fewer demands on their time than non-volunteers. In terms of the categorization scheme of Wymer, Riecken, and Yavas (1996), senior-volunteers have fewer contextual barriers impeding their volunteer activity than non-volunteers.

Senior Volunteers and Non-Senior Volunteers

The regression results in Table 3a show the standardized and unstandardized parameter estimates of variables which were significant differentiators

TABLE 3a. Regression Results: Senior Volunteers/Non-Senior Volunteers[a]

Independent Variables	b	Std. Error	Beta	T
Employment[b]	−.425	.024	−.419	−17.8***
Size of household	.098	.008	−.287	−11.7***
Home ownership[c]	.251	.029	.215	8.6***
Gender[d]	−.135	.026	−.124	−5.1***
Mature love	−.054	.013	−.108	−4.3***
Church attendance[e]	.010	.003	.081	3.1**
Number of org.[f]	.032	.010	.075	3.2**
World at peace	.051	.013	.103	3.9***
Empathy	−.045	.017	−.067	−2.7**
Church membership[g]	.080	.028	.073	2.8**
Income	−.018	.007	−.068	−2.5*
Equality	−.030	.013	−.060	2.3*
Sense of accomp.	.026	.012	.053	2.3*

$R^2 = .484$

$R^2_{adj} = .477$

$N = 1,013$

a ☞ dep. variable = senior vol (1)/non-senior vol (0) dummy.
b ☞ full-time = 1, other = 0.
c ☞ rent home = 1, own home = 0.
d ☞ female = 1, male = 0.
e ☞ average monthly church service attendance.
f ☞ number of organizations volunteer works for.
g ☞ 1 = yes, 0 = no.
*$p < .05$
**$p < .01$
***$p < .001$

of senior volunteering from non-senior volunteering sub-groups. As shown in the table, the predictors account for a substantial proportion of the variance between senior volunteers and non-senior volunteers ($R^2 = 48\%$).

In contrast to the first regression in which empathy was not a significant predictor, in this regression empathy is a negative predictor of senior volunteering. Non-senior volunteers appear to have significantly higher levels of emotional empathy than seniors.

In examining the value differences between senior and non-senior volunteers, the two groups are differentiated by four values: mature love, a world at peace, equality, and a sense of accomplishment. Senior volunteers place a greater importance on a sense of accomplishment (making a lasting contribution) and a world at peace (free of war & conflict), whereas younger volunteers place a greater importance on mature love (spiritual & sexual intimacy) and equality (brotherhood & equal opportunity for all).

In regards to demographic and lifestyle variables, several are significant in this regression. As shown in Table 3b, senior volunteers attend church more regularly than their younger co-volunteers. Senior volunteers attend church about five times in an average month, compared to about three attendances

TABLE 3b. Descriptive Statistics of Senior Volunteers and Non-Senior Volunteers

Predictor Variable	N	Range			Std Dev
		Min	Max	Mean	
Church attendance[1]	363	0	34	4.76	4.90
	(577)	(0)	(30)	3.01	3.54
Church member[2]	388	0	1	.82	.39
	(601)	(0)	(1)	(.68)	(.47)
Employment[3]	379	0	1	.06	.24
	(602)	(0)	(1)	(.55)	(.50)
Gender[4]	381	0	1	.65	.48
	(603)	(0)	(1)	(.77)	(.42)
Income	358	1	7	3.28	1.70
	(578)	(1)	(7)	(4.04)	(1.93)
Home ownership	378	0	1	.88	.33
	(581)	(0)	(1)	(.70)	(.46)
Organizations	384	1	7	2.27	1.19
	(603)	(1)	(7)	(1.84)	(1.08)
Size of household	364	0	6	1.38	.91
	(587)	(0)	(8)	(2.49)	(1.57)

Note: Values in parentheses represent non-senior volunteers. Values not in parentheses represent senior volunteers.

1 → Ave monthly church attendance.
2 → 0 = no, 1 = yes.
3 → 0 = p/t, 1 = f/t.
4 → 0 = male, 1 = female.

for younger volunteers. Seniors are also more likely to be church members than non-senior volunteers. Senior volunteers report an 82 percent church membership rate, whereas non-seniors report a 68 percent church membership rate. These two significant predictors, church attendance and membership, indicate that senior volunteers tend to be more committed to their churches than non-senior volunteers.

Senior volunteers are also differentiated from non-seniors by the number of nonprofit organizations in which they donate their time. Seniors volunteer in a larger number of organizations, an average of 2.3 compared to 1.4 for non-senior volunteers.

Gender is a significant predictor in this regression. While females make up the majority of volunteers, this gender difference is significantly more balanced for senior volunteers. Men are more likely to volunteer when they are seniors.

Senior volunteers are more likely to rent their homes than non-senior volunteers. Seniors are more likely to live in smaller households than non-seniors. In regards to their respective income levels, senior volunteers appear to have lower annual income levels than non-senior volunteers. Finally, seniors are less likely to be employed on a full-time basis than non-senior volunteers. As shown in Table 3c, 87 percent of senior volunteers are retired or not employed, compared to 16 percent for non-senior volunteers. More than 50 percent of non-senior volunteers are employed on a full-time basis.

These findings suggest that senior volunteers have available time (retired) and use it by volunteering in multiple organizations. They appear to be motivated by their religious beliefs, a sense of duty, a desire to be useful, a desire for social contact, and a desire to make a contribution with their lives. The proportion of male volunteers is significantly greater with the senior volunteer group. Men, with former occupational and familial responsibilities no longer exerting their influences, find volunteer work more desirable or feasible.

Influences on the Depth and Breadth of Senior Volunteer Service

Just as paid employees' job performances differ, volunteers work performances also differ. One dimension of performance investigated here is the average monthly hours seniors volunteer. Many NPOs have a core subgroup of volunteers which are most heavily relied upon. It is important for managers to better understand their most dedicated volunteers.

The issue is complicated by the fact that volunteers may serve in a single organization or in multiple organizations. There may be a commitment to a primary organization and its purpose, or a volunteer may feel a duty to "volunteer" in a general sense and may more equally distribute time in two or more NPOs. Seniors reported volunteering a monthly average of 17.7

TABLE 3c. Employment Status: Senior/Non-Senior Volunteers

Employment Category	Senior Vols.		Non-Senior Vols.	
	Freq.	Percent	Freq.	Percent
Self-employed full-time	8	2.1	41	6.8
Self-employed part-time	9	2.3	26	4.3
Work for someone else: full-time	15	3.9	292	48.3
Work for someone else, part-time	9	2.3	66	10.9
Not employed	20	5.1	69	11.4
Retired	318	81.7	31	5.1
Full-time student	0	0.0	77	12.7
Missing	10	2.6	3	0.5
Total	389	100.0	605	100.0

hours for their primary organization (non-senior volunteers, 13.6 hours/month). They reported volunteering a monthly average of 25.9 hours in all NPOs (non-seniors, 18.4).

To take into account the complexity of multi-organizational volunteerism, three separate regressions were performed. First, the predictor variables previously described were regressed on a variable representing the average number of hours senior volunteers reported volunteering in all organizations in which they serve. Second, the dependent variable was changed to one representing the average monthly hours donated for the organization in which senior volunteers reported feeling the most commitment (i.e., primary organization). Third, the dependent variable was changed to one representing the total number of organizations for which the senior volunteer donates time. The results of these regressions are shown in Table 4.

Hours in All Organizations

In the first regression three variables were significant. They were two values, a sense of accomplishment and salvation, and gender. Senior volunteers who donate more hours in multiple NPOs desire a sense of accomplishment

TABLE 4. Regression Results: Senior Vol. Performance

Independent Variables	b	Std. Error	Beta	T
1st Regression[a]				
Constant	25.943	.959		27.1***
Sense of accomp.	3.131	1.038	.156	3.0**
Salvation	2.167	.992	.112	2.2*
Gender[b]	−4.282	2.002	−.108	−2.1*
$R^2 = .044$ $R^2_{adj} = .037$ $N = 389$				
2nd Regression[c]				
Constant	30.984	4.296		7.2***
Gender	−4.948	1.573	−.159	−3.2**
Education	−.644	.257	−.127	−2.5*
Social recognition	1.803	.766	.118	2.4*
$R^2 = .048$ $R^2_{adj} = .048$ $N = 389$				
3rd Regression[d]				
Constant	.893	.347		2.6**
Education	.072	.020	.177	3.6***
Comfortable life	−.142	.062	−.119	2.3*
Exciting life	.176	.061	.146	2.9**
Church member	.342	.154	.111	2.2*
Wisdom	.124	.061	.102	2.0*
$R^2 = .096$ $R^2_{adj} = .084$ $N = 384$				

a ☞ dep. variable = hours in all organizations.

b ☞ female = 1, male = 0.

c ☞ dep. variable = hours in primary organization.

d ☞ dep. variable = number of organizations.

*p < .05

**p < .01

***p < .001

from their volunteer work. Wymer, Riecken, and Yavas (1996) reported that some senior volunteers seek to enhance their sense of efficacy. Other studies have found that seniors view volunteer work as a means to feel more useful and productive (Okun & Eisenberg, 1992; Fischer & Schaffer, 1993; Okun, 1994). The findings of this present study suggest that the number of hours senior volunteers donate across NPOs is positively associated with the relative importance they place on a sense of accomplishment in their value systems.

In addition to a sense of accomplishment, salvation was a value which was positively associated with the number of hours seniors donate in all their organizations. Reported previously, senior volunteers are about twice as likely as non-volunteers to be church members. They are significantly differentiated from non-senior volunteers by higher levels of both church membership and church attendance. Senior volunteers appear to be more religious than the two comparison groups, non-volunteers and non-senior volunteers. The number of hours seniors volunteer in multiple NPOs is positively related to the importance seniors give to the salvation value. Not only do senior volunteers appear to be religious, those donating the most time in a number of NPOs appear to be the more religious among this group.

Gender is also associated with the number of hours volunteers give. Previously reported, senior volunteers are more likely to be male than non-senior volunteers. Given that the average age of senior volunteers was about 70 years, and given the commonly-known gender differential in life expectancy rates, this finding is surprising. The findings support the conclusion that the more likely a senior volunteer is to give substantial amounts of time in multiple organizations, the more likely that volunteer is going to be male, religious, and seeking a sense of accomplishment from volunteer service.

Hours in Primary Organization

Whereas the previous analysis examined senior volunteering in multiple organizations, this analysis examines senior volunteering in the NPO to which the senior volunteer reports feeling the greatest commitment (i.e., primary organization). Three variables were significantly associated with greater numbers of hours volunteered in primary organizations. Two demographic variables, gender and education, were negatively related to higher numbers of hours volunteered in primary organizations. One value, social recognition, was positively associated with volunteering more hours in primary organizations. Senior volunteers who donate the most time in their primary NPOs are more likely to be male, have fewer years of formal education than other volunteers, and feel that social recognition is a more important value than other senior volunteers.

Number of NPOs

In the third regression, the dependent variable is the number of NPOs for which the senior volunteer reported volunteering. The significant variables were one demographic variable (education), a lifestyle variable (church membership), and three values (a comfortable life, an exciting life, and wisdom). Volunteering in a greater number of NPOs is positively associated with higher levels of education, and higher rates of church membership. Senior volunteers who donate their time in a greater number of organizations are more likely to place a relatively higher level of importance on the values of an exciting life and wisdom, and to place a relatively lower level of importance on the value of a comfortable life.

While education was a negative predictor of hours volunteered in a senior volunteer's primary organization, it was positively related to the number of organizations for which the volunteer donates time. One theoretical explanation given for an association between higher socio-economic status and volunteerism is that volunteers in higher socio-economic groups perceive themselves as having greater resources of use to an NPO (Fischer & Schaffer, 1993). A person, under this argument, weighs the costs and benefits of volunteering while deciding whether or not to volunteer. The greater the perceived level of resources, the relatively lower the perceived costs associated with volunteering. Thus, people in what society considers to be more prestigious socio-economic categories (dominant social statuses) should be expected to volunteer more frequently. The findings in this study are not entirely consistent with this rationale. Variables which significantly predicted higher rates of volunteer service in multiple NPOs were related to religious beliefs, gender, and a desire to derive a sense of accomplishment from volunteer service. The significant predictors of higher service levels for a volunteer's primary organization were gender, lower levels of education, and a desire to receive social recognition. These results do not support previous interpretations of findings which propose dominant social statuses indicate perceived greater resources, reduced personal costs, and greater volunteer activity. In the case of predicting volunteers' hours in a volunteer's primary organization, education was a negative predictor of volunteer activity. Only in the case of predicting the number of organizations for which a volunteer donates time was one variable, which could be considered a dominant status indicator, significant. Education was positively associated with volunteering in greater numbers of NPOs. These findings corroborate an interpretation of perceived portability of personal resources, not a reduced personal cost of volunteering.

Senior volunteers who serve in a substantially greater number of NPOs are distinguished (in addition to their higher levels of education) by higher rates of church membership. Both the increased rate of church membership among these seniors and the higher importance they give to the value wisdom suggests a higher level of religious beliefs which they may be expressing through their volunteer work (Wymer, 1997). Senior volunteers working in a number of organizations feel that an exciting life is an important value. These active senior volunteers, with an average age of 70, feel that their volunteer work provides them with a means of having a more dynamic lifestyle. This finding is consistent with previous research suggesting that seniors volunteer in order to regain a lost sense of usefulness they had prior to reaching their current (senior) life stage (Fischer & Schaffer, 1993; Okun, 1994; Okun & Eisenberg, 1992). Generally, the findings here suggest that more active senior volunteers are desiring to act in ways consistent with their religious beliefs (cf. Wood & Hougland, 1990) while also seeking positive rewards from their more intense volunteer involvement: a sense of accomplishment, social recognition, and an exciting life.

DISCUSSION

Summary of Findings

One purpose of this study was to determine if senior volunteers could be differentiated from non-volunteers. The determinant variables used are from five different areas: demographic, lifestyle, personality, social, and personal values. Senior volunteer group membership is predicted by nine significant variables. Senior volunteers report having greater social ties to persons who are themselves volunteers and who are able to provide information and support regarding volunteer service. Senior volunteers are not differentiated by the personality variable used, emotional empathy. They are not differentiated by having had parents who were themselves volunteers. Among the demographic and lifestyle variables, senior volunteers are differentiated from non-volunteers by being more likely to be retired or underemployed, by living in households with fewer family members, by being more likely to rent their homes, and by higher rates of church attendance. In terms of their respective core values, senior volunteers are differentiated by assigning three values significantly less importance than non-volunteers: pleasure, mature love, and a comfortable life.

Another purpose of this study was to determine if senior volunteers could be differentiated from non-senior volunteers using the determinant variables previously described. Senior volunteers are retired/underemployed. They live in smaller households, are more likely to rent their homes, and receive smaller annual incomes than non-senior volunteers. Senior volunteers, compared to non-senior volunteers, are more likely to be male, and they are more likely to volunteer in a larger number of nonprofit organizations.

Senior volunteers report higher rates of church membership and church attendance than non-senior volunteers. They score significantly lower on the emotional empathy scale then non-senior volunteers. In terms of their values, seniors feel that equality and mature love are significantly less important and that a sense of accomplishment and a world at peace are significantly more important than non-senior volunteers.

Senior volunteers appear to volunteer from a sense of duty or to act in accordance with their religious beliefs. Senior volunteers are less ego-centric than non-senior volunteers. However, senior volunteers do seek benefits from their volunteer work, chiefly in the form of deriving a sense of accomplishment from their service.

Another purpose of this study was to determine if the determinant variables used could be helpful in predicting higher performing senior volunteers, as measured by average monthly hours volunteered. The findings, given the lower proportion of variances accounted for in the final series of analyses, indicate that the determinant variables used in this study are more helpful in differentiating volunteer subgroups than in accounting for performance differences. Yet, these variables may serve as a basis from which future replications and extensions of this work can increase our knowledge of volunteer performance.

The findings show that seniors volunteering the greatest time in a variety of organizations are more likely to be male. They are differentiated from seniors donating less time in multiple organizations by their core values. These seniors assign greater importance to the values salvation and a sense of accomplishment than senior volunteers donating less time in multiple organizations.

Senior volunteers donating the greatest amount of time in their primary organizations are also more likely to be male. They report relatively fewer years of formal education and place a significantly higher importance on the value social recognition than seniors giving lower amounts of time in their primary organization.

Seniors volunteering in a greater number of organizations tend to have more years of formal education. They are more religious than seniors volunteering in a smaller number of NPOs. Seniors volunteering in the greatest number of organizations were more likely to be church members and were more likely to feel that wisdom is a core value. They are less egoistic (gave the value comfortable life a significantly lower position among core values) than other senior volunteers. However, seniors volunteering in a relatively large number of organizations desire an exciting lifestyle and perhaps view volunteer service as a means to achieve this end.

MANAGERIAL IMPLICATIONS

The findings reported here have important implications for NPO managers. While future research is needed to replicate and extend this initial work, our understanding of senior volunteers is enriched by using the framework described in this study.

Smith (1994) developed a literature review of volunteerism over the previous 20 years. One of his chief recommendations for future research was that determinant variables from different conceptual domains were needed to obtain a more comprehensive understanding of volunteerism. The findings of this study support the efficacy of Smith's recommendation. The profile of senior volunteers in this study is richer as a result of including variables representing social, personality, demographic, lifestyle, and value domains. Managers who want to profile important groups of volunteers may benefit from using determinant variables from these areas.

Another important contribution of this study was that it demonstrated the distinctiveness of a relatively homogeneous group of volunteers–senior volunteers. Seniors are an attractive segment of the population for target marketing efforts (Cnaan & Cwikel, 1992). The more managers know about this market segment, the better equipped they will be to develop effective marketing strategies to *recruit* new volunteers, *retain* current volunteers, and *return* former volunteers to active service (the 3 R's of volunteer marketing). For example, seniors in this study are differentiated by their employment status, home ownership status, household size, church membership, and church attendance. The preponderance of female volunteers among non-senior volunteers is more balanced among seniors. Among senior volunteers, males tend to donate more time. Senior volunteers are distinguished by having higher levels of religious beliefs. They are more altruistic than younger volunteers, but still desire achievement and recognition from their work.

Just as managers in commercial organizations would like to know how to identify their most profitable customers, nonprofit managers need to know how to identify their most dedicated volunteers. One way to assess productivity is by examining the hours volunteers give. Results in this study show that among senior volunteers, those who give more of their time were more likely to be male, were more likely to have fewer years of education, and were more likely to have social recognition as a core value.

Although most NPO managers are responsible for recruiting volunteers for their own organizations, some managers work in umbrella organizations whose mission it is to stimulate volunteer recruitment/placement into other organizations. The Retired Senior Volunteer Program (RSVP), as an example, is funded by the federal government. Through local agencies, RSVP recruits seniors and places them with NPOs requesting volunteer assistance. Findings from this study are important to managers of volunteer umbrella organizations because this study examined senior volunteering in a multi-organizational context. The results show that senior volunteers who donate the most time in multiple organizations tend to be male, religious, and desire a sense of accomplishment from their work. Senior volunteers who served in the greatest number of organizations (indicating a commitment to service in general rather than to a single organization or mission) tend to have more formal education, are religious, are altruistic to a point, but feel that volunteer service adds a level of excitement to their lives. Thus, the analysis described in this study not only provides managers with demographic and lifestyle descriptors, it also provides NPO managers with possible insights into the motives and the desired benefits of senior volunteers.

CONCLUSION

This study was not only useful in demonstrating a methodology for better understanding important segments of volunteers, it also has important implications for future research. First, the population of volunteers should not be thought of as a monolithic, homogenous group. The total market of volunteers is composed of diverse sub-strata. There are many ways to categorize volunteers. Wymer (1997) described a volunteer typology based on the roles volunteers serve and the type of volunteer organization in which they serve. In this study, age was used as a means of differentiating one group of volunteers from another group. Because volunteers are a multi-faceted population, future research would add to our knowledge in this area by exploring diverse volunteer segments in greater depth.

Second, this study is important because it demonstrates the efficacy of understanding one's target market (in this case, senior volunteers) by learning how it differs from other market segments. Our understanding of volunteers can be enhanced by learning how a particular volunteer segment differs from other segments. Few studies of volunteerism have used comparison groups. Those few that have used a comparison group of volunteers have generally used a group of non-volunteers (Cnaan & Goldberg-Glen, 1991). This study demonstrates the added insights provided by using multiple comparison groups. In this study, two comparison groups (i.e., non-volunteers and non-senior volunteers) provided both interesting findings and insights into interpreting the results. Future studies would produce richer findings by using multiple comparison groups.

Third, this study demonstrates the usefulness of examining volunteerism using a multidimensional approach (i.e., using determinant variables from multiple conceptual domains). Reviewing 20 years of previous research in this area, Smith (1994) made a recommendation for future research to begin taking a multidimensional approach. Smith commented on the shortfalls of a narrower approach (e.g., relying exclusively on demographic variables) and noted the dearth of research taking a more comprehensive approach. This study demonstrates the increased understanding of an important subgroup of volunteers by learning how it differs from other groups in terms of demographic variables, lifestyle variables, social influences, personality, and values. The findings reported here support Smith's recommendation.

Finally, this study is important because it demonstrates the utility of using a non-matched sample. The comparison groups in this study were not matched to the group of senior volunteers and this non-matching appears to have been beneficial. Independent Sector performs bi-annual national surveys of volunteerism. In doing so, it forces its samples to match the demographic profile of the U.S., potentially removing interesting differences between volunteers and non-volunteers from its data (e.g., gender imbalances). Cnaan, Kasternakis, and Wineburg (1993) did not match their sub-groups to census data and reported the gender disparity among volunteers found in this study. However, their comparison group of non-volunteers was selected by the group of volunteers. Survey respondents who were volunteers were asked to select a non-volunteer friend to participate in the study. Since members of the same social groups are likely to share similar beliefs and values, this matching procedure brought into question the results of the study whose purpose was to examine the religious beliefs of volunteers. In regards to the present study, even given its limitations, the methodology of using comparison groups which have not been matched appear to yield richer data. If a researcher is specifically interested in controlling certain variables, then it may be a better procedure to control those variables statistically in the data analysis rather than to control for them by attempting to match sample comparison groups.

REFERENCES

Allen, Natalie J. and J. Philippe Rushton (1983), "Personality Characteristics of Community Mental Health Volunteers: A Review," *Journal of Voluntary Action Research* 12 (1), 36-49.

Bryman, Alan and Duncan Cramer (1990), *Quantitative Data Analysis for Social Scientists*. London: Routledge.

Clary, E. Gil and Mark Snyder (1991), "A Functional Analysis of Altruism and Prosocial Behavior: The Case of Volunteerism," In *Review of Personality and Social Psychology, vol 12*, ed. M.S. Clark, 119-148. Newbury Park, CA: Sage.

Cnaan, Ram A. and J. Cwikel (1992), "Elderly Volunteers: Assessing Their Potential as an Unmapped Resource," *Journal of Aging and Social Policy*, 4 (1-2), 125-147.

_____ and Roben S. Goldberg-Glen (1991), "Measuring Motivation to Volunteer in Human Services," *Journal of Applied Behavioral Sciences*, 27 (3), 269-284.

_____ Amy Kasternakis, and Robert J. Wineburg (1993), "Religious People, Religious Congregations, and Volunteerism in Human Services: Is There a Link?" *Nonprofit & Voluntary Sector Quarterly* 22 (1), 33-51.

Fahey, Maureen (1986), "Lay Volunteers Within an American Catholic Parish: Personality and Social Factors," Doctoral diss., University of San Francisco.

Fischer, Lucy Rose and Kay Banister Schaffer (1993), *Older Volunteers: A Guide to Research and Practice*. Newbury Park, CA: Sage.

Gillespie, David F. and Anthony E. O. King I. (1985), "Demographic Understanding of Volunteerism," *Journal of Sociology and Social Welfare* 12 (4), 798-816.

Herzog, A. R., and House, J. S. (1991), "Productive Activities and Aging Well," *Generations*, 15, 49-54.

Independent Sector (1996), *Volunteering and Giving in the United States: Findings From a National Survey.* Washington, D.C.: Author.

Kouri, M. K. (1990), *Volunteerism and Older Adults: Choices and Challenges.* Santa Barbara, CA: ABC-CLIO.

Marriott Senior Living Services (1991), *Marriott's Seniors Volunteerism Study.* Washington, D.C.: Author.

Mehrabian, Albert and Norman Epstein (1972), "A Measure of Emotional Empathy," *Journal of Personality* 40, 525-543.

Moody, H. R. (1988), *Abundance of Life: Human Development Policies for an Aging Society.* New York: Columbia University Press.

Okun, Morris A. (1994), "The Relation Between Motives for Organizational Volunteering and the Frequency of Volunteering by Elders," *The Journal of Applied Gerontology* 13 (2), 115-126.

_____ and Nancy Eisenberg (1992), "Motives and Intent to Continue Organizational Volunteering Among Residents of a Retirement Community Area," *Journal of Community Psychology* 20 (3), 183-187.

Rokeach, Milton (1973), *The Nature of Human Values.* New York: The Free Press.

_____ (1968), *Beliefs, Attitudes, and Values: A Theory of Organization and Change.* San Francisco: Jossey-Bass.

Schwartz, Shalom H. and Judith A. Howard (1984), "Internalized Values as Motivators of Altruism," in *Development and Maintenance of Prosocial Behavior,* ed. E. Staub, D. Bar-Tal, and J. Karylowski, 229-255. New York: Plenum.

Smith, David Horton (1994), "Determinants of Voluntary Association Participation and Volunteering: A Literature Review," *Nonprofit and Voluntary Sector Quarterly* 23 (3), 243-264.

Wood, James R. and James G. Hougland, Jr. (1990), "The Role of Religion in Philanthropy," in *Critical Issues in American Philanthropy,* ed., Jon Van Til and Associates, 29-33. San Francisco: Jossey-Bass.

Wright, Newell D., Val Larson, and Roger Higgs (1995), "Marketing of Volunteerism: The Case of Appalachian Mountain Housing," *Journal of Consumer Satisfaction, Dissatisfaction, and Complaining Behavior,* 8, 188-197.

Wymer, Walter W., Jr. (1997), "Formal Volunteering as a Function of Values, Self-Esteem, Empathy, and Facilitation," *Journal of Nonprofit & Public Sector Marketing* 5 (2), in press.

_____ Glen Reicken, and Ugur Yavas (1996), "Determinants of Volunteerism: A Cross-Disciplinary Review and Research Agenda," *Journal of Nonprofit & Public Sector Marketing* 4 (4), 3-26.

Segmenting Subgroups of Volunteers for Target Marketing: Differentiating Traditional Hospice Volunteers from Other Volunteers

Walter W. Wymer, Jr.
Becky J. Starnes

SUMMARY. The research objective was to investigate if hospice volunteers could be differentiated from other volunteers using determinant variables from multiple conceptual domains (i.e., personality variables, social/lifestyle variables, demographic variables, and terminal values). Another purpose was to determine if higher performing hospice volunteers could be differentiated from lower performing hospice volunteers.

Lifestyle, demographic, personality, social influence, and terminal value measures were obtained from a sample of 63 hospice volunteers and 950 volunteers from other organizations. Survey respondents were derived from over 40 nonprofit organizations in two Midwestern cities.

In comparing hospice volunteers to volunteers serving in other types of organizations, hospice volunteers are differentiated by 11 determinant

Walter W. Wymer, Jr., DBA, is Assistant Professor of Marketing, Christopher Newport University.

Becky J. Starnes, MBA, is Marketing and Management Instructor and PhD student at Auburn University Montgomery.

Address correspondence to: Walter W. Wymer, Jr., DBA, Management & Marketing Department, Christopher Newport University, Newport News, VA 23606 (Email: wwymer@cnu.edu).

[Haworth co-indexing entry note]: "Segmenting Subgroups of Volunteers for Target Marketing: Differentiating Traditional Hospice Volunteers from Other Volunteers." Wymer, Walter W. Jr., and Becky J. Starnes. Co-published simultaneously in *Journal of Nonprofit & Public Sector Marketing* (The Haworth Press, Inc.) Vol. 6, No. 2/3, 1999, pp. 25-50; and: *Volunteerism Marketing: New Vistas for Nonprofit and Public Sector Management* (ed: Donald R. Self and Walter W. Wymer, Jr.) The Haworth Press, Inc., 1999, pp. 25-50. Single or multiple copies of this article are available for a fee from The Haworth Document Delivery Service [1-800-342-9678, 9:00 a.m. - 5:00 p.m. (EST). E-mail address: getinfo@haworthpressinc.com].

variables. One demographic variable (age), one social/lifestyle variable (the number of organizations to which the volunteer donates time for), and one personality variable (self-esteem) were significant. The remaining eight significant predictors of hospice volunteering were values.

An aspect of performance examined in this study is the average monthly hours hospice volunteers serve in their organizations. Because volunteers may serve in either single or multiple organizations, multiple analyses were performed using three different dependent variables (time volunteered in all organizations, time volunteered in primary organization, and number of organizations for which volunteer serves). *[Article copies available for a fee from The Haworth Document Delivery Service: 1-800-342-9678. E-mail address: getinfo@haworthpressinc.com <Website: http://www.haworthpressinc.com>]*

INTRODUCTION

Volunteer labor is an important resource for nonprofit organizations. In 1995, the estimated annual labor volunteers donated to nonprofit organizations (NPOs) was 20.3 billion hours (Independent Sector, 1996). Many NPOs are highly dependent upon donated labor from volunteers willing to forego alternative consumption activities to expend some of their time in volunteer service.

A marketing-oriented approach to volunteer recruitment would be to view volunteers as a customer group (Yavas and Riecken, 1981). Wright and Higgs (1995) conducted a study of volunteering in a charitable organization which builds low-cost homes for the poor. They concluded that this organization's volunteers represented its most important group of customers because the supply of volunteers was scarce whereas the supply of people needing the organization's services was plentiful. While volunteers in hospice organizations may not be *the* most important customer group (all constituent groups are important), volunteers are essential. Effective marketing of volunteers, then, is an important task for NPO managers.

Hospices are organizations which rely upon volunteer services. Hospice volunteers serve terminally ill patients and their family by providing (1) personal care, (2) patient support, (3) spiritual support, (4) homemaking, and (5) family support (Stephany, 1989). Bunn (1984) states that volunteers are the backbone and sustaining force behind a successful hospice program. Lafer (1991) calls hospice volunteers a " . . . key element in the provision of service to dying patients and their families" (p. 161).

Hospices need volunteers to function and to accomplish their missions. One study of 53 hospices found that for every paid worker, there were two volunteers (Briggs, 1987). However, in the U.S. hospice organizations are also *required* to use volunteers. Federal legislation has been enacted which sets minimum numbers of patient care hours which must be made by volunteer workers in order to qualify for federal funding or Medicare payments (Silbert, 1985).

The modern hospice movement began when Dr. Cicely Saunders founded St. Christopher's Hospice in England in 1967. Since then there has been a dramatic growth in hospices. In 1993, there were 1,800 such programs in the U.S. (Hegeman, 1994) attempting to serve some of the eight million Americans who lose a relative to death each year (Craig, 1994). As of 1996, there were 37,382 full-time volunteers providing services to 400,000 patients in approximately 3,000 organizations within the U.S. (Hospice Association of America, 1997). The growth in hospice volunteer demand is even more of a managerial challenge given that hospice volunteers must possess a specific set of personal characteristics to be suitable as well as complete a six-to-eight-week training program to prepare them to serve the terminally ill and surviving family members (Hall and Marshall, 1996).

Unfortunately, volunteerism in America is not robust. According to Independent Sector, which conducts biannual national surveys on volunteerism, from 1989 to 1996 the total number of U.S. adults who volunteer declined from 98.4 million to 93 million (Independent Sector, 1996). While volunteerism in America is waning in popularity, a burgeoning hospice movement is in need of an increasing number of qualified volunteers. Factors such as the aging of the American population, inclusion of hospice care as a Medicaid benefit, expanded private insurance coverage, and the managed care revolution have stimulated demand for hospice care (Neigh, 1995; Self and Starnes, 1998). Managers of hospice organizations must more effectively recruit and retain their volunteers.

Adopting a marketing-oriented approach, a hospice manager would first try to understand his or her volunteers in order to (1) develop a volunteer experience which would approximate an equal value exchange with the volunteer, and (2) develop the most effective message to appeal to the potential volunteer. Nonprofit managers can make better informed decisions regarding the recruitment and management of their volunteers when they have a better understanding of not only why and what type of people volunteer in general, but why and what type of people volunteer for their particular type of organization. Heidrich (1988) states:

> From a marketing point of view, it is important for voluntary organizations to know their type of volunteer and how they differ from others. A competitive advantage would accrue to an organization tailoring its recruitment message to a specific group having more or less homogeneous characteristics and a demonstrated likelihood to volunteer for certain roles or organizations. (p. 10)

While prior studies of hospice volunteers have added to our knowledge, more needs to be known. The purpose of this study is to increase our understanding of hospice volunteers to assist marketing decision-making by (1) differentiating hospice volunteers from other subgroups of volunteers, and (2) by differentiating more active hospice volunteers from less active hospice volunteers.

LITERATURE REVIEW

Traditional Hospices and AIDS Hospices

Prior research has categorized hospice organizations as two basic types. First, there are the traditional hospices. While both types of hospices serve terminally ill people, their families and loved ones, traditional hospice patients tend to be cancer victims. Because traditional hospices have been in existence longer, and because they are greater in number, people usually think of traditional hospices when the term "hospice" is used. However, there are also AIDS hospice organizations. AIDS hospice organizations serve terminally ill persons, their families, and their companions.

There are reasons to believe that AIDS hospice volunteers and traditional hospice volunteers may represent two distinct groups. Shuff, Horne, Westberg, Mooney, and Mitchell (1991) compared 40 volunteers from a traditional hospice with 60 volunteers from an AIDS hospice and reported that the two groups differed significantly on 8 of 16 demographic variables. AIDS hospice volunteers appear to be younger. They are more homogenous in terms of demographic variables than traditional hospice volunteers. AIDS hospice volunteers are more likely to be gay, lesbian, or bisexual. Traditional hospice volunteering is represented by a majority female gender imbalance (70 to 80% female, typically). Whereas AIDS hospices attract a more equal representation from each gender (Paradis and Usui, 1987).

While volunteers serving in the two types of hospice organizations appear to be differentiated by demographic characteristics, they may not be as different in terms of personality and motivation. In an analysis of the data mentioned previously in Shuff et al. (1991), Mitchell and Shuff (1995) compared the group of AIDS hospice volunteers with the group of traditional hospice volunteers using the Myers-Briggs Type Indicator to measure personality dimensions. The authors reported no significant differences between the two groups.

In terms of motivation, Murrant and Strathdee (1995) conducted a study in which they examined the motivations of 62 AIDS hospice volunteers. They concluded " . . . it appears that the primary motivation of AIDS hospice volunteers is not unlike that of volunteers from the traditional hospice setting" (p. 35).

Scope of study. This scope of this study is limited to traditional hospice volunteers.

Prior Research

Our understanding of hospice volunteers has been increased by several prior studies. Most prior research on hospice volunteering has focused on two areas. First, several studies have provided demographic descriptions of hospice volunteers. Second, a smaller number of studies have examined personality characteristics and motives of hospice volunteers. This section will present some of these findings, then discuss gaps in the literature, and then frame the focus of this study.

Demographic characteristics. Table 1 presents demographic information from several studies of traditional hospice volunteers. The most frequently reported information related to the sample size, the number of hospice organizations from which the sample was taken, and the gender profile of the sample. Education and age were sometimes reported. However each was reported in different formats, making comparisons difficult. For example, sometimes the sample's mean age was reported, and other times age was reported in categorical ranges (e.g., 50% of the sample between the ages of 40 and 50). Education was reported in differing formats also. The marital status and race/ethnicity of a sample in a given study was seldom reported.

Conclusions we can make regarding the demographic profile of most traditional hospice volunteers is that they tend to be white, females, with some college education. Most tend to be between the ages of 40 to 59 years old.

One interesting observation from examining prior research in this area is that the overrepresentation of females lessens as the age of the volunteer increases. The gender difference with volunteers over 60 years of age is more balanced than with younger volunteers. For example, in his sample of 401 volunteers from 33 hospices, Hoad (1991) found that about 85 percent of his sample was female. However, Hoad found that 72 percent of the male volunteers were older than 60, whereas only 41 percent of female volunteers were older than 60. Field and Johnson (1993) reported similar results from their study of 276 volunteers from an English hospice organization. Field and Johnson found that 88 percent of the volunteers were females. However, 76 percent of males and 38 percent of females were older than 60 years. Future research into this issue would be helpful.

Personality characteristics. Two studies used the Myers-Briggs Type Indicator (MBTI) to assess the personality types of hospice volunteers. The MBTI is a 94-item instrument which assesses four separate personality indices: extroversion-introversion, sensing-intuitive, thinking-feeling, and judging-feeling (See Mitchell and Shuff [1995] for a more detailed description of the MBTI.) Mitchel and Shuff (1995) reported that their sample was characterized by

TABLE 1. Demographic Findings from Prior Research

Study	Size (Orgs/N)	Percent female	Percent married	Race (% white)	Education (in years)	Age (years)
Briggs (1987)	2/166	86	62	96	note f	note f
Caty and Tamlyn (1983)	1/41	note e	note e	nr	note e	note e
Chevrier, Steur, & MacKenzie (1994)	1/100	77	nr	nr	nr	note a
Field & Johnson (1993)	1/276	88	nr	nr	nr	note b
Hayslip & Walling (1985)	1/29	90	nr	nr	16.1	38.8
Hoad (1991)	33/401	85	nr	nr	nr	note d
Lafer (1989)	10/75	100	nr	100	note g	46
Robbins (1992)	6/320	84	nr	nr	nr	nr
Scott & Caldwell (1996)	28/156	87	73	95	14.6	55.6
Shuff et al. (1991)	1/40	83	nr	nr	note c	50.2
Wilkinson & Wilkinson (1986)	1/41	72	65	nr	nr	nr

unless otherwise noted, values represent group means.

nr = not reported

note a–39% between ages 20 to 39, 46% between ages 40 to 59, 15% older than 59 years.

note b–8% below 40, 50% between 40 to 59, 41% older than 59 years.

note c–80% reported some college or higher.

note d–72% of men over 60 years old, 53% of women were in 40s and 50s.

note e–majority are middle-aged, married females, with some college education.

note f–43% had attended college; 21% between 42-49 years old, 22% over 65 years old.

note g–67% had some college.

extroversion, intuition, feeling (judging-feeling dimension not significant). Caldwell and Scott (1994) did an analysis on females and males separately, reporting that females were extroverted, sensing, feeling, and judging. Males were introverted, sensing, feeling, and judging personality types.

Motives. Three motives are found consistently in prior literature. They are a desire to help others, religious/spiritual beliefs, and an experience with the death of a loved one. Murrant and Strathdee (1995) examined the motivations of a sample of hospice volunteers. They reported that volunteers were motivated by a general desire to contribute, and a desire for interaction and growth. Briggs (1987) surveyed 166 hospice volunteers and reported that religious beliefs and having a friend or relative die alone and afraid were motivating factors for becoming a volunteer. In their study of 259 hospice volunteers, Kovacs and Black (1997) reported "Overall, the greatest number of persons learned about the volunteer opportunity (29.8%) through a personal experience with hospice" (p. 48).

Gaps in Literature

Comparing hospice volunteers with other volunteers. While there have been several prior studies adding to our knowledge of hospice volunteering, more remains to be known. For example, prior research has used samples of hospice volunteers solely. No studies could be found which compared hospice volunteers with volunteers serving in different organizations. Such a comparison would be useful because it would help hospice managers develop a sharper image, or a more refined profile, of hospice volunteers. One of the fundamental principles of marketing is that an organization ought to understand its customers as thoroughly as possible in order to develop the most effective marketing mix. The first step in developing a marketing strategy is to define a target market. Differentiating hospice volunteers from other volunteers is a step in this process if one accepts the assumption that potential hospice volunteers are likely to be similar to current hospice volunteers.

Volunteer values. No studies of hospice volunteers could be found which added to our understanding of their values. This gap in the hospice volunteering literature is surprising given the importance values have been given in the volunteer literature. Previous research on volunteer motivations consistently finds that people who volunteer do so as a means of demonstrating or giving expression to strongly-held beliefs. In their national survey of AIDS volunteers, Omoto and Snyder (1990, 1993) took attitude measures of survey respondents. The reported attitudes were then aggregated to a higher level of abstraction to determine what functions attitudes served for the volunteer. The strongest function was interpreted to be "value expressive." The respondents felt that volunteering allowed them to act upon their underlying values, to be their true selves (Snyder and Debono, 1987). Okun and Eisenberg (1992) used a similar methodology to study the motives of 262 senior citizen volunteers. After factor analyzing 13 scale items onto three factors, they interpreted one of the three as "value expressive."

The use of values has proven to discriminate volunteers from nonvolunteers (Heidrich, 1988; Manzer, 1974). Volunteers tend to place more importance on prosocial values (Killeen and McCarrey, 1986; McClintock and Allison, 1989). For example, Hobfoll (1980) found that volunteers were significantly discriminated by social responsibility. Mahoney and Pechura (1980) compared responses on the Rokeach Value Survey (RVS) between telephone hotline volunteers and a control group and found that twelve values discriminated the two groups. Williams (1987) also used the RVS to measure values. In his study of volunteers working with people with mental retardation, Williams found that values were a useful variable to use in differentiating volunteers assisting the mentally retarded from the general public. Other studies have also found values to be good discriminators of volunteers with non-volunteers (Hougland and Christenson, 1982; Williams and Ortega, 1986).

Volunteer intensity. While a small number of studies have examined the issue of hospice volunteer satisfaction, none could be found which examined volunteer intensity. Volunteer intensity refers to the quantity of time a volunteer serves on a regular basis. It is operationalized as the average monthly number of hours a hospice volunteer serves in the organization.

Many managers understand that while the roster may show a large number of volunteers, in practice a smaller number of volunteers represent the more dependable, committed core group upon which the manager relies. Having a better understanding of higher performing volunteers would be useful information to a manager. While volunteer performance is a multidimensional construct, volunteer intensity is one of its dimensions and learning more about who the more intensive hospice volunteers are would add to our present knowledge.

Discussion. Three gaps in the literature on hospice volunteers have been identified: (1) comparing hospice volunteers with other volunteers, (2) developing a better understanding of their values, and (3) identifying correlates of hospice volunteer intensity. While responding to these gaps will make a contribution to the research literature, it will also make practical contributions. By differentiating hospice volunteers from other volunteers, including differentiating the values of hospice volunteers with other volunteers, hospice managers can develop a richer understanding of their volunteers. An improved understanding of hospice volunteers will help the manager develop more persuasive messages in recruitment appeals. A better understanding of the core values of hospice volunteers and how their value systems differ from other volunteers will help managers know what values to emphasize in recruitment appeals and what values to help volunteers express in order to enhance retention. A better understanding of correlates of volunteer intensity may help the manager select and screen volunteers.

METHODOLOGY

Research Questions

In Smith's (1994) review of the prior literature on voluntary participation over the previous 20 years, he recommends that future studies could substantially add to our knowledge by (1) including a comparison group in addition to the study's target group, and (2) by using determinant variables from multiple domains to differentiate the groups. This study responds to both of these recommendations. First, the target group of traditional hospice volunteers is being differentiated from a comparison group of volunteers from other organizations. Second, determinant variables used are from multiple domains: (1) demographic, (2) social-lifestyle, (3) personality, and (4) personal values.

Demographic. Yavas and Reicken (1985) conducted a telephone survey of 329 male volunteers to determine if demographic correlates to volunteering (in general) could be identified. They reported that occupation, age, and education were significant correlates of volunteering. As previously discussed, prior research has added to our knowledge regarding the basic demographic profile of hospice volunteers. However, we do not know if there are demographic variables which help to differentiate hospice volunteers from other volunteers.

H1: Demographic variables should be helpful in differentiating hospice volunteers from other volunteers.

Social and lifestyle variables. In their cross-disciplinary literature review, Wymer, Riecken, and Yavas (1996) discuss previous research which shows the importance of social influences on volunteering. "Social influences provide incentives or disincentives for an individual's volunteer behavior by supporting, failing to support, or discouraging the behavior of volunteering" (p. 11). Church is an important social/religious institution for many people. Church attendance/membership has been consistently and positively correlated with volunteering (Cnaan, Kastemakis, and Wineburg, 1993; Fischer and Schaffer, 1993; Gerard, 1985; Hodgkinson, Weitzman, and Kirsch, 1990). While the causal link between church attendance and volunteerism has been a debated in prior research (cf. Wymer, 1997a), the literature shows that volunteers are more likely to be frequent church attenders or church members.

Facilitation is a variable which has been used in prior research to represent the degree of social support and connectedness between individuals and volunteers or volunteer organizations. Facilitation represents those activities which provide a potential volunteer with information and/or social support (Wymer, 1997b). Prior research has found that a person who is asked by someone to volunteer (typically asked by an associate in an organization to which both belong), is about five time more likely to volunteer than people not personally asked to volunteer (Independent Sector, 1996).

While facilitation accounts for current social influences, it is reasonable to believe that parental attitudes/behaviors regarding volunteering might exert a lasting influence on their children. In their literature review, Wymer, Riecken, and Yavas (1996) identify two studies which support the argument that parents influence their children's future adult volunteer service.

H2: Social-lifestyle variables should be helpful in differentiating hospice volunteers from other volunteers.

Personality. Wymer, Riecken, and Yavas (1996) report that many previous studies which attempted to account for volunteer behavior using personality variables were largely unsuccessful. However, volunteers have been found to exhibit higher levels of emotional empathy than nonvolunteers (Allen & Ruston, 1983; Fahey, 1986; Wymer, 1997b). Empathy is thought to be a motivating dimension underlying an altruistic personality. People with higher levels of emotional empathy are more concerned about the welfare of others, and are more likely to provide help by voluntary assistance than people with lower levels of emotional empathy.

In addition to emotional empathy, there is reason to believe that self-esteem may differentiate hospice volunteers. Self-esteem refers to people's perceptions of their own bundles of skills, talents, and competencies–their self-worth.

Volunteers tend to have positive self-images, feeling capable and competent (Fischer and Schaffer, 1993; Gerard, 1985; Okun, 1994). Miller (1985) reported that volunteers' participation was influenced by the extent to which they felt in control of their lives. In a British national survey which interviewed over 1,000 volunteers, Gerard (1985) wrote " . . . the voluntary workers studied reported better health, found greater meaning in life, and expressed a greater preference for active pursuits. The interviewers assessed them as self-assured" (p. 238).

H3: Self-esteem and empathy should be helpful in differentiating hospice volunteers from other volunteers.

Personal values. While studying the motivations of volunteers, it is important to include values or beliefs in addition to other variables (Schwartz and Howard, 1984). A value is defined as "an enduring belief that a specific mode of conduct or end-state of existence is personally and socially preferable to alternative modes of conduct or end-states of existence" (Rokeach, 1968, p. 160). Fahey (1986) studied motivations in a sample of volunteers and nonvolunteers. She found that "volunteers were guided significantly more by internalized principles and motivations than are nonvolunteers who are more susceptible to peer pressure" (p. 88). Clary and Snyder (1991) wrote that volunteering "helps individuals remain true to their conception of self and allows the expression of deeply held values . . . " (p. 125). Mahoney and Pechura (1980) compared responses of the Rokeach Value Survey (RVS, see Table 2 for listing of 18 terminal values) between telephone hotline volunteers and a control group. They reported that volunteers ranked inner harmony, equality, and self-respect significantly higher in their personal value systems than the control group. Control group subjects ranked a comfortable life and an exciting life significantly higher than volunteers. Mahoney and Pechura concluded that " . . . effective recruitment of volunteers appears to require some understanding of the values of potential volunteers" (p. 1008). As discussed previously, no studies could be found that examined the values of hospice volunteers, and one contribution of this study is that it provides insights into this important group's core values.

H4: Values should be helpful in differentiating hospice volunteers from other volunteers.

Intensity of volunteer service. For an NPO manager, a desirable volunteer performance attribute would be a relatively generous amount of time donated

TABLE 2. Eighteen Terminal Values from Rokeach Value Survey

A Comfortable Life (a prosperous life)	An Exciting Life (a stimulating, active life)
A Sense of Accomplishment (lasting contribution)	A World at Peace (free of war and conflict)
A World of Beauty (beauty of nature & the arts)	Equality (brotherhood, equal opport.)
Family Security (taking care of loved ones)	Freedom (independence, free choice)
Happiness (contentedness)	Inner Harmony (freedom from inner conflict)
Mature Love (sexual & spiritual intimacy)	National Security (protection from attack)
Pleasure (an enjoyable, leisurely life)	Salvation (saved, eternal life)
Self-Respect (self-esteem)	Social Recognition (respect, admiration)
True Friendship (close companionship)	Wisdom (mature understanding of life)

on a regular basis. Although the amount of time a volunteer donates to his/her organization(s) does not capture the complete conceptual domain of "performance," the amount of time volunteered is one important dimension of the domain. Managers would likely be interested in identifying or better understanding volunteers who donate greater numbers of hours compared to those volunteers who give very little of their time. Because no prior studies could be found to assist in predicting important variables associated with hospice volunteering intensity, this relationship will be examined in an exploratory manner.

H5: The determinant variables selected in this study should be useful in differentiating hospice volunteers by volunteer intensity.

Procedures

Measures. Consistent with the approach of previous studies of volunteers, demographic and lifestyle variables were obtained. These included church membership, church attendance, age, gender, education, income, home ownership, marital status, employment status, parental volunteerism, family volunteerism, and family size. Empathy was measured using the Emotional Empathy Scale (Mehrabian and Epstein, 1972).

This study used the Rokeach Value Survey instrument (Rokeach, 1973; see Table 1) to measure terminal values. The RVS has been used in previous research on volunteers (Heidrich, 1988; Mahoney and Pechura, 1980; Williams, 1986, 1987). The instrument instructs respondents to rank 18 terminal values by order of perceived importance. The RVS has been in use and revised several times since its initial development in 1967. Feather (1975) and Braithwaite and Scott (1991) discuss the psychometric properties of the RVS and provide evidence of the instrument's reliability and validity.

The ranking procedure of the RVS is simple to administer, and captures the concept of a hierarchy of values based upon subjects' own comparisons. The main disadvantage of the ranking procedure, ordinal data, can be overcome by data transformation. The ranks from 1 to 18 are transformed to standard scores (Z scores). This transformation is based on the assumption that differences between ranks at the extremes offer greater discrimination than differences between ranks nearer the middle. This is a common assumption in ranking procedures (Meddis 1984). Hollen (1967) provided support for this assumption. He found that values rated most and least important changed the least, whereas values rated near the middle changed the most, between test and retest (Feather, 1975; Hays, 1967).

Facilitation was measured using five 9-point Likert scales which assess the degree to which respondents had access to information or social support linked to an NPO (Cronbach alpha reliability coefficient .70; Wymer, 1997b).

Sample and data acquisition. Approximately 40 NPOs in two midwestern cities (Bloomington and Indianapolis, Indiana) agreed to participate in the study. The participating NPOs represented a diversity of missions. Volunteers serving in these organizations were mailed a survey which contained a cover letter, a questionnaire, and a business reply return envelope. No incentives were offered to respondents.

There were 1,016 completed questionnaires (of 3,400 delivered) from volunteers. The response rate was approximately 30 percent. This response rate is similar to that reported by Gillespie and King (1985). They conducted a mail survey of Red Cross volunteers, reporting 1,346 returned question-naires for a 26.9 response rate.

Because a sample frame for the volunteer populations in the two cities was not available, a nonprobability sample was taken. Therefore, sample repre-sentativeness was a concern. Collecting data from a number of NPOs in two cities to comprise a relatively large sample helps to reduce the likelihood that the sample will differ in some important way from the population of interest (Bryman and Cramer, 1990). Also, as a representativeness check, administra-tors familiar with their volunteers in 10 participating organizations were contacted after the sample was collected. They were asked to describe the demographic characteristics of their volunteers. Then the administrators were asked to describe the demographic characteristics of volunteers in other orga-nizations with which they were familiar. Finally, the administrators were given a description of the sample and asked to comment on the degree of similarity to volunteers in their organizations. Results of this check supported the representativeness of the sample.

Hospice volunteers were identified from their answer to a question which asked them to print the name of their primary volunteer organization. It was recognized that respondents could volunteer for multiple organizations. Therefore, having respondents print the name of their primary organizations served as a control. There were 63 hospice volunteers and 953 volunteers from other organizations. Hospice volunteers ranged from 23 to 86 years of age (mean = 54). The comparison group of volunteers ranged from 16 to 93 years of age (mean = 51). Hospice volunteers tended to be female (75 percent female) as did the comparison group of volunteers (72 percent female). This gender imbalance is similar to that of other studies discussed previously.

In terms of employment status, 41 percent of hospice volunteers were employed on a full-time basis (36% for other volunteers). In terms of marital status, 53 percent of hospice volunteers were married (66% for other volun-teers). In regards to home ownership status, 77 percent of both hospice and other volunteers rented their homes. Hospice volunteers reported receiving an average of 16 years of education (15.6 years for other volunteers). All volunteers tended to be members of religious institutions (78%, hospice;

73%, other volunteers). Hospice volunteers reported attending an average of 5.8 religious services each month (3.6 for other volunteers). Hospice volunteers volunteer, on average, in 1.75 organizations (2.01 for other volunteers). They work a monthly average of 13.86 hours in their primary organization (15.35, other volunteers) and 20.20 hours in all of the organizations for which they volunteer (21.53, other volunteers).

Analysis. Logistic regression was used to assess the contribution of the variables described previously as predictors of hospice volunteering. Logistic regression is the appropriate method of analysis in predicting a dichotomous dependent variable such as a dummy variable representing hospice volunteers and other volunteers (Aldrich and Nelson, 1984).

In examining the association of the independent variables with volunteer intensity, the statistical analysis involved a series of stepwise multiple regression procedures. First, the independent variables were regressed on the average monthly number of hours hospice volunteers donated in all organizations for which they gave time. Second, the independent variables were regressed on the average monthly number of hours hospice volunteers served in their primary volunteer organization. In the final analysis, the independent variables were regressed on a dependent variable representing the number of NPO organizations in which hospice volunteers reported serving. Data set diagnostics included examining the correlation matrix, Cook's distance statistics, and variance inflation factors (VIF). One outlier was detected and removed.

FINDINGS

Differentiating Hospice Volunteers from Other Volunteers

The logistic regression results are shown in Table 3. The model was accurate in predicting group differences in 93% of the cases. The -2 log likelihood (391) is statistically significant. The first column shows the variables which were found to be significant predictors of hospice volunteering. The second column shows the logistic coefficients (ß). These coefficients are not easily interpreted. In the case of the first significant variable, age, the coefficient means that for every 1 year increase in age, the log odds of the probability of the dependent variable increases by .0187. The third column lists the standard errors of the variables. The forth column lists the Wald statistic with degree of significance indicated by asterisks.

The fifth column lists *R*. This is a statistic used to examine the partial correlation between the dependent variable and each of the independent variables. The "R" value is constrained to be between -1 and $+1$. The magnitude of "R" indicates the contribution of the independent variable to the model.

TABLE 3. Logistic Regression Results: Hospice Volunteers vs. Other Volunteers

Variable	β	Std Err.	Wald	R	Exp (β)	Sig of Log L.R.
Age	.0187	.0082	5.2491*	.0847	1.0189	.0220
Number[a]	−.4008	.1400	8.1985**	−.1170	.6698	.0016
Self-Esteem Score	−.4957	.2405	4.2503*	−.0705	.6091	.0206
Sense of Accomp.[b]	.5946	.1967	9.1364**	.1255	.5518	.0018
World at Peace	.3621	.1724	4.4148*	.0730	.6962	.0356
Family Security	.4721	.2051	5.2994*	.0854	.6237	.0166
Inner Harmony	.7499	.2123	12.4798***	.1521	.4724	.0001
Mature Love	.4835	.1633	8.7632**	.1222	.6166	.0023
Salvation	.3987	.1118	12.7217***	.1539	.6712	.0002
True Friendship	.6452	.2307	7.8172**	.1133	.5246	.0035
Wisdom	.5955	.1956	9.2679**	.1267	.5513	.0015
Constant	−3.9522	.7104	30.9481***			

Dependent variable = Hospice volunteer (1)/Other volunteer (0).
−2 Log Likelihood = 391
Goodness of Fit = 826, Model Chi-Square = 63 (11 df), $p < .001$.
Total number of cases = 1,013 (rejected because of missing data = 102).
Classification accuracy of model: 93% of cases.
a = Number of organizations for which person volunteers time.
b = A Sense of Accomplishment.
* $p < .05$; ** $p < .01$; *** $p < .001$.

The sixth column lists *Exp* (ß). This is the factor by which the odds change from a one unit change in the associated independent variable. For example, if we increase age by one unit (1 year), the odds of hospice volunteering increase by a factor of 1.0189.

The seventh and final column lists *Sig of Log L.R.*, which represents the significance of the log likelihood ratio. This statistic is helpful in understanding the usefulness of a variable to the model. For example, if the value "salvation" were removed from the model, it would get significantly worse because the log likelihood ratio is statistically significant.

One demographic variable is a significant predictor of hospice volunteering-Age. Hospice volunteers are older, on average, than volunteers in other types of nonprofit organizations. The average age of hospice volunteers, as previously reported, is about three years older than the comparison group of other volunteers.

One social-lifestyle variable was included in the model. Hospice volunteers serve, on average, in fewer volunteer organizations than do other volunteers (group means reported previously).

One of the two personality variables was included in the model-self-esteem. Hospice volunteers were found to have lower average levels of self-esteem than other volunteers.

Values are useful in predicting hospice volunteering. In examining the value differences between hospice volunteers and other volunteers, the two groups are differentiated by eight values: a sense of accomplishment, a world at peace, family security, inner harmony, mature love, salvation, true friendship, and wisdom. Hospice volunteers placed significantly more importance on these values within their personal value systems than did other volunteers.

Influences on the Intensity and Breadth of Hospice Volunteering

Obviously, volunteers differ in terms of their performance. One dimension of performance investigated here is the average monthly hours hospice volunteers serve in their organizations. A complicating factor is that people can either volunteer for a single organization or for multiple organizations. There may be a commitment to a primary organization and its purpose, or a person may feel a duty to "volunteer" in a general sense and may more equally distribute donated time in two or more NPOs.

To take into account the complexity of multiple organization volunteering, three separate stepwise multiple regressions were performed. First, the predictor variables previously described were regressed on a variable representing the average number of hours hospice volunteers reported volunteering in all organizations in which they serve. Second, the dependent variable was changed to one representing the average monthly hours donated for the organization in which hospice volunteers reported feeling the most commitment (i.e., their primary organization). Third, the dependent variable was changed to one representing the total number of organizations for which hospice volunteers donate time. The results of these regressions are shown in Table 4.

Hours in multiple NPOs. In the first regression four variables are significant. They are one demographic variable (employment status), one personality variable (self-esteem), and two values, "a sense of accomplishment" and "true friendship." Hospice volunteers who donate relatively larger numbers of hours

TABLE 4. Regression Results: Hospice Volunteer Performance

Independent Variables	b	Std. Error	Beta	t
1st Regression[a]				
Constant	8.413	6.403		1.3
Employment[b]	− 17.479	3.773	− .463	− 4.6***
Self-Esteem	13.236	4.118	.326	3.2**
Sense of Accomp.[c]	5.868	1.968	.301	3.0**
True Friendship	6.271	2.534	.246	2.5*
R^2 = .418 R^2_{adj} = .378 N = 63				
2nd Regression[d]				
Constant	− 5.507	4.182		− 1.3
Age	0.366	0.075	.503	4.9***
Sense of Accomp.[c]	3.402	1.168	.298	2.9**
Pleasure	3.721	1.340	.287	2.8**
R^2 = .373 R^2_{adj} = .341 N = 63				
3rd Regression[e]				
Constant	− .480	.333		− 1.4
Church attendance	.066	.014	.431	4.7***
Hours, all orgs	.026	.005	.463	5.3***
Income	.133	.048	.235	2.8**
Family vol[f]	.802	.202	.369	4.0***
Wisdom	.339	.112	.261	3.0**
Gender[g]	.454	.220	.185	2.1*
R^2 = .615 R^2_{adj} = .574 N = 63				

a ☞ Dep. variable = hours in all organizations.

b ☞ Employment status. 1 = full-time. 0 = part-time.

c ☞ A sense of accomplishment.

d ☞ Dep. variable = hours in primary organization.

e ☞ Dep. variable = number of organizations.

f ☞ Family volunteers together.

g ☞ Female 1, male = 0.

* $p < .05$; ** $p < .01$; *** $p < .001$

in multiple NPOs are less likely to be fully employed compared to hospice volunteers who give less time across organizations. The more giving hospice volunteers have higher levels of self-esteem, which may be an enabling factor. Persons with higher levels of self-esteem may find volunteering in a number of organizations less stressful than persons with comparatively low self-esteem.

In terms of values which separate hospice volunteers by the time they serve in their volunteer organizations, the more giving volunteers place significantly less importance on "true friendship." These volunteers appear less concerned about achieving a close, intimate friendship with another individual than their counterparts. They also appear to be achievers, seeking to derive "a sense of accomplishment" from their volunteer work.

Hours in primary organization. Whereas the previous analysis examined hospice volunteering in multiple organizations, this analysis examines hospice volunteering in the volunteer's primary organization. Three variables are significantly associated with greater numbers of hours volunteered in primary organizations. One demographic variable, age, is associated with greater numbers of hours volunteered in primary organizations. Two values, "a sense of accomplishment," and "pleasure," are also associated with volunteering more hours in primary organizations.

Hospice volunteers who serve the most hours in their organizations are older than other volunteers, and they feel that "a sense of accomplishment" and "pleasure" are more important values than other volunteers. In addition to be older, on average, the more intensive volunteers seek to derive a sense of accomplishment from their work. They may also enjoy their volunteer work more, compared to other volunteers.

Number of NPOs. In the third regression, the dependent variable represents the number of organizations in which the hospice volunteer donates his or her time. There are six significant, positive predictors of volunteering in greater numbers of organizations. They are frequency of church attendance, average monthly hours donated in all organizations, income, family volunteers together, "wisdom," and gender.

In terms of demographic variables, hospice volunteers working in a greater number of volunteer organizations are more likely to be female and have comparatively higher incomes. In terms of social/lifestyle variables, these volunteers appear to attend church more regularly, work more hours in their volunteer organizations, and volunteer more often with their family members than other volunteers. One value predicted more multiorganizational volunteering–"wisdom."

DISCUSSION

One purpose of this study was to determine if hospice volunteers could be differentiated from other volunteers using various determinant variables. The determinant variables used were from multiple conceptual domains: demographic, social/lifestyle, personality, and personal values. The hypothesis that hospice volunteers could be differentiated from other volunteers using these determinant variables was supported. The logistic regression analysis resulted in 11 significant predictors of hospice volunteering.

Another purpose of this investigation was to determine if values were useful in differentiating hospice volunteering. We report that values appear to be a useful determinant factor in differentiating hospice volunteering. In Table 3 we show that 8 of the 11 significant predictor variables are values.

A final purpose of this study was to account for variations of volunteer intensity using the determinant variables also used to differentiate hospice volunteers from other volunteers. A series of three regression procedures were performed. In the first regression, the dependent variable was the average monthly hours volunteers serve in all organizations for which they donate time. The analysis resulted in four significant predictor variables with about 42 percent of the variance accounted for by the regression equation.

In the second regression analysis, the dependent variable was the average monthly number of hours the hospice volunteer serves in his or her primary organization. This analysis produced a regression equation explaining about 37 percent of the variance in the dependent variable, finding three significant predictor variables.

The dependent variable for the final multiple regression was the total number of organizations in which the volunteer serves. The procedure produced a regression equation explaining about 62 percent of the variance, resulting in six significant predictor variables.

In summary, the purposes of this study were largely fulfilled. This investigation has responded to gaps in the literature identified previously and added to our knowledge by: (1) demonstrating that hospice volunteers are able to be differentiated from other types of volunteers using determinant variables from multiple conceptual domains, (2) adding to our understanding about the values of hospice volunteers and how their values differ from other volunteers' values, and (3) by using determinant variables to account for three variations of volunteer intensity.

Managerial Implications

The findings reported here have important implications for hospice managers. While future research is needed to replicate and extend this initial work, our understanding of hospice volunteers is enriched by using the methodology described in this study.

A contribution of this study is that it demonstrates the distinctiveness of an important subgroup of volunteers–hospice volunteers. The more managers of hospice organizations know about their volunteers, the better equipped they will be to develop effective tactics to *recruit* new volunteers, *retain* current volunteers, and *return* former volunteers to active service (the 3 R's of volunteer marketing management).

The manager of a hospice organization's first step in recruiting volunteers is to first research them, attempting to better understand them. Kotler and Scheff (1997) state: "This means understanding who the volunteers are, why they volunteer, and how to 'speak' to them" (p. 424).

A first step in developing a deeper understanding of hospice volunteers is to "segment" them. Segmenting in this sense means to aggregate individual hospice volunteers into a common grouping, and then to differentiate them from other groups of volunteers. The hospice manager must find appropriate bases upon which to segment his or her volunteers. This study used variables from demographic, social/lifestyle, personality, and personal values bases. The bases found to be most useful were personal values, followed by demographic variables. Finding other bases upon which to segment hospice volunteers or finding other important variables within the conceptual domains used in this study would be productive areas of future research.

Once the group is adequately segmented (differentiated from other volunteers), the manager can then develop a profile of his or her volunteers. The variables found to predict hospice volunteers can be useful in developing such a profile. In our initial work here, we reported that hospice volunteers were older, volunteered in fewer organizations, and had lower levels of self-esteem than other types of volunteers. In addition, eight values were reported which hospice volunteers placed a significantly greater importance upon than other volunteers.

Significant variables from demographic, social-lifestyle, personality, and value domains may be useful in helping a manager identify who current volunteers are, their interests and activities, and their core values. Assuming that current volunteers are similar to potential volunteers most likely to be attracted to the hospice organization and most likely to derive a satisfying experience, potential volunteers in the community who are similar to current volunteers represent an attractive target group for recruitment. A profile from these conceptual domains can help a manager identify prospective volunteers and communicate a message that will appeal to their interests and values.

In a manager's efforts to retain current hospice volunteers, knowing something of their values can be important. Managers should understand if volunteers are seeking to express their religious beliefs in their volunteer work, or if they are attempting to derive a feeling of accomplishment, or if they are seeking meaningful interpersonal relationships. Unmet fulfillment of core values can produce an ambivalence to volunteering and stimulate a search for alternatives for value expression. Managers with an understanding in these areas can attempt to provide volunteers with meaningful, satisfying, value expressive experiences.

In the introduction, volunteers were presented as an important group of customers of nonprofit organizations. Just as managers in commercial organizations would like to know how to identify their most profitable customers, nonprofit managers need to know how to identify their potentially more productive volunteers.

One simple way to assess productivity is by examining the hours volunteers serve. (Obviously, there are multiple factors to consider when assessing volunteer productivity.) The methodology used in this study produced significant variables which differentiated volunteers on the amount of time they donated. One productive area for future research would be to better understand the dimensionality of volunteer performance and to discover predictors of superior volunteer performance. The ability to better predict volunteer performance would enable NPO managers to more effectively select and place volunteers.

Although most NPO managers are responsible for recruiting volunteers for their own organizations, some NPO managers serve in umbrella organizations (supporting other NPOs) whose mission it is to increase the supply of volunteers and to refer them to recruiting organizations. The Retired Senior Volunteer Program (RSVP), as an example, is such an umbrella organization. RSVP agencies recruit senior citizens and place them with other NPOs requesting volunteers. Findings from this study are important to managers of umbrella organizations because this study examined volunteering in a multiple organization context. The findings showed that there are volunteers who donate time in a number of organizations and that these volunteers can be differentiated from other volunteers. Umbrella organizations would be interested in identifying potential volunteers who are willing to donate time in a number of NPOs.

Limitations

Since this study is among the first to differentiate hospice volunteers from other volunteers, its findings are generally exploratory and descriptive in nature. The methodology used is intended to be an initial step in adding to our knowledge of how to differentiate subgroups of volunteers in general. It is hoped that future research will build upon this initial work. Furthermore, while the sample was derived from many organizations, it was not randomly drawn and was limited to two cities within a single midwestern state. Generalizations to other populations should be made with this limitation in mind.

CONCLUSION

This study was not only useful in demonstrating a methodology for better understanding a largely overlooked group of volunteers, it also has important implications for future research. First, the population of volunteers should not be thought of as a monolithic, homogenous group. The total population of volunteers is composed of diverse subgroups.

Second, this study is important because it demonstrates the efficacy of understanding one's target market (in this case, hospice volunteers) by learning how it differs from other market segments. Our understanding of volunteerism can be enhanced by learning how a particular volunteer segment differs from other segments. Few studies of volunteerism have used comparison groups. Those that have used comparison groups have generally used nonvolunteers (Cnaan and Goldberg-Glen, 1991). This study demonstrates the added insights provided by using a comparison group of other types of volunteers.

Third, this study demonstrates the utility of examining volunteerism using a multidimensional approach (i.e., using determinant variables from multiple conceptual domains). Reviewing 20 years of previous research on voluntary participation, Smith (1994) made a recommendation for future research to begin using such a multidimensional approach. Smith commented on the shortfalls of a narrower approach (e.g., relying exclusively on demographic variables) and noted the dearth of research taking a more comprehensive approach. This study demonstrates the increased understanding of an important subgroup of volunteers by learning how it differs from other groups in terms of demographic variables, social/lifestyle variables, personality, and values.

AUTHOR NOTE

Walter W. Wymer, Jr.'s area of interests are marketing management of nonprofit organizations, volunteer segmentation/psychology, church marketing, professional services marketing, and service marketing performance.

Becky J. Starnes is also a retired U.S. Air Force officer where she specialized in administration and Total Quality Management. Her research interests include the management and marketing of nonprofit organizations.

REFERENCES

Aldrich, J.H., and Nelson, F.D. (1984), *Linear Probability, Logit, and Probit Models* (Sage University Papers Series on Quantitative Applications in the Social Sciences, No. 07-045). Beverly Hills, CA: Sage.

Allen, N.J. and Rushton, J.P. (1983), "Personality Characteristics of Community Mental Health Volunteers: A Review," *Journal of Voluntary Action Research*, 12 (1), 36-49.

Braithwaite, V.A. and Scott, W.A. (1991), "Values," in Robinson, J.P., Shaver, P.R., and Wrightsman (eds), *Measures of Personality and Social Psychological Attitudes*, vol. 1. New York: Academic Press.

Briggs, J.S. (1987), "Volunteer Qualities: A Survey of Hospice Volunteers," *Oncology Nursing Forum*, 14 (1), 27-31.

Bryman, A. and Cramer, D. (1990), *Quantitative Data Analysis for Social Scientists*. London: Routledge.

Bunn, E. (1984), "Volunteers as the Backbone," *American Journal of Hospice Care*, 1 (1), 34-36.

Caldwell, J. and Scott, J.P. (1994), "Effective Hospice Volunteers: Demographic and Personality Characteristics," *The American Journal of Hospice & Palliative Care*, 11 (2), 40-45.

Caty, S. and Tamlyn, D. (1983), "Hospice Volunteers: A Recruitment Profile," *Dimensions in Health Service*, 60 (12), 22-23.

Chevrier, F., Steuer, R. and MacKenzie, J. (1994), "Factors Affecting Satisfaction Among Community-Based Hospice Volunteer Visitors," *The American Journal of Hospice & Palliative Care*, 11 (4), 30-37.

Clary, E.G. and Snyder, M. (1991), "A Functional Analysis of Altruism and Prosocial Behavior: The Case of Volunteerism," in Clark, M.S. (ed), *Review of Personality and Social Psychology*, vol 12. Newbury Park, CA: Sage.

Cnaan, R.A., Kasternakis, A., and Wineburg, R.J. (1993), "Religious People, Religious Congregations, and Volunteerism in Human Services: Is There a Link?" *Nonprofit & Voluntary Sector Quarterly*, 22 (1), 33-5 1.

Cnaan, R.A., and Goldberg-Glen, R. (1991), "Measuring Motivation to Volunteer in Human Services," *Journal of Applied Behavioral Sciences*, 27 (3), 269-284.

Craig, M. (1994), "Volunteer Services," *The American Journal of Hospice & Palliative Care*, 11 (2), 33-35.

Fahey, M. (1986), "Lay Volunteers Within an American Catholic Parish: Personality and Social Factors," doctoral dissertation, University of San Francisco.

Feather, N.T. (1975), *Values in Education and Society*. New York: The Free Press.

Field, D. and Johnson, I. (1993), "Satisfaction and Change: A Survey of Volunteers in a Hospice Organisation," *Social Science Medicine*, 36 (12), 1625-1633.

Fischer, L.R., and Schaffer, K.B. (1993), *Older Volunteers: A Guide to Research and Practice*. Newbury Park, CA: Sage.

Gerard, D. (1985), "What Makes a Volunteer?" *New Society*, 74 (Nov 8), 236-238.

Gillespie, D.F., and King, A.E. (1985), "Demographic Understanding of Volunteerism," *Journal of Sociology and Social Welfare*, 12 (4), 798-816.

Hall, S.E. and Marshall, K. (1996), "Enhancing Volunteer Effectiveness," *The American Journal of Hospice & Palliative Care*, 13 (May/June), 22-25.

Hays, W.L. (1967), *Quantification in Psychology*. Belmont, CA: Brooks-Cole.

Hayslip, B. and Walling, M.L. (1985), "Impact of Hospice Volunteer Training on Death Anxiety and Locus of Control," *Omega*, 16 (3), 243-254.

Hegeman, M.T. (1994), "A book review of 'In the Light of Dying: The Journals of a Hospice Volunteer'," *Catholic World*, 237 (1421), 241-242.

Heidrich, K.W. (1988), "Lifestyles of Volunteers: A Market Segmentation Study," Ph.D. dissertation, University of Illinois at Urbana-Champaign.

Hoad, P. (1991), "Volunteers in the Independent Hospice Movement," *Sociology of Health & Illness*, 13 (2), 231-248.

Hobfoll, S.E. (1980), "Personal Characteristics of the College Volunteer," *American Journal of Community Psychology*, 8 (4), 503-506.

Hodgkinson, V.A., Weitzman, M.S., and Kirsch, A.D. (1990), "From Commitment to Action: How Religious Involvement Affects Giving and Volunteering," in Wuthnow, R., Hodgkinson, V.A., and Associates (eds.), *Faith and Philanthropy in America: Exploring the Role of Religion in America's Voluntary Sector.* San Francisco: Jossey-Bass, 1990.

Hollen, C.C. (1967), "The Stability of Values and Value Systems," M.A. thesis, Michigan State University.

Hospice Association of America (1997), *Hospice Facts & Statistics.* Washington, D.C.: author.

Hougland, J.G. and Christenson, J.A. (1982), "Voluntary Organizations and Dominant American Values," *Journal of Voluntary Action Research*, 11 (4), 6-26.

Independent Sector (1996), *Volunteering and Giving in the United States: Findings From a National Survey.* Washington, D.C.: author.

Killeen, J. and McCarrey, M. (1986), "Relations of Altruistic Versus Competitive Values, Course of Study, and Behavioral Intentions to Help or Compete," *Psychological Reports*, 59 (2), 895-898.

Kotler, P. and Scheff, J. (1997), *Standing Room Only: Strategies for Marketing the Performing Arts.* Boston, MA: Harvard Business School Press.

Kovacs, P.J. and Black, B. (1997), "Differentiating Recruitment Strategies for Direct Patient Care, Clerical, and Fundraising Hospice Volunteers," *The Hospice Journal*, 12 (4), 43-56.

Lafer, B. (1989), "Predicting Satisfactoriness and Persistence in Hospice Volunteers," Ph.D. dissertation, Seton Hall University.

Lafer, B. (1991). "The Attrition of Hospice Volunteers," *Omega*, 23 (3), 161-168.

Mahoney, J. and Pechura, C.M. (1980), "Values and Volunteers: Axiology of Altruism in a Crisis Center," *Psychological Reports*, 47 (3), 1007-1012.

Manzer, L.L. (1974), "Charitable Health Organization Donor Behavior: An Empirical Study of Value and Attitude Structure," Ph.D. dissertation, Oklahoma State University.

McClintock, C.G. and Allison, S.T. (1989), "Social Value Orientation and Helping Behavior," *Journal of Applied Psychology*, 19 (4), 353-362.

Meddis, R. (1984), *Statistics Using Ranks: A Unified Approach.* New York: Basil Blackwell.

Mehrabian, A., and Epstein, N. (1972), "A Measure of Emotional Empathy," *Journal of Personality*, 40, 525-543.

Miller, L.E. (1985), "Understanding the Motivation of Volunteers: An Examination of Personality Differences and Characteristics of Volunteers' Paid Employment," *Journal of Voluntary Action Research*, 1985, 14 (2-3), 112-122.

Mitchell, C.W. and Shuff, I.M. (1995), "Personality Characteristics of Hospice Volunteers as Measured by Myers-Briggs Type Indicator," *Journal of Personality Assessment*, 65 (3) 521-532.

Murrant, G. and Strathdee, S.A. (1995), "Motivations for Service Volunteer Involvement at Casey House AIDS Hospice," *The Hospice Journal*, 10 (3), 27-37.

Neigh, J.E. (1995), "Surviving and Keeping the Heart in Hospice–Not Mutually Exclusive," *Caring Magazine*, 14 (Oct), 12-18.

Okun, M.A. (1994), "The Relation Between Motives for Organizational Volunteering and the Frequency of Volunteering by Elders," *The Journal of Applied Gerontology*, 13 (2), 115-126.

Okun, M.A. and Eisenberg, N. (1992), "Motives and Intent to Continue Organizational Volunteering among Residents of a Retirement Community Area," *Journal of Community Psychology*, 20 (3), 183-187.

Omoto, A.M. and Snyder, M. (1990), "Basic Research in Action: Volunteerism and Society's Response to AIDS," *Personality and Social Psychology Bulletin*, 16 (1), 152-165.

Omoto, A.M. and Snyder, M. (1993), "AIDS Volunteers and Their Motivations: Theoretical Issues and Practical Concerns," *Nonprofit Management & Leadership*, 4 (2), 157-176.

Paradis, L.F., and Usui, W.M. (1987), "Hospice Volunteers: The Impact of Personality Characteristics on Retention and Job Performance," *The Hospice Journal*, 3 (1), 3-30.

Robbins, R.A. (1992), "Death Competency: A Study of Hospice Volunteers," *Death Studies*, 16 (6), 557-569.

Rokeach, M. (1973), *The Nature of Human Values*. New York: The Free Press.

Rokeach, M. (1968), *Beliefs, Attitudes, and Values: A Theory of Organization and Change*. San Francisco: Jossey-Bass.

Schwartz, S.H., and Howard, J.A. (1984), "Internalized Values as Motivators of Altruism," in Staub, E., Bar-Tal, D., and Karylowski, J. (eds.), *Development and Maintenance of Prosocial Behavior*. New York: Plenum.

Scott, J.P. and Caldwell, J. (1996), "Needs and Program Strengths: Perceptions of Hospice Volunteers," *The Hospice Journal*, 11 (1), 19-30.

Self, D.R. and Starnes, B.J. (1998), "Strategic Marketing Alliances for Hospices: Horizontal Alliances," *Health Marketing Quarterly*, 16 (3), forthcoming.

Shuff, I.M., Horne, A.M., Westberg, N.G., Mooney, S.P., and Mitchell, C.W. (1991), "Volunteers Under Threat: AIDS Hospice Volunteers Compared to Volunteers in a Traditional Hospice," *The Hospice Journal*, 7 (1/2), 85-107.

Silbert, D. (1985). "Assessing Volunteer Satisfaction in Hospice Work," *American Journal of Hospice Care*, 2 (2), 36-40.

Smith, D.H. (1994), "Determinants of Voluntary Association Participation and Volunteering: A Literature Review," *Nonprofit and Voluntary Sector Quarterly*, 23 (3), 243-264.

Snyder, M. and Debono, K.G. (1987), "A Functional Approach to Attitudes and Persuasion," in *Social influence: The Ontario Symposium*, vol. 5, ed. M.P. Zanna, J.M. Olson, and C.P. Herman, 107-125. Hillsdale, NJ: Lawrence Erlbaum.

Stephany, T. (1989), "Identifying Roles of Hospice Volunteers," *Home Healthcare Nurse*, 7 (3), 51-52.

Wilkinson, H.J. and Wilkinson, J.W. (1986), "Evaluation of a Hospice Volunteer Training Program," *Omega*, 17 (3), 263-27.

Williams, J.A. and Ortega, S.T. (1986), "The Multidimensionality of Joining," *Journal of Voluntary Action Research*, 15, 35-44.

Williams, R.F. (1986), "The Values of Volunteer Benefactors," *Mental Retardation*, 24, 163-168.

Williams, R.F. (1987), "Receptivity to Persons with Mental Retardation: A Study of Volunteer Interest," *American Journal of Mental Retardation*, 92 (3), 299-303.

Wright, N.D., Larson, V., and Higgs, R. (1995), "Marketing of Voluntarism: The Case of Appalachian Mountain Housing," *Journal of Consumer Satisfaction, Dissatisfaction, and Complaining Behavior*, 8, 188-197.

Wymer, W.W. (1997a), "A Religious Motivation to Volunteer? Exploring the Linkage Between Volunteering and Religious Values," *Journal of Nonprofit & Public Sector Marketing*, 5 (3), 3-17.

Wymer, W.W. (1997b), "Segmenting Volunteers Using Values, Self-esteem, Empathy, and Facilitation as Determinant Variables," *Journal of Nonprofit & Public Sector Marketing*, 5 (2), 3-28.

Wymer, W.W., Riecken, G., and Yavas, U. (1996), "Determinants of Volunteerism: A Cross Disciplinary Review and Research Agenda," *Journal of Nonprofit & Public Sector Marketing*, 4 (4), 3-26.

Yavas, U. and Riecken, G. (1981), "Volunteer Recruitment: A Marketing Approach," in Bernhardt et al. (eds.), *The Changing Marketing Environment: New Theories and Applications*. Chicago: American Marketing Association.

Yavas, U. and Riecken, G. (1985), "Can Volunteers be Targeted?" *Journal of the Academy of Marketing Science*, 13 (2), 218-228.

Hospital Volunteers as Customers: Understanding Their Motives, How They Differ from Other Volunteers, and Correlates of Volunteer Intensity

Walter W. Wymer, Jr.

SUMMARY. The research objectives were to better understand the motives of hospital volunteers, determine if hospital volunteers could be differentiated from other volunteers using determinant variables from multiple conceptual domains, and to discover correlates which may predict more intensive volunteering.

Social lifestyle, demographic, personality, and terminal value measures were obtained from a sample of 105 hospital volunteers and 908 volunteers serving in other organizations. Survey respondents were derived from over 40 nonprofit organizations in two midwestern cities.

In comparing hospital volunteers to volunteers serving in other types of organizations, hospital volunteers are differentiated by two demographic variables (age and average hours volunteered each month), two social lifestyle variables (the number of volunteer organizations in which they serve and the frequency of attendance at religious services), one personality variable (self-esteem), and one value (a world of beauty).

Determinates of three facets of volunteer intensity were examined: the number of hours worked in all volunteer organizations, the number of hours worked for the volunteer's primary organization, and the number of organizations in which the volunteer serves.

Walter W. Wymer, Jr., DBA, is Assistant Professor of Marketing, Christopher Newport University, Newport News, VA 23606 (E-mail: wwymer@ cnu.edu).

[Haworth co-indexing entry note]: "Hospital Volunteers as Customers: Understanding Their Motives, How They Differ from Other Volunteers, and Correlates of Volunteer Intensity." Wymer, Walter W., Jr. Co-published simultaneously in *Journal of Nonprofit & Public Sector Marketing* (The Haworth Press, Inc.) Vol. 6, No. 2/3, 1999, pp. 51-76; and: *Volunteerism Marketing: New Vistas for Nonprofit and Public Sector Management* (ed: Donald R. Self and Walter W. Wymer, Jr.) The Haworth Press, Inc., 1999, pp. 51-76. Single or multiple copies of this article are available for a fee from The Haworth Document Delivery Service [1-800-342-9678, 9:00 a.m. - 5:00 p.m. (EST). E-mail address: getinfo@haworthpressinc.com].

51

A qualitative section of this article provides insights into events leading to hospital volunteering, influences on volunteer retention, and perceived benefits and rewards of hospital volunteering. Managerial implications of the findings are discussed. *[Article copies available for a fee from The Haworth Document Delivery Service: 1-800-342-9678. E-mail address: getinfo@haworthpressinc.com <Website: http://www.haworthpressinc. com>]*

INTRODUCTION

. . . the world of volunteering is like a marketplace, . . . unfilled volunteer assignments are like unsold products, .·. . alternative activities are like competitors, . . . volunteers are like buyers, and . . . volunteer administrators are like marketers.

Heidrich, 1988

Volunteering in America is an important component of our society in general and especially important to the thousands of nonprofit organizations (NPOs) which rely on their generosity. In 1995, the Independent Sector (1996) commissioned the Gallup Organization to conduct a national study on giving and volunteering in America. They reported that, in 1995, 93 million Americans volunteered 20.3 billion hours of labor. Many NPOs are highly dependent upon donated labor from volunteers willing to forego alternative consumption activities to expend some of their time in volunteer service.

A marketing oriented approach to volunteer recruitment would be to treat them as a customer group (Yavas and Riecken, 1981). Wright and Higgs (1995) conducted a study of volunteering in a charitable organization which builds low cost homes for the poor and concluded that this organization's volunteers were their most important group of customers because the supply of volunteers was scarce whereas the supply of consumers needing the organization's services (low cost homes) was plentiful.

One of the key principles in managing volunteers, according to Canada-based Heart and Stroke Foundation, is to treat them as customers (Adams and Shepherd 1996). While volunteers in hospitals may not be *the* most important customer group, they are essential. Dickerson (1985) states: "Volunteers are needed in every hospital in the country" (p. 73). The effective marketing of volunteers is an important task for hospital managers and hospital volunteer coordinators.

Hospital Volunteers

In regard to hospital volunteers, Edward Hodges (1993), former chairman of the American Hospital Association's Congress of Hospital Trustees, stated:

Hospitals have long depended on volunteers to fill vital roles in patient care and support services. Volunteers provide many extra services that add to the comfort, care and happiness of patients, their families, and visitors. Working with patients or behind the scenes with health care professionals, volunteers improve the quality of care and help contain medical expenses. It is unlikely that hospitals can find better goodwill ambassadors than those in their volunteer departments. (p. 28)

Volunteers are helpful in constraining hospital's operating expenses. In Botsford General Hospital, in Farmington, Michigan, 364 volunteers worked over 85,000 hours in 1992, saving the hospital from adding 40 full-time employees (Hodges, 1993). Not only do volunteers save hospitals money, they also benefit hospitals by working in fund-raising campaigns and by extending their hospitals' goodwill throughout their communities.

Given the importance of volunteers to hospitals, it is surprising that relatively little is known about them. This is unfortunate. Pforzheimer and Miller (1996) state: "To appropriately recruit, train and make best use of their volunteers' time, it is critical that hospitals get to know their volunteers" (p. 80). The purpose of this article is to increase our understanding of hospital volunteers.

LITERATURE REVIEW

Hospital Volunteerism

Hospital volunteerism is changing. First, in efforts to control expenses, hospitals are looking for volunteers who can serve in non-traditional roles. Pforzheimer and Miller state: "While volunteers still perform the traditional roles of gift shop operator, desk greeter and benefit chair, many are using their professional skills and taking on important responsibilities . . . " (p. 80). Second, traditional hospital volunteers used to be women whose children were in school. This is changing as more and more women are entering the paid work force. Fortunately, this change is being countered by favorable demographic trends. The population is getter older, many people are retiring younger, and many retired professionals are seeking to use their skills for their communities (Hodges, 1993; Pforzheimer and Miller, 1996).

Unfortunately, volunteerism in America is not robust. According to Independent Sector, which conducts biannual national surveys on volunteerism, from 1989 to 1996 the total number of U.S. adults who volunteered during the survey year declined from 98.4 million to 93 million (Independent Sector, 1996). While volunteerism in America is waning in popularity, hospital administrators are finding that competition for volunteers is increasing. "Volunteers are now in the desirable position of selecting where and with whom they will contribute the gift of involvement" (Pforzheimer and Miller, 1996, p. 80).

Hospital Volunteerism and the Marketing Concept

Bagozzi (1974, 1978) argued that the exchange relationship is the essence of marketing. The exchange relationship in the context of hospital volunteerism suggests that before people will give their time/skills to an organization, they must perceive that what they will receive from the experience is worth the time and effort to volunteer. The benefits volunteers may receive might be a feeling of satisfaction from helping others, a sense of achievement, the development of friendships, and so forth.

One primary benefit volunteers seek is the opportunity to express their core values and beliefs. In their national survey of AIDS volunteers, Omoto and Snyder (1990, 1993) took attitude measures of survey respondents. The attitudes were then aggregated to a higher level of abstraction in order to determine what functions attitudes served for the volunteers. The strongest function was interpreted to be "value expressive." Volunteers felt that their service allowed them to act upon their underlying values, to be their true selves (Snyder and Debono, 1987). Okun and Eisenberg (1992) used a similar analysis to study the motives of 262 senior citizen volunteers. After factor analyzing 13 scale items onto three factors, they interpreted one of the three as "value expressive." Values conducive to volunteering may be a sense of civic duty, religious beliefs that encourage benevolence, or a desire to help others. Understanding what volunteers hoped to derive from their service is important because it gives marketers information regarding what they must offer potential volunteers to persuade them to enter into exchange relationships with the organization.

While the exchange concept was originally thought of as a discrete transaction, the exchange concept has evolved to the context of a long-term, on-going relationship (Bejou 1997). This broadening of the concept of exchange has served as the basis for relationship marketing, defined by Berry (1983) as "attracting, maintaining, and enhancing customer relationships" (p. 25). The goal of relationship marketing is to help the parties involved in the relationship (i.e., hospital and volunteer) meet their goals and objectives by a "mutual exchange and fulfillment of promises" (Gronroos 1991, p. 8).

In adopting a marketing-oriented approach, a hospital manager (e.g., director of volunteer services) should first try to understand his or her volunteers in order to (1) develop a volunteer experience which would approximate an equal value exchange with the volunteer, and (2) develop the most effective recruitment message to persuade the potential volunteer to give his or her time, talents, and skills. Nonprofit managers can make better informed decisions regarding the recruitment and management of their volunteers when they have a better understanding of not only why and what type of people volunteer in general, but why and what type of people volunteer for their particular type of organization. Heidrich (1988) states:

> From a marketing point of view, it is important for voluntary organizations to know their type of volunteer and how they differ from others. A competitive advantage would accrue to an organization tailoring its recruitment message to a specific group having more or less homogeneous characteristics and a demonstrated likelihood to volunteer for certain roles or organizations. (p. 10)

The purpose of this study is to increase our understanding of hospital volunteers to assist marketing decision-making by: (1) differentiating hospital volunteers from other sub-groups of volunteers; (2) by differentiating more active hospital volunteers from less active hospital volunteers; and (3) by better understanding events leading to their volunteer work, motivations for their retention, and perceived benefits and rewards from their volunteer service.

RESEARCH QUESTIONS

In Smith's (1994) review of the prior literature on voluntary participation over the previous 20 years, he recommends that future studies could substantially add to our knowledge by (1) including a comparison group in addition to the study's target group, and (2) by using determinant variables from multiple domains to differentiate the groups. This study responds to both of these recommendations. First, the target group of hospital volunteers from four hospitals is being differentiated from a comparison group of volunteers from other organizations. Second, determinant variables used are from multiple domains: (1) demographic, (2) social-lifestyle, (3) personality, and (4) personal values.

Demographic Variables

Yavas and Reicken (1985) conducted a telephone survey of 329 volunteers to determine if demographic correlates to volunteering (in general) could be identified. They reported that occupation, age, and education were significant correlates of volunteering. Demographic variables may offer utility in differentiating and identifying hospital volunteers.

H1: Demographic variables should be helpful in differentiating hospital volunteers from other volunteers.

Social and Lifestyle Variables

In their cross-disciplinary literature review, Wymer, Riecken, and Yavas (1996) discuss previous research which shows the importance of social influences on volunteering. "Social influences provide incentives or disincentives for an individual's volunteer behavior by supporting, failing to support, or discouraging the behavior of volunteering" (p. 11). Church is an important social/religious institution for many people. Church attendance/membership has been consistently and positively correlated with volunteering (Cnaan, Kastemakis, and Wineburg, 1993; Fischer and Schaffer, 1993; Gerard, 1985; Hodgkinson, Weitzman, and Kirsch 1990). While the causal link between church attendance and volunteerism has been a debated in prior research (cf. Wymer, 1997a), the literature shows that volunteers are more likely to be frequent church attenders or church members.

Facilitation is a variable which has been used in prior research to represent the degree of social support and connectedness between individuals and volunteers or volunteer organizations. Facilitation represents those activities which provide a potential volunteer with information and/or social support (Wymer, 1997b). Prior research has found that a person who is asked by someone to volunteer (typically asked by an associate in an organization to which both belong), is about five times more likely to volunteer than people not personally asked to volunteer (Independent Sector, 1996).

H2: Social-lifestyle variables should be helpful in differentiating hospital volunteers from other volunteers.

Personality Variables

Wymer, Riecken, and Yavas (1996) report that many previous studies which attempted to account for volunteer behavior using personality variables were largely unsuccessful. However, volunteers have been found to exhibit higher levels of emotional empathy than non-volunteers (Allen & Ruston, 1983; Fahey, 1986; Wymer, 1997b). Empathy is thought to be a motivating dimension underlying an altruistic personality. People with higher levels of emotional empathy are more concerned about the welfare of others, and are more likely to provide help by voluntary assistance than people with lower levels of emotional empathy.

In addition to emotional empathy, there is reason to believe that self-esteem may differentiate hospital volunteers. Self-esteem refers to a person's perceptions of his or her own bundle of skills, talents, and competencies–his or her self-worth.

Volunteers tend to have positive self-images, feeling capable and competent (Fischer and Schaffer, 1993; Gerard, 1985; Okun, 1994). Miller (1985) reported that volunteers' participation was influenced by the extent to which they felt in control of their lives. In a British national survey which interviewed over 1,000 volunteers, Gerard (1985) wrote " . . . the voluntary workers studied reported better health, found greater meaning in life, and expressed a greater preference for active pursuits. The interviewers assessed them as self-assured" (p. 238).

H3: Self-esteem and empathy should be helpful in differentiating hospital volunteers from other volunteers.

Personal Values

While studying the motivations of volunteers, it is important to include values or beliefs in addition to other variables (Schwartz and Howard, 1984). A value is defined as "an enduring belief that a specific mode of conduct or end-state of existence is personally and socially preferable to alternative modes of conduct or end-states of existence" (Rokeach, 1968, p. 160).

Fahey (1986) studied motivations in a sample of volunteers and non-volunteers. She found that "volunteers are guided significantly more by internalized principles and motivations than are non-volunteers who are more susceptible to peer pressure" (p. 88). Clary and Snyder (1991) wrote that volunteering "helps individuals remain true to their conception of self and allows the expression of deeply held values . . . " (p. 125). Mahoney and Pechura (1980) compared responses of the Rokeach Value Survey (RVS) between telephone hotline volunteers and a control group. They reported that volunteers ranked "inner harmony," "equality," and "self-respect" significantly higher in their personal value systems than the control group. Control group subjects ranked "a comfortable life" and "an exciting life" significantly higher than volunteers. Mahoney and Pechura concluded that " . . . effective recruitment of volunteers appears to require some understanding of the values of potential volunteers" (p. 1008). No studies could be found which examined the values of hospital volunteers, and one contribution of this study is that it provides insights into this important group's values.

H4: Values should be helpful in differentiating hospital volunteers from other volunteers.

Intensity of Volunteer Service

From the perspective of a director of volunteer services, a desirable volunteer performance attribute would be a relatively generous amount of time donated on a regular basis. Although the amount of time a volunteer donates to his/her organization(s) does not capture to complete conceptual domain of "performance," the amount of time volunteered is one important dimension of the concept. Zweigenhaft, Armstrong, Quintis, and Riddick (1996) surveyed 96 volunteers in a North Carolina community hospital. They used two dimensions, rated by the volunteers' supervisor, in assessing performance: dependability and impact on the volunteer program. They reported that females with strong religious beliefs who worked the greatest number of hours/month made the greatest impact on the program. In predicting impact, the average monthly hours volunteers served had the largest regression coefficient.

H5: The determinant variables should be useful in differentiating hospital volunteers by their volunteering intensity.

Qualitative Assessment

In order to enrich the data, assist in interpreting the results and benefit our overall understanding of hospital volunteers, they were asked a series of open-ended questions regarding events leading to their volunteer work, rewards/benefits of volunteering, and reasons for continuing their volunteer work. This part of the study is considered descriptive and exploratory.

METHOD

Sample and Data Acquisition

Approximately 40 NPOs in two midwestern cities (one large, one small) agreed to participate in the study. The participating NPOs represented a diversity of missions (human service, religion, education, health, youth development, and arts/culture). Volunteers were mailed a survey which contained a cover letter, a questionnaire, and a business reply return envelope. No incentives were offered to respondents. There were 1,013 completed questionnaires (of 3,400 delivered) from volunteers. The response rate was approximately 30 percent. This response rate is similar to that reported by Gillespie and King (1985). They conducted a mail survey of Red Cross volunteers, reporting 1,346 returned questionnaires for a 26.9 response rate.

It was recognized that volunteers can serve in multiple organizations. Therefore, survey respondents were instructed (in the multiple NPO case) to print the name of the organization for which they felt a primary commitment. Hospital volunteers were identified by their response to this question (i.e., printing the name of the hospital and indicating it was their primary volunteer organization). There were 105 hospital volunteers from four participating hospitals and 908 volunteers from other types of organizations.

Hospital volunteers ranged from 18 to 82 years of age (mean = 63). The comparison group of volunteers ranged from 16 to 93 years of age (mean = 50). Hospital volunteers tended to be female (73 percent female). Our comparison group of volunteers was 72 percent female. This gender imbalance is similar to that reported by Cnaan, Kasternakis, and Wineburg (1993). Using a similar methodology, they collected data from a sample of 871 persons from over 60 NPOs in three cities. They reported that 71.2 percent of volunteers in their sample were female. In their study of 152 hospital volunteers from two hospitals, Miller, Powell, and Seltzer (1990) reported that 91 percent of their sample was female and that 56 percent of the sample checked the "over 60 years of age" category.

In terms of employment status, only 12 percent of hospital volunteers reported being employed on a full-time basis, whereas 39 percent of other volunteers reported being employed on a full-time basis. Given the age differential between hospital volunteers and other volunteers, it is likely that more hospital volunteers are retired. In their study of 98 volunteers from one hospital, Zweigenhaft et al. (1996) reported that 80 percent of their sample was not employed.

As one might expect from the employment status of the sample, hospital volunteers reported lower incomes than other volunteers. There were seven incremental income categories for volunteers to indicate appropriate for themselves. Hospital volunteers averaged (on a 1 to 7 scale) an income level of 3.18. Other volunteers averaged an income level of 3.79.

In terms of marital status, 73 percent of hospital volunteers reported being married compared to 64 percent for other volunteers. Hospital volunteers averaged 13.8 years of education, compared to 15.9 years for other volunteers. Of the hospital volunteers, 82 percent were church members (attending an average 4.7 services/month), compared to other volunteers, 73 percent of whom were church members (attending an average of 3.6 services/month).

In terms of their participation in volunteer organizations, hospital volunteers serve in an average of 1.7 organizations. Hospital volunteers work, on average, 25.6 hours/month for their hospital and 29.8 hours/month for all volunteers organizations combined. Our comparison group of volunteers serve in an average of 2.0 volunteer organizations. These volunteers work, on average, 14.1 hours/month for their primary organization and 20.5 hours/month for all their volunteer organizations combined.

Because a sample frame for the volunteer populations in the two cities was not available, a non-probability sample was taken. Therefore, sample representativeness was a concern. Collecting data from a number of NPOs in two cities to comprise a relatively large sample helps to reduce the likelihood that the sample will differ in some important way from the population of interest (Bryman and Cramer 1990). Also, as a representativeness check, administrators familiar with their volunteers in 10 participating organizations were contacted after the sample was collected. They were asked to describe the demographic characteristics of their volunteers. Then the administrators were asked to describe the demographic characteristics of volunteers in other organizations with which they were familiar. Finally, the administrators were given a description of the sample and asked to comment on the degree of similarity to volunteers in their organizations. Results of this check supported the representativeness of the sample.

Measures

Consistent with the approach of previous studies of volunteers, data for demographic and lifestyle variables were obtained. These included church membership, church attendance, age, gender, education, income, home ownership, marital status, employment status, parental volunteerism, family volunteerism, and family size.

Two personality variables were measured: empathy and self-esteem. Empathy was measured using the Emotional Empathy Scale (Mehrabian and Epstein, 1972). Self-esteem was measured using the Self-Esteem Scale (Coopersmith, 1967).

This study used the Rokeach Value Survey instrument (Rokeach, 1973; see Table 1) to measure terminal values. The RVS has been used in previous research on volunteers (Heidrich, 1988; Mahoney and Pechura, 1980; Williams, 1987). The instrument instructs respondents to rank 18 terminal values by order of perceived importance. The RVS has been in use and revised several times since its initial development in 1967. Feather (1975) and Braithwaite and Scott (1991) discuss the psychometric properties of the RVS and provide evidence of the instrument's reliability and validity.

The ranking procedure of the RVS is simple to administer and captures the concept of a hierarchy of values based upon subjects' own comparisons. The main disadvantage of the ranking procedure, ordinal data, can be overcome by data transformation. The ranks from 1 to 18 are transformed to standard scores (Z scores). This transformation is based on the assumption that differences between ranks at the extremes offer greater discrimination than differences between ranks nearer the middle. This is a common assumption in ranking procedures (Meddis, 1984). Hollen (1967) provided support for this assumption. He found that values rated most and least important changed the least, whereas values rated near the middle changed the most, between test and retest (Feather, 1975; Hays, 1967).

Facilitation was measured using five 9-point Likert scales which assess the

TABLE 1. Eighteen Terminal Values from Rokeach Value Survey

A Comfortable Life (a prosperous life)	An Exciting Life (a stimulating, active life)
A Sense of Accomplishment (lasting contribution)	A World at Peace (free of war and conflict)
A World of Beauty (beauty of nature & the arts)	Equality (brotherhood, equal opport.)
Family Security (taking care of loved ones)	Freedom (independence, free choice)
Happiness (contentedness)	Inner Harmony (freedom from inner conflict)
Mature Love (sexual & spiritual intimacy)	National Security (protecfion from attack)
Pleasure (an enjoyable, leisurely life)	Salvation (saved, eternal life)
Self-Respect (self-esteem)	Social Recognition (respect, admiration)
True Friendship (close companionship)	Wisdom (mature understanding of life)

degree to which respondents had access to information or social support linked to an NPO (Cronbach alpha reliability coefficient .70; Wymer, 1997b).

Analysis. Logistic regression was used to assess the contribution of the variables described previously as predictors of hospital volunteering. Logistic regression is the appropriate method of analysis in predicting a dichotomous dependent variable such as a dummy variable representing hospital volunteers (1) and other volunteers (0) (Aldrich and Nelson, 1984).

In examining the association of the independent variables with our measure of volunteer performance, the statistical analysis involved a series of stepwise multiple regression procedures. First, the independent variables were regressed on the average monthly number of hours hospital volunteers donated in all organizations in which they serve. Second, the independent variables were regressed on the average monthly number of hours hospital volunteers serve in their primary organization (i.e., their hospital). In the final analysis, the independent variables were regressed on a dependent variable representing the number of NPO organizations in which respondents reported serving. Data set diagnostics included examining the correlation matrix, Cook's distance statistics, and variance inflation factors (VIF). One outlier was detected and removed.

RESULTS

Hospital Volunteers and Other Volunteers

The logistic regression results are presented in Table 2. The model was accurate in predicting group differences in over 90% of the cases. The −2 log likelihood (457) is statistically significant. The first column shows the variables which were found to be significant predictors of hospital volunteering. The second column shows the logistic coefficients (ß). These coefficients are not easily interpreted. In the case of the first significant variable, age, the interpretation of the coefficient is that for every 1 year increase in age, the log

TABLE 2. Logistic Regression Results: Hospital Volunteers vs. Other Volunteers

Variable	ß	S.E.	Wald	ρ	R	Exp (β)
Age	0.0382	.0070	29.99	.0000	.2282	1.0389
Hours[a]	0.0249	.0054	21.64	.0000	.1912	1.0252
Number[b]	− 0.3758	.1254	8.97	.0027	− .1139	0.6868
RelServ[c]	0.0100	.0049	4.06	.0440	.0619	1.0100
Self-Esteem	0.2809	.1322	4.52	.0336	.0684	1.3243
World at Beauty	− 0.4282	.1835	5.44	.0196	− .0801	1.5344
Constant	− 5.0711	.5459	86.29	.0000		

Dependent variable = Hospice volunteer (1)/Other volunteer (0).
−2 Log Likelihood = 457
Goodness of Fit = 961, Model Chi-Square = 80 (6 df), ρ < .001.
Total number of cases = 1,013 (rejected because of missing data = 102).
Classification accuracy of model: 91% of cases.
a = Ave. monthly hours served in primary organization.
b = Number of organizations for which person volunteers time.
c = Ave. monthly religious service attendance frequency.

odds of the probability of a volunteer being a hospital volunteer increases by .0382. The third column lists the standard errors of the variables. The forth column lists the Wald statistics for the logistic coefficients. The forth column lists the p values (levels of significance) for the Wald statistics.

The fifth column lists *R*. This represents the partial correlation between the dependent variable and each of the independent variables. The R value is constrained to be between −1 and +1. The magnitude of R indicates the contribution of the independent variable to the model.

The sixth column lists *Exp* (ß). This is the factor by which the odds of group membership change from a one unit change in the associated independent variable. For example, if we increase age by one unit (1 year), the odds that a volunteer in the sample is a hospital volunteer increase by a factor of 1.0389.

One demographic variable is a significant predictor of hospital volunteering–age. Hospital volunteers are older, on average, than volunteers in other types of nonprofit organizations as previously reported.

Three social-lifestyle variables are significant in the model. They are the average number of hours served in a volunteer's primary organization, the number of volunteer organizations in which the volunteer serves, and the frequency of attending religious services. Compared to other volunteers, hospital volunteers are differentiated by working more hours for their hospital (than other volunteers do in their primary organizations), volunteering in fewer organizations, and attending church more often. Hospital volunteers appear to be more committed to their hospitals, their primary organizations (because they serve in fewer organizations and work more hours in their primary organizations). They also appear to be more committed to their churches, or perhaps, more religious than other volunteers. Another plausible explanation for the significance of church attendance is that hospital volunteers are more socially engaged than other volunteers, and church is an institution through which they engage in social interactions and relations. Prior research, however, provides greater support for the religious interpretation (Wymer 1997a).

In Zweigenhaft et al.'s (1996) study, the sample of 98 hospital volunteers reported that their religion was important to them. Of the sample, 19 percent said their religion was important to themselves, and 70 percent said their religion was very important. Only 10 percent said their religion was not important, neutral, or unimportant. While Zweigenhaft et al.'s study did not use a comparison group, this present study did. The findings reported here suggest that hospital volunteers are not only religious in general, but may be more religious than other types of volunteers.

One personality variable and one value were significant in the model. Hospital volunteers reported higher levels of self-esteem. In terms of their personal values, hospital volunteer felt that the value "a world of beauty" was significantly less important than other volunteers.

Hospital Volunteer Intensity

Obviously, volunteers differ in terms of their performance. One dimension of performance investigated here is the average monthly hours hospital volunteers serve in their organizations. A complicating factor is that people can either volunteer for a single organization or for multiple organizations. There may be a commitment to a primary organization and its purpose, or a person may feel a duty to "volunteer" in a general sense and may more equally distribute donated time in two or more NPOs.

To take into account the complexity of multi-organizational volunteering, three separate stepwise multiple regressions were performed. First, the predictor variables previously described were regressed on a variable representing the average number of hours hospital volunteers reported working in all organizations for which they serve. Second, the dependent variable was changed to one representing the average monthly hours served in their hospitals (i.e., their primary organizations). Third, the dependent variable was changed to one representing the total number of organizations for which the hospital volunteers donates time. The results of these regressions are shown in Table 3.

Hours in Multiple NPOs

In the first regression four variables are significant. One demographic variable and three values are associated with hospital volunteers donating greater numbers of hours across volunteer organizations. Income was negatively associated with working more hours across organizations. Reasons for this association with income is speculative at best, but it may be that these more intensive volunteers are less concerned with money, personal comfort/security, and themselves in general, than other volunteers. The association between income and volunteer intensity needs to be examined further in future research.

Three values, "salvation," "a sense of accomplishment," and "self-respect," were positively associated with more intensive volunteering across organizations. Volunteers who give more time across organizations feel that these three values are more important than do other hospital volunteers. There is an obvious linkage between the value "salvation" and religion. Perhaps these hospital volunteers are among the more religious hospital volunteers. Zweigenhaft et al. (1996) reported that religion was significantly associated with a volunteer's impact on the organization (a measure they used for performance).

TABLE 3. Regression Results: Hospital Vol. Performance

Independent Variables	b	Std. Error	Beta	t
1st Regression[a]				
Constant	34.586	3.578		9.7***
Salvation	7.417	1.892	.361	3.9***
Sense of accomp.[b]	6.072	2.043	.277	3.0**
Self-respect	4.907	1.974	.220	2.5*
Income	−2.316	.973	−.211	−2.4*
$R^2 = .241$ $R^2_{adj} = .211$ $N = 105$				
2nd Regression[c]				
Constant	23.107	1.647		14.0***
Salvation	6.096	1.715	.318	3.6**
Self-respect	5.192	1.865	.250	2.8**
Freedom	−3.823	1.531	−.222	−2.5*
$R^2 = .199$ $R^2_{adj} = .175$ $N = 105$				
3rd Regression[d]				
Constant	−.543	.409		−1.3
Education	.160	.029	.475	5.5***
$R^2 = .225$ $R^2_{adj} = .218$ $N = 105$				

a ☞ Dep. variable = hours in all organizations.

b ☞ A sense of accomplishment.

c ☞ Dep. variable = hours in primary organization.

d ☞ Dep. variable = number of organizations.

* $p < .05$; ** $p < .01$; *** $p < .001$

Two other values, "a sense of accomplishment" and "self-respect" were also positive predictors of more intensive volunteering across organizations. This suggests that these more intensive volunteers view volunteering as a means of deriving esteem-enhancement rewards. This would be consistent with anecdotal experiences of two practitioners, Pforzheimer and Miller (1996), who stated:

> As volunteers undertake new roles in the hospital, hospitals must find new ways to show their appreciation. Today's professionals may not need a year-end certificate of thanks so much as they need to see the

results of their work. . . . it is important for volunteers to see their efforts come to fruition. (p. 80)

Hours in Primary Organization

Whereas the previous analysis examined hospital volunteering in multiple organizations, this analysis examines hospital volunteering in volunteers' primary organizations (i.e., their hospitals). Three variables are significantly associated with the average monthly hours hospital volunteers serve in their hospitals. All three are values.

The more intensive hospital volunteers felt that the values "salvation" and "self-respect" were significantly more important than other hospital volunteers. They also felt that "freedom" was significantly less important than other hospital volunteers. As previously discussed, salvation is associated with religion, and religions emphasize altruism and dedication (Wymer, 1997a). The more intensive in-hospital volunteers, like the more intensive cross-organizational hospital volunteers, appear to be among the more religious volunteers. Also, the more intensive in-hospital volunteers also appear to derive an egoistic benefit from volunteering (self-respect).

This interpretation is consistent with prior research on volunteers which has found that volunteers want to help others, but they also want personal benefits as well. Cnaan and Goldberg-Glen (1991) asked volunteers in their study to rank 28 motives for volunteering identified from previous research. They concluded that volunteers are both altruistic and egoistic, and that they do not distinguish between these motives but act on both. In their study of 98 hospital volunteers, Zweigenhaft et al. (1996) reported that their volunteers' motives were both altruistic ("to help others" and "to give something back because I am so fortunate") and egoistic ("to feel needed" and "it gives me a good feeling or a sense of satisfaction to help others").

The value "freedom" was negatively associated with intensive in-hospital volunteering. That is, more intensive hospital volunteers felt that freedom was significantly less important than other hospital volunteers. It appears that the more dedicated volunteers are less concern about their independence and autonomy than others.

Number of NPOs

In the third regression, the dependent variable represents the number of organizations for which the hospital volunteer donates his or her time. There is one significant variable in the regression equation–education. Those persons volunteering in relatively more organizations reported higher levels of formal education. The most typical reason given for positive associations between upper socioeconomic demographic variables, like education, and volunteerism is that people in more dominant social strata believe they have more resources of use to an NPO (Fischer and Schaffer, 1993). A person making the decision to volunteer weighs the perceived costs and benefits of service. The greater the perceived level of personal resources, the relatively lower the perceived net cost of volunteering. People, in what society considers to be dominant social echelons, under this argument, would be expected to volunteer more frequently because the perceived cost of volunteer is relatively low. The findings in this study are consistent with this rationale only if the argument is modified to mean that perceived personal resources as indicated by dominant social statuses are related to the number of organizations for which a person volunteers, not the quantity of time a volunteer donates. In prior research, this distinction has not been made.

Qualitative Assessment of Hospital Volunteers

To better understand the motives and perceived rewards of hospital volunteering, to develop a richer profile of hospital volunteers, and to possibly obtain new insights regarding hospital volunteers, qualitative data was collected. Specifically, volunteers were asked a series of three open-ended questions at the end of the questionnaire. The first question asked volunteers about events leading to their volunteer work. The second question asked volunteers to explain why they continue volunteering. The final question asked volunteers to describe benefits/rewards they receive from their volunteer work.

Events Leading to Volunteer Work

The most prevalent event leading to hospital volunteering was a significant life change or change in a person's life stage. The most frequently reported life-stage transition was retirement. One volunteer wrote, "After retirement wanted some structure in my life." Other comments regarding retirement were similar. "Retirement, time to give to other." "Retirement." "Retirement–Did not want to live in the past; desire for new horizons. Desire to work w/public in busy friendly environment where there was a need and desire for volunteers; wanted active not passive participation." "Retirement, leisure time, feeling of helping necessary."

Another frequently reported life-stage transition event was the death of a loved one. Volunteers wrote, "Retirement and widowhood." "I worked a long time and enjoyed working; my husband died just before retired and I like to keep busy." "I lost my husband and needed to be busier. I had a friend who volunteered at St. Francis." "Retired from work–death of husband–children left home–I do this to help me stay healthy." "Husband died. Wanted to contribute to community."

There were a few other events, such as children leaving home or a divorce, which influenced a person's decision to volunteer.

In addition to changes in life stage to retirement or widow-hood, some volunteers reported social reasons for volunteering. "Had too many hours by myself. Needed to get out of house to meet other people." "Lonesome, did not know what to do with myself, talking to other volunteers." "Visited facility, open house. Encouragement from friend. Filled out volunteer card." "Wife has volunteered for years." "Several of my friends were involved and I wished to participate."

There were several other types of comments. Most frequently in the "other" category was the comment that the person became a volunteer in order to help others. A few other volunteers mentioned employer expectations of community service. One volunteer mentioned hospital volunteering as a means of getting into a medical training program and a college student mentioned hospital volunteering satisfied a school requirement.

In synthesizing the meaning of these comments, it appears that in many cases, multiple events placed a person in a state in which volunteering appeared to satisfy a need. Whether it was retirement and a husband's death or retirement and a need to feel useful, these events appear to combine with a desire to help others and interact with others socially. Some people volunteer to alleviate loneliness or adjust to the next phase of their lives. In a small number of cases, hospital volunteering was instrumental in satisfying an employer's expectations for community involvement, or satisfying a school requirement.

Why They Continue Volunteering

In considering reasons for their retention as hospital volunteers, a variety of comments were given. Reasons for continuing their volunteer work ranged from being satisfied with the work to social benefits of volunteering.

A primary reason for retention as a hospital volunteer was that the volunteer enjoyed helping other people or felt a need to help others. "The need is there." "I like helping others." "Need to be doing something for others."

A major reason given for continuance in hospital volunteering was enjoying the work itself. "I enjoyed working. The people are interesting and pleasant." "Self-satisfying, enjoyable." "I very much enjoy my volunteer work. It is very rewarding."

Other important reasons for retention in hospital volunteering were intrinsic rewards from the experience. These rewards varied. "Satisfied life style." "Love of people. A need to feel useful." "Feel I am doing something worthwhile." "Enjoyment of new experience and helping people." "I derive a sense of personal satisfaction in helping others." "Need to be of help to others."

There was also a social component of the volunteer experience that helps retain volunteers. "To help others, to make new friends, to use my time meaningfully." "I enjoy keeping with people. It is a good reason to get out of the house." "Helping others, meeting new people, staying active." "Bored. Enjoy being with people." "There is much self satisfaction in being with other people."

While there were a smaller proportion of "other" responses, it appears that multiple factors influence retention of hospital volunteers. These volunteers have a need to help others, a need to be with other people, and a need to be active. While these needs, if met, stimulate retention, several comments related to the contextual environment of volunteering, influenced the satisfaction of the experience. These included the friendliness of the people the volunteer interacted with and the perceived degree of interest in the work itself.

Rewards and Benefits of Volunteering

The final open-ended question hospital volunteers answered involved identifying rewards and benefits derived from their volunteer work. As in previous questions, responses were varied. However, the comments indicate that when volunteers feel a need to help others, and feel they are really helping other people, they derive a feeling of accomplishment and satisfaction from expressing the values and beliefs which stimulated volunteering in the first place. These values/beliefs may involve helping others, paying back the community for their good fortune or health, or a sense of civic duty.

Examples of responses are: "An internal peace with myself." "Feel good about helping others." "I like to help others." "Peace." "Helping other people." "Feel you are helping others." "Happiness." "I feel this is why God created me, not to be served, but to serve." "Satisfaction of helping people. Receiving appreciative comments." "A feeling that I am doing something to help someone else."

Hospital volunteers also perceive feeling appreciated as a reward/benefit of their work. "Just to know that I am needed in a job that needs doing." "Most rewards from volunteerism are of an intangible nature. The opportunity for service to families of the community is almost always repaid with brief words of appreciation." "The smiles and thank you's are reward enough." "Reminded that your service is appreciated."

There are also social benefits to hospital volunteering. When asked what benefits and rewards they receive, some made comments similar to these: "Friendship." "Sense of contributing to my community, becoming acquainted with new persons in my community, and doing good." "Provide opportunity for direct interaction w/public, learning of new skills, development of good friendship with co-worker who has similar interest, opens doors to volunteer services available in other organizations." "Being with people, feeling a need to serve others, keeping busy." "A feeling of self-worth. New friendships of others." "Made some new friends. Feel good helping people."

There were some varied responses related to a sense of accomplishment or a sense of well-being from volunteering. There were also a few other extrinsic rewards that hospital volunteers reported. "Free parking, free meal at annual recognition dinner, feeling of helping others." "Discount at hospital. Free lunch." "Lunch ticket, senior promise parking."

DISCUSSION

Summary of Findings

A purpose of this study was to determine if hospital volunteers could be differentiated from other volunteers using the determinant variables selected. The determinant variables selected were from multiple conceptual domains: demographic, social-lifestyle, personality, and personal values. The results showed that hospital volunteers are relatively older than other volunteers. Hospital volunteers work more hours each month, on average, than other volunteers. They tend to serve in fewer volunteer organizations. Hospital volunteers attend religious services more frequently than other volunteers. They have higher levels of self-esteem, and they feel that the value "a world of beauty" is significantly less important in their value systems than other volunteers.

Compared to other types of volunteers, hospital volunteers are older and more committed and dedicated to their organizations. They tend to be more religious, and they have a healthy sense of self-worth. Values were not very helpful in differentiating hospital volunteers from other volunteers.

Another purpose of this study was to determine if the determinant variables used are helpful in differentiating higher performing hospital volunteering, as measured by average monthly hours volunteered. The findings showed that hospital volunteers donating the greatest time in a variety of organizations were differentiated from other hospital volunteers by three values and one demographic variable. These more intensive cross-organizational volunteers felt that "salvation," "a sense of accomplishment," and "self-respect" were important core values. They also reported significantly lower income levels than less intensive cross-organizational volunteering.

In regards to hospital volunteers who work the greatest number of monthly hours for their hospitals, they are differentiated from other hospital volunteers by three values: "salvation," "self-respect," and "freedom." Hospital volunteers who are the most involved, as indicated by working more hours for their hospitals, appear to be among the most religious hospital volunteers. However, in addition to acting on their religious beliefs through their volunteer work, they also desire esteem-enhancement rewards from their volunteer experience. The more intensive in-hospital volunteers felt that "freedom" was a significantly less important value than did other hospital volunteers. This may suggest that volunteers who work the most hours in their hospitals regard personal independence and autonomy as less important than other hospital volunteers.

In differentiating hospital volunteers who serve in the greatest number of volunteer organizations, one variable was significant–education. As discussed previously, the association between higher levels of education and serving in a greater variety of organizations may suggest that volunteers with higher levels of education perceive themselves as having more skills of use to NPOs. More educated volunteers may also perceive the cost of volunteering to be lower than other volunteers.

In the qualitative assessment of hospital volunteering, it appears that there are three basic modalities, intertwined and overlapping, through which a person becomes a hospital volunteer. In the most prevalent case, persons who are in a life-stage transition and who become aware of the volunteer opportunity, view hospital volunteering as a means of coping and adjusting to their new life stage. Life stage is a general term, but in the specific cases of hospital volunteers, most were dealing with retirement or with the death of a loved one (usually a husband). Obviously, people have to become aware of the opportunity before volunteering. Most learned of the opportunity through friends, church affiliations, or experiences with hospital volunteers when relatives were being treated in the hospital.

In her commentary, Gelb (1994) recommends recruiting hospital volunteers by "turning patients into volunteers." Statements of hospital volunteers in this study suggest that another approach would be to have current hospital volunteers interact with patients' loved ones, possibly stimulating subsequent interest in becoming a hospital volunteer.

In addition to being asked about events leading to their hospital volunteer work, they were also asked about benefits and rewards received and about why they continue to volunteer. Volunteers gave a variety of responses. It appears that reasons for volunteering and rewards are multidimensional. Many volunteers want to help others. They want social contact as well. They want to act on their religious beliefs or a need to be civic-minded or to "give back" to the community for their good fortune. Hospital volunteers enjoy a friendly work climate and perks, such as free parking and free lunches. They also want to feel that they are making a meaningful difference to others in need. Hospital volunteers view expressions of appreciation from patients and their families, as well as hospital staff, as rewards. These components: acting on their values, having positive social interactions, feeling needed, and being appreciated, help to provide the hospital volunteer with a rewarding experience. Rewarding volunteer experiences stimulate retention. Volunteers who are enjoying their experience are more likely to have a positive attitude, engage in more positive work behaviors, and interact with others in more positive ways.

Managerial Implications

The findings reported here have important implications for NPO managers. While future research is needed to replicate and extend this initial work, our understanding of hospital volunteers is enriched by using the methodology described in this study.

A contribution of this study is that it demonstrates the distinctiveness of an important subgroup of volunteers–hospital volunteers. The more hospitals' directors of volunteer services know about their volunteers, the better equipped they will be to develop effective tactics to *recruit* new volunteers, *retain* current volunteers, and *return* former volunteers to active service (the 3 R's of volunteer marketing management).

The volunteer coordinator's first step in recruiting volunteers is to learn more about them, attempting to better understand them. Kotler and Scheff (1997) state: "This means understanding who the volunteers are, why they volunteer, and how to 'speak' to them" (p. 424).

A first step in developing a deeper understanding of an organization's volunteers is to "segment" them. Segmenting in this sense means to aggregate hospital volunteers into a common grouping, then to differentiate them from other groups of volunteers. The administrator or volunteer coordinator must find appropriate bases upon which to segment his or her volunteers. This study used variables from demographic, social-lifestyle, personality, and personal values as bases for segmentation. Finding other bases upon which to segment hospital volunteers or finding other important variables within the bases used in this study would be productive areas of future research.

Once the group is adequately segmented (differentiated from other volunteers), the manager or marketer can then develop a profile of his or her volunteers. The variables found to predict hospital volunteer group membership can be used in developing such a profile. Profiling a hospital's volunteers gives the organization more information with which to identify, construct recruitment appeals, design recruitment tactics, and influence volunteers' experiences.

Qualitative research can be a useful tool in better understanding volunteers. The qualitative information provided by hospital volunteers in this study added new information and insights. The profile of these volunteers was made more complete. Our understanding of hospital volunteers was enhanced. Both quantitative and qualitative methods, working in a complementary manner, appear to produce the best results.

In the introduction, volunteers were presented as an important group of customers of nonprofit organizations. Just as managers in commercial organizations would like to know how to identify their most profitable customers, nonprofit managers need to know how to identify their potentially most productive volunteers.

One simple way to assess productivity is by examining the hours volunteers serve. (Obviously, there are multiple factors to consider when assessing volunteer productivity.) The methodology used in this study produced significant variables which differentiated volunteers on the amount of time they donated. One productive area for future research would be to better understand the dimensionality of volunteer performance and to discover predictors of superior volunteer performance. The ability to better predict volunteer performance would enable NPO managers to more effectively select and place volunteers.

Limitations

Since this study is among the first to differentiate hospital volunteers from other volunteers, its findings need to be supported by replication and extension. It is hoped that future research will build upon this initial work. Furthermore, while the sample was derived from many organizations, it was not randomly drawn and was limited to two midwestern cities. Generalizations to other populations should be made with this limitation in mind.

CONCLUSION

This study was not only useful in demonstrating a methodology for better understanding a largely overlooked group of volunteers, it also has important implications for future research. First, the population of volunteers should not be thought of as a monolithic, homogenous group. The total population of volunteers is composed of diverse subgroups.

Second, this study is important because it demonstrates the efficacy of understanding one's target market (in this case, hospital volunteers) by learning how it differs from other market segments. Our understanding of volunteerism can be enhanced by learning how a particular volunteer segment differs from other segments. Few studies of volunteerism have used comparison groups. Those that have used comparison groups have generally used non-volunteers (Cnaan and Goldberg-Glen, 1991). This study demonstrates the added insights provided by using a comparison group of other types of volunteers.

Third, this study demonstrates the utility of examining volunteerism using a multidimensional approach (i.e., using determinant variables from multiple conceptual domains). Reviewing 20 years of previous research on voluntary participation, Smith (1994) made a recommendation for future research to begin using such a multidimensional approach. Smith commented on the shortfalls of a narrower approach (e.g., relying exclusively on demographic variables) and noted the dearth of research using a more comprehensive methodology. This study demonstrates the increased understanding of an important subgroup of volunteers by learning how it differs from other groups in terms of demographic variables, social-lifestyle variables, personality, and values.

REFERENCES

Adams, C. H. and Shepherd, G. J. (1996), "Managing Volunteer Performance: Face Support and Situational Features as Predictors of Volunteers' Evaluations of Regulative Messages," *Management Communication Quarterly*, 9 (4), 363-388.

Aldrich, J. H., and Nelson, F. D. (1984), *Linear Probability, Logit, and Probit Models* (Sage University Papers Series on Quantitative Applications in the Social Sciences, No. 07-045). Beverly Hills, CA: Sage.

Allen, N. J. and Rushton, J. P. (1983), "Personality Characteristics of Community Mental Health Volunteers: A Review," *Journal of Voluntary Action Research*, 12 (1), 36-49.

Bagozzi, R. P. (1974), "Marketing as an Organized Behavioral System of Exchange," *Journal of Marketing*, 43, 69-75.

Bagozzi, R. P. (1978), "Marketing as Exchange: A Theory of Transactions in the Marketplace," *American Behavioral Scientists*, 21, 535-555.

Bejou, D. (1997), "Relationship Marketing: Evolution, Present State, and Future," *Psychology & Marketing*, 14 (8), 727-735.

Berry, L. L. (1983), "Relationship Marketing," in L. L. Berry, G. L. Shostack, & G. D. Upah (eds.), *Emerging Perspectives on Services Marketing* (pp. 25-28). UT: American Marketing Association.

Braithwaite, V. A. and Scott, W. A. (1991), "Values." In Robinson, J.P., Shaver, P.R., and Wrightsman (eds), *Measures of Personality and Social Psychological Attitudes*, vol. 1. New York: Academic Press.

Bryman, A. and Cramer, D. (1990), *Quantitative Data Analysis for Social Scientists*. London: Routledge.

Clary, E. G. and Snyder, M. (1991), "A Functional Analysis of Altruism and Prosocial Behavior: The Case of Volunteerism," in Clark, M.S. (ed), *Review of Personality and Social Psychology*, vol 12. Newbury Park, CA: Sage.

Cnaan, R. A., Kasternakis, A., and Wineburg, R. J. (1993), "Religious People, Religious Congregations, and Volunteerism in Human Services: Is There a Link?" *Nonprofit & Voluntary Sector Quarterly*, 22 (1), 33-5 1.

Cnaan, R. A., and Goldberg-Glen, R. A. (1991), "Measuring Motivation to Volunteer in Human Services," *Journal of Applied Behavioral Sciences*, 27 (3), 269-284.

Coopersmith, S. (1967), *The Antecedents of Self-Esteem*. California: W.H. Freeman and Company.

Dickerson, J. (1985), "Why I Spent Time as a Hospital Volunteer," *Medical Laboratory Observer*, 17 (2), 73-75.

Fahey, M. (1986), "Lay Volunteers Within an American Catholic Parish: Personality and Social Factors," doctoral dissertation, University of San Francisco.

Feather, N. T. (1975), *Values in Education and Society*. New York: The Free Press.

Fischer, L. R., and Schaffer, K. B. (1993), *Older Volunteers: A Guide to Research and Practice*. Newbury Park, CA: Sage.

Gelb, B. D. (1994), "Turning Volunteers into Patients–and Vice Versa," *Journal of Health Care Marketing*, 14 (1), 8-10.

Gerard, D. (1985), "What Makes a Volunteer?" *New Society*, 74 (Nov 8), 236-238.

Gillespie, D. F., and King, A. E. O. (1985), "Demographic Understanding of Volunteerism," *Journal of Sociology and Social Welfare*, 12 (4), 798-816.

Gronroos, C. (1991), "The Marketing Strategy Continuum: Toward a Marketing Concept for the Services Marketing," *Management Decision*, 29, 7-13.

Hays, W. L. (1967), *Quantification in Psychology*. Belmont, CA: Brooks-Cole.

Heidrich, K. W. (1988), "Lifestyles of Volunteers: A Market Segmentation Study," Ph.D. dissertation, University of Illinois at Urbana-Champaign.

Hodges, E. N., III, (1993), "The Importance of Being a Volunteer," *Trustee*, February, 28.

Hodgkinson, V. A., Weitzman, M. S., and Kirsch, A. D. (1990), "From Commitment to Action: How Religious Involvement Affects Giving and Volunteering," in Wuthnow, R., Hodgkinson, V. A., and Associates (eds.), *Faith and Philanthropy in America: Exploring the Role of Religion in America's Voluntary Sector*. San Francisco: Jossey-Bass.

Hollen, C. C. (1967), "The Stability of Values and Value Systems," M.A. thesis, Michigan State University.

Independent Sector (1996), *Volunteering and Giving in the United States: Findings From a National Survey*. Washington, D.C.: Independent Sector.

Kotler, P. and Scheff, J. (1997), *Standing Room Only: Strategies for Marketing the Performing Arts*. Boston, MA: Harvard Business School Press.

Mahoney, J. and Pechura, C. M. (1980), "Values and Volunteers: Axiology of Altruism in a Crisis Center," *Psychological Reports*, 47 (3, pt. 1), 1007-1012.

Meddis, R. (1984), *Statistics Using Ranks: A Unified Approach*. New York: Basil Blackwell.

Mehrabian, A., and Epstein, N. (1972), "A Measure of Emotional Empathy," *Journal of Personality*, 40, 525-543.

Miller, L. E. (1985), "Understanding the Motivation of Volunteers: An Examination of Personality Differences and Characteristics of Volunteers' Paid Employment," *Journal of Voluntary Action Research*, 14 (2-3), 112-122.

Miller, L. E., Powell, G. N., and Seltzer, J. (1990), "Determinants of Turnover Among Volunteers," *Human Relations*, 43 (9), 901-917.

Okun, M. A. (1994), "The Relation Between Motives for Organizational Volunteering and the Frequency of Volunteering by Elders," *The Journal of Applied Gerontology*, 13 (2), 115-126.

Okun, M. A. and Eisenberg, N. (1992), "Motives and Intent to Continue Organizational Volunteering Among Residents of a Retirement Community Area," *Journal of Community Psychology*, 20 (3), 183-187.

Omoto, A. M. and Snyder, M. (1990), "Basic Research in Action: Volunteerism and Society's Response to AIDS," *Personality and Social Psychology Bulletin*, 16 (1), 152-165.

Omoto, A. M. and Snyder, M. (1993), "AIDS Volunteers and Their Motivations: Theoretical Issues and Practical Concerns," *Nonprofit Management & Leadership*, 4 (2), 157-176.

Pforzheimer, E. S. and Miller, A. R. (1996), "Hospital Volunteerism in the '90s," *Hospitals & Health Networks*, Feb 20, 80.

Rokeach, M. (1973), *The Nature of Human Values*. New York: The Free Press.

Rokeach, M. (1968), *Beliefs, Attitudes, and Values: A Theory of Organization and Change*. San Francisco: Jossey-Bass.

Schwartz, S. H., and Howard, J. A. (1984), "Internalized Values as Motivators of Altruism," in Staub, E., Bar-Tal, D., and Karylowski, J. (eds.), *Development and Maintenance of Prosocial Behavior*. New York: Plenum.

Smith, D. H. (1994), "Determinants of Voluntary Association Participation and Volunteering: A Literature Review," *Nonprofit and Voluntary Sector Quarterly*, 23 (3), 243-264.

Snyder, M., and Debono, K. G. (1987), "A Functional Approach to Attitudes and Persuasion," in Zanna, M. P., Olson, J. M., and Herman, C. P. (eds.), *Social influence: The Ontario Symposium*, vol. 5. Hillsdale, NJ: Lawrence Erlbaum.

Williams, R. F. (1987), "Receptivity to Persons with Mental Retardation: A Study of Volunteer Interest," *American Journal of Mental Retardation*, 92 (3), 299-303.

Wright, N. D., Larson, V., and Higgs, R. (1995), "Marketing of Voluntarism: The Case of Appalachian Mountain Housing," *Journal of Consumer Satisfaction, Dissatisfaction, and Complaining Behavior*, 8, 188-197.

Wymer, W. W., Jr. (1997a), "A Religious Motivation to Volunteer? Exploring the Linkage Between Volunteering and Religious Values," *Journal of Nonprofit & Public Sector Marketing*, 5 (3), 3-17.

Wymer, W. W., Jr. (1997b), "Segmenting Volunteers Using Values, Self-esteem, Empathy, and Facilitation as Determinant Variables," *Journal of Nonprofit & Public Sector Marketing*, 5 (2), 3-28.

Wymer, W. W., Jr. Riecken, G., and Yavas, U. (1996), "Determinants of Volunteerism: A Cross Disciplinary Review and Research Agenda," *Journal of Nonprofit & Public Sector Marketing*, 4 (4), 3-26.

Yavas, U. and Riecken, G. (1981), "Volunteer Recruitment: A Marketing Approach," in Bernhardt et at. (eds.), *The Changing Marketing Environment: New Theories and Applications*. Chicago: American Marketing Association.

Yavas, U. and Riecken, G. (1985), "Can Volunteers be Targeted?" *Journal of the Academy of Marketing Science*, 13 (2), 218-228.

Zweigenhaft, R. L., Armstrong, J., Quintis, F., and Riddick, A. (1996), "The Motivations and Effectiveness of Hospital Volunteers," *The Journal of Social Psychology*, 136 (1), 25-34.

Encouraging Human Organ Donation: Altruism versus Financial Incentives

Thomas J. Cossé
Terry M. Weisenberger

SUMMARY. A major concern of the organ procurement and transplantation community is finding ways to increase organ donation. Over 72,000 patients were on the national waiting lists for organs in the United States during 1996, but less than 18,000 organs were actually transplanted. Furthermore, over 4,000 patients died in 1996 while awaiting suitable organs for transplantation. Financial incentives have been proposed as a method to increase donation. This paper provides an overview of the organ procurement and allocation system in the United States; reviews the proposals to introduce financial incentives into the system; and presents the findings of a four-year study that gauged public attitudes toward such incentives in a medium-size, southeastern U.S. metro area. *[Article copies available for a fee from The Haworth Document Delivery Service: 1-800-342-9678. E-mail address: getinfo@haworthpressinc. com <Website: http://www.haworthpressinc.com>]*

INTRODUCTION

Although organ transplantation is one of the most remarkable chapters in medical history, the biggest obstacle transplant science faces today is the

Thomas J. Cossé is Professor of Marketing and Terry M. Weisenberger is Associate Professor of Marketing, both at E. Claiborne Robins School of Business, University of Richmond.

This paper is an extension of a paper presented at the 1997 Atlantic Marketing Association Conference.

[Haworth co-indexing entry note]: "Encouraging Human Organ Donation: Altruism versus Financial Incentives." Cossé, Thomas J., and Terry M. Weisenberger. Co-published simultaneously in *Journal of Nonprofit & Public Sector Marketing* (The Haworth Press, Inc.) Vol. 6, No. 2/3, 1999, pp. 77-94; and: *Volunteerism Marketing: New Vistas for Nonprofit and Public Sector Management* (ed: Donald R. Self and Walter W. Wymer, Jr.) The Haworth Press, Inc., 1999, pp. 77-94. Single or multiple copies of this article are available for a fee from The Haworth Document Delivery Service [1-800-342-9678, 9:00 a.m. - 5:00 p.m. (EST). E-mail address: getinfo@haworthpressinc.com].

severe shortage of suitable organs to transplant (Perry 1995). According to data from the United Network for Organ Sharing (UNOS), 72,386 patients were listed on the national waiting lists during 1996 (see Exhibit 1). Though there are more than 2,000,000 deaths annually in the U.S., there were only 5,420 cadaveric donors during 1996. While the number of cadaveric donors in the U.S. has increased by nearly a third since 1988 (4,083 donors), the number is far short of the potential given the number of deaths (UNOS 1998a).

There are many opinions as to the reasons for the disparity between supply and demand and what can be done to reduce it. Some have theorized that, in general, there is no incentive to be an organ donor, while others have battled the dilemma of whose choice should weigh most heavily, the deceased or the deceased's family (Tamelleo 1993)? Similarly, suggestions to increase the number of organs recovered have ranged from public and professional education via formal programs (Partnership Organ Donation 1996a, 1996b) and promotional activities (Anonymous 1996) to some form of compensation system. While the use of financial incentives in the donation process is the

EXHIBIT 1. Selected Data from the Organ Procurement and Transplantation Network and The National Scientific Registry

Type of Organ	Total Patients Waiting List in 1996[b]	Cadaveric Donors in 1996[c]	Organs Transplanted in 1996[d]	Reported Patient Deaths While Awaiting Organs in 1996
Kidney	45,513	10,017	8,782	1,797
Liver	12,814	4,335	4,013	953
Heart	7,171	2,459	2,368	744
Lung	3,557	1,385	1,256	386
Kidney-Pancreas	2,441			91
Pancreas	543	1,300	1,019	3
Heart-Lung	347			48
Total	72,386	5,420	17,438	4,022

[a]These figures include multiple registrations.

[b]Adjusted for multiple registrations.

[c]This is the number of cadaveric donors; living donors are not included. Donors refers to the number of persons whose organs were donated, not to the actual number of organs recovered. Further, some organs are not used for transplantation; some are used in research and others are discarded for medical reasons.

[d]Includes transplants of organs recovered from living donors.

Source: UNOS (1998).

focus of this paper, before addressing this issue some background on the cultural acceptability of organ donation, the legal framework of organ donation and allocation, the donation process, and methods of identifying donors is necessary.

CULTURAL ACCEPTABILITY
OF ORGAN DONATION IN THE U.S.

Given the low level of donations in the U.S., it is tempting to assume that organ donation is not culturally acceptable. National surveys, however, indicate that such is not the case. In fact, most surveys conducted in Western countries show that over 50% of those polled favor organ donation (Sanner 1994a). In the U.S., a 1984 survey reported that a majority expressed positive attitudes toward donation (Prottas and Batten 1986, Prottas 1993) (see Exhibit 2). Similar results were obtained in a 1993 nationwide survey conducted by The Gallup Organization (see Exhibit 3).

Differences in attitude among ethnic/racial groups is evident in both studies–whites are generally more positive than Hispanics, who in turn are more positive than blacks. Although not shown in Exhibit 2, Prottas (1993) found that controlling for race reveals that better educated individuals are more supportive than less educated individuals, and that wealthier individuals are more supportive than poorer individuals. It should also be noted that in both studies, participants expressed greater willingness to donate a relative's organs than their own organs. The generally positive attitudes toward organ donation in the U.S. are similar to those found in a Swedish study; but contrary to U.S. findings, the Swedish respondents were far less likely to donate a relative's organs than their own (Sanner 1994b, Lundberg 1994).

EXHIBIT 2. Public Attitudes: Percent Expressing Willingness/Support

	Percent Expressing Willingness/Support		
	Total	White	Black
I strongly approve of organ donation.	90	91	79
I'd donate my own organs.	72	74	51
If my kin had expressed a willingness, I'd permit donation.	94	94	85
If my kin had not expressed a preference and I knew he/she was brain dead, I'd permit donation.	77	79	58

Source: Prottas and Batten (1986). Differences between whites and blacks significant (p < .05) for each statement.

EXHIBIT 3. Public Attitudes Toward Organ Donation and Transplantation

	Percent Very or Somewhat Likely			
	Total	White	Black	Hispanic
How likely are you to want to have your organs donated after your death?	69	72	52	57
Would you be willing to sign a donor card giving permission for your organs to be donated upon your death (or have you already signed a donor card)?	55	56	34	49
If you had not discussed organ donation with a family how likely would you be to donate their organs upon death?	47	48	39	43
If a family member had requested that their organs be donated upon death, how likely would you be to donate their organs upon death?	93	93	88	83

Source: The Gallup Organization, Inc. (1993). Significance levels not reported.

LEGAL FRAMEWORK

The legal framework for organ donation in the U.S. is the National Organ Transplant Act (NOTA) of 1984 (as amended in 1988 and in 1990), the Uniform Anatomical Gift Act (UAGA), and the Sixth Omnibus Budget Reconciliation Act (SOBRA). NOTA, which specifically outlaws the buying or selling of human organs or tissue (Prottas 1993), established the National Organ Transplantation Network (OPTN). The OPTN's responsibilities include improving the effectiveness of cadaver organ procurement and distribution, increasing patient access to state-of-the-art transplantation technology, improving the system for sharing organs, assuring quality control, and maintaining the skills of those involved in procurement and transplantation activities (UNOS 1996). UNOS is a private, non-profit organization that has the Federal contract to operate the OPTN. UNOS has specific policies regarding standards of membership, organ allocation and data management. At this time the policies and standards are not enforceable by law and are considered *voluntary guidance* to OPTN members. UNOS also has the Federal contract to maintain the U.S. Scientific Registry of Transplant Recipients. The Scientific Registry collects and maintains data for ongoing evaluation of the clinical and scientific status of transplantation in the U.S. (UNOS 1996).

UAGA, which specifically precludes the introduction of a market presence into individual donation decisions, explicitly authorizes the voluntary gifting of body parts upon death and delineates a hierarchy of rules governing how the gift may be stipulated and who may commit the gift. The method of commitment with which most persons are most familiar is the Organ Donor Card (ODC), which is routinely the back side of state driver's licenses. An individual's wishes, as demonstrated on an executed ODC, is a binding, legal authorization to remove organs regardless of the wishes of the individual's family. In the absence of an ODC, the UAGA specifies which family members have a right to authorize a donation-generally, the spouse of an adult or the parents of a minor.

While NOTA and the UAGA are aimed at the protection of the individual's rights without imposing any specific obligation on the physicians or medical profession in general, passage of the Sixth Omnibus Budget Reconciliation Act in 1986 (SOBRA) substantially altered the responsibilities of the medical profession by introduction of *required request*. SOBRA states that families have the right to decide whether to permit organ donation. When there is no executed ODC, physicians and hospitals are required to present organ donation as an option to the family of patients judged to be dying or who have just died. This is referred to as *required request* (Farrell and Greiner 1993).

ORGAN RECOVERY AND DISTRIBUTION SYSTEM

Recovery and distribution of organs is conducted by Organ Procurement Organizations (OPOs). NOTA requires that all OPOs as well as transplant hospitals be OPTN members. Currently there are 65 OPOs in the U.S. Of those, 53 are independent and the others are affiliated with hospital transplant centers. OPOs conduct their activities in specific geographic regions. The tasks facing OPOs are difficult for three reasons. First, although laws require doctors/hospitals to cooperate (required request), doctors and hospitals have considerable control over patient information and only a doctor can determine that a patient is medically suitable for donation, or declare a patient dead. Laws cannot coerce either judgment and there may be no true motivation for a doctor to cooperate. Second, although not required by law, OPOs seek family permission even if a valid, executed ODC exists. Third, recovery is a complex task, involving numerous technical and administrative steps as well as geographic considerations.

While organs are allocated using the UNOS computer system and following the allocation rules, policies, and procedures of the OPTN (UNOS 1997), equity issues may be raised because of the geographic areas that OPOs serve. Some OPOs' service areas may include a portion of a state, an entire state, or even multiple states. Geographic areas can differ by race, social class, education, income, or other demographic variables which can have an effect on individuals' willingness to donate as well as on donor/recipient compatibility (Davidson and Devney 1991, Novello 1992, Wheeler and Cheung 1996). Adding to the problem is the fact that some groups that have a higher incidence of need for transplants also donate at a lower rate (Farrell and Greiner 1993). Simply stated, the type of transplant needed, where a patient lives and the number and type of hospitals in an area can add months or years to the waiting time for an organ (Fernández et al. 1991; McMenamin 1996; Tokarski 1994).

In April 1998, the Department of Health and Human Services published a rule requiring standardized criteria to list patients on the organ waiting lists and to determine medical status. The new rule eliminates the current practice of first searching for recipients within the recovering OPO's service area and it requires a nationwide search to find the person most in need. The rule was scheduled to go into effect July 1998 (see HHS 1998a, 1998b). However, considerable opposition was expressed by members of the procurement and transplantation community. In October 1998, the 1999 Omnibus Appropriations Act was passed. Included in the act is a provision that places a one year moratorium on the new rule. During the moratorium year, the act requires the Institute of Medicine of the National Academy of Sciences to conduct a study of the impact of the OPTN current policies and of the new rule on procurement and transplantation activities (UNOS 1998b). The study must be completed by May 1999 and is to be submitted to appropriate Congressional Committees for review.

Explicit Consent

The current system in the U.S. is based on a practice referred to as *explicit consent*. Under explicit consent, individuals (adults) must decide for themselves whether or not they wish to become organ donors. Executing an ODC is the method used most often to document the decision. Despite the ease of completing an ODC and the general support for the practice of organ donation expressed by the public, the number of individuals who actually take the time to do so is much smaller than the number who express support for the concept of organ donation (Gallup 1993). Legally the wishes of the deceased must be honored and in the event no declaration exists, the family should decide. However, even in the face of a signed ODC, OPOs typically honor the wishes of the family not to recover organs.

Mandated Choice

The limited participation under explicit consent has led to significant discussion of a practice referred to as *mandated choice*. Under this program, all competent adults would be required to decide and record prospectively whether or not they wish to become organ donors when they die, and their decision would be controlling, unable to be overridden by their families. (Theoretically, under the current system of explicit consent, an individual's decision to be a donor is legally binding; in practice, however, the family's wishes not to donate are respected.) This mandated choice could be accomplished by asking about organ donation on drivers' license applications or tax returns. In order to obtain a license or have the return accepted, the question would have to be answered. A change of mind could easily be communicated at any time with a written directive (Spital 1995). This proposal would remove the hurdle of individuals failing to complete an advance directive, but it does not ensure an increase in the number of organs recovered. If a majority of respondents declined to be donors, mandated choice will not have helped alleviate the organ shortage.

Presumed Consent

A final approach that has been suggested is *presumed consent*. Under presumed consent, it is assumed that people consent to be cadaveric (deceased) organ donors unless they or their family members register an objection (Glasson et al. 1994). This is almost the mirror image of the current practice as only those with strong feelings either way will elect to complete an ODC or other advance directive indicating an affirmative or negative preference. If the directive is negative, the potential donor is lost; if it is affirmative or missing, the OPO will look to the family as is the current practice under explicit consent. The greatest hope for improved organ recovery under this method is that more families will be asked. This is unlikely to have an impact on the number of organs recovered as SOBRA stipulates required request. Under presumed consent, the laws effectively will not have changed the situation.

ALTRUISM VERSUS FINANCIAL INCENTIVES

Altruism suggests that individuals give in non-reciprocal situations and do not seek any direct return. The belief is that the individual considers the benefits that accrue to society as a whole from their behavior. The only direct benefit the individual receives is from membership in the social system (Prottas 1992, 1993). Organ donation is an extreme form of such altruism. Individuals willing to donate most often express a desire to help an unknown member of the community; the hope of using organ donation to salvage something positive (life) from something negative (death), or allowing a loved one to live on through a recipient.

The counter argument comes primarily from the allocation of available resources. The prevailing philosophy is that donated organs are "public property" and that individual doctors and hospitals merely provide stewardship of the organs. The actual allocation of the organs is controlled principally by the appropriate OPO. As previously stated, there may be inequities in the allocation process because of the demographic composition of the people in geographic areas served by each OPO.

A classic chicken and egg situation may result. Are individuals reluctant to give because they have no opportunity to receive in return, or are these individuals unable to receive due to an overall insufficient number of donors? Prottas (1993) argues that gift giving, especially gift giving involving a "sacred object," both builds and defines communities. If categories of people are excluded from receiving a transplant, they are excluded from a community in which gifts are given and accepted. The present system is contradictory in that all families may be asked to donate organs, but the Americans that are uninsured or underinsured are pragmatically ineligible to receive a transplant regardless of need–except in the case of kidneys which are covered by Medicare (Hagen 1995). Despite what appears to be overwhelming support for the practice of organ donation and the willingness to donate one's own organs as well as the those of a loved one, the number of organs actually recovered for transplantation remains unacceptably low.

Some have pointed to a lack of incentives as the root cause. Proponents of a compensation-based system of organ procurement suggest that the problem is two-fold. First, there is no incentive for donors to give, and second, there is no incentive for the medical profession or procurement coordinators to ask them to give (Barnett, Blair, and Kaserman 1992). Barnett et al. state that the principle cause of the current organ shortage is a widespread failure to request donation from potential organ suppliers, not a refusal to donate. They feel that the failure to request stems from there being no incentive for the physicians, nurses or OPOs to ask; and because the task of asking is so inherently unpleasant that those who do ask generally do so only half-heartedly.

It should be noted that the claim that there is no incentive to ask is not completely accurate. OPOs receive organ acquisition fees that at least recoup their organ recovery costs. Some doctors get consultation fees for evaluating the donor once permission to recover the organs is secured and hospitals get payment from the OPOs in seven to ten days for all hospital costs associated with the donation. Further, the OPO personnel that typically seek permission from the family to recover organs, organ procurement coordinators, are highly trained professionals who rarely ask in a "half-heartedly" manner as claimed by Barnett, Blair, and Kaserman (1992).

Although NOTA outlaws the buying or selling of human organs and tissues, several proponents of compensation based systems have provided arguments that deserve consideration. Two in particular that cover most available arguments are for the establishment of either (1) a futures market, or (2) a market-based procurement system.

Futures Market

Under a futures market, individuals would be compensated for the promise of their donated organs at some later date, or the deceased's estate would in some way benefit from the pre-arranged recovery of the deceased's organs upon death. The proposal would seek to eliminate any family role in the decision process at time of death and place further liability on physicians to obtain relevant information and to preserve or make available the organs (Glasson et al. 1994). Similar arguments have been made to provide some compensation for the completion of affirmative advance directives.

Market Based System

Barnett, Blair, and Kaserman (1992) go a step further in proposing a "market-based system of organ procurement with a profit incentive for organ procurement firms to actively seek out potential organ donors and negotiate a mutually agreeable supply contract." Their proposal would remove the OPOs from the practice of coordinating the recovery of organs and would introduce an independent, profit motivated party to conduct transactions. This party would fill requests for needed organs, or seek buyers for available organs, presumably at current market prices. They further argue that such a market system would correct the problems of both the lack of incentive to donate and the lack of incentive to ask, whereas compensation just to the donor, only addresses the former problem. Even strong proponents of incentives and compensation-based systems recognize that the idea may be so objectionable to the general public that the availability of organs and the number of organs transplanted may actually decrease.

Two recent studies shed some light on the opinions of the general public and of the "gatekeepers" in the organ procurement system. According to the previously cited Gallup study (1993), a majority of the participants indicate that the presence of financial incentives would have no effect on donating their own or a family member's organs (see Exhibit 4). While the proportions differ by race/ethnic group, a majority say that such incentives would have no effect.

Altshuler and Evanisko (1992) examined the gatekeepers' views on (1) whether financial incentives should be offered to encourage families to donate after the individual is deceased, and (2) the gatekeeper's level of comfort in presenting donation as an option if financial incentives were part of the package.

EXHIBIT 4. The Effect of Financial Incentives on Willingness to Donate Own or Family Member's Organs

| | | Percent Responding No Effect | | | |
		Total	White	Black	Hispanic
Would financial incentives like these					
[assistance in paying funeral	**Own Organs:**	81	83	70	67
expenses, a cash award to					
the donor's estate, or a cash award	**Family Members**				
to a charity of the family's choice]	**Organs:**	78	80	62	66
make you more or less likely to					
donate your organs or a family					
member's organs, or would it have					
no effect?					

Source: The Gallup Organization, Inc. (1993). Significance levels not reported.

The results are presented in Exhibit 5. Overwhelmingly, respondents felt incentives should not be offered to encourage families to donate. More importantly, gatekeepers are simply uncomfortable presenting the option to families once financial incentives are introduced. As low requestor comfort has been shown to be related to low consent rates (Hoffman and Malecw 1987), the addition of financial incentives may make requestor (gatekeeper) comfort levels even lower, and thus could make the situation worse. For example, many of those polled stated they would not participate in donation if they were required to offer incentives. Financial incentives could actually decrease, instead of increase, the number of organ donors (Altshuler and Evanisko 1992).

ANNUAL TRACKING STUDY

As part of a larger tracking study on attitudes toward organ donation and transplantation in a medium-size southeastern city, four telephone surveys of metro area adults were conducted approximately 12 months apart beginning in July 1994. Telephone numbers were randomly selected from the residential listings of the local telephone directory and the +1 technique was employed (Churchill 1991, p. 329). Respondents were screened to ensure that neither they nor any other member of the household were employed in the medical/ health care industry. Interviews were completed with 161 persons in 1994, 126 in 1995, 142 in 1996, and 141 in 1997. The research question addressed

EXHIBIT 5. Gatekeeper Attitudes

A. Should Financial Incentives Be Offered to Encourage Families to Donate?	Percent Responding		
	Yes	Unsure	No
Chaplain	5	16	79
Critical Care Nurse	8	13	79
Neurosurgeon	10	12	78
Organ Procurement Coordinator	16	31	53
Social Worker	9	21	70

B. Level of Comfort Presenting Donation Option Currently vs. With Financial Incentives[a]	Percent Very or Somewhat Comfortable:	
	Without Financial Incentives	With Financial Incentives
Chaplain	85	22
Critical Care Nurse	59	17
Neurosurgeon	80	20
Organ Procurement Coordinator	99	52
Social Worker	80	41

[a]For each category of gatekeeper, the difference between very/somewhat comfortable without financial incentives and very/somewhat comfortable with financial incentives is significant at $p < .001$.
Source: Altshuler and Evanisko (1992).

in this paper is to determine the extent to which the general public believes that financial incentives should be employed and whether feelings about such incentives have changed over time.

To examine consumer feelings about financial incentives, three Likert-type statements were employed (see Table 1). Statements 1 and 2 deal directly with financial incentives (contribution to funeral expenses, cash payments, etc.), while statement 2 addresses concerns over the possibility of extra medical expenses, and therefore, deals indirectly with financial issues. Respondents indicated if they *strongly agreed, agreed, neither agreed nor disagreed, disagreed, or strongly disagreed* with each of the statements. Standard demographic data also were obtained.

Analysis

Sample Equivalency. Prior to analyzing the responses to the three statements, the samples were tested for equivalency on demographic variables (see Table 2). The samples do not differ by, education (p. = .166), race (p. =

TABLE 1. Attitudes Toward the Use of Financial Incentives: 1994, 1995, 1996, 1997

		Study	Percent Responding[bc]					Percent Agreeing, Neither, Disagreeing[c]			Sample
	Statement[a]	Year	SA	A	AnD	D	SD	SA+A	AnD	D+SD	$\bar{x}$[d]
1.	A contribution should be made	1994	2	34	22	39	3	36	22	42	2.92
	toward the funeral costs of an	1995	4	31	22	41	2	35	22	43	2.94
	organ donor.	1996	5	36	23	31	5	41	23	36	3.05
		1997	4	30	22	41	3	34	22	44	2.89
2.	Financial incentives, such as	1994	1	31	13	47	9	32	13	56	2.68
	cash payments, to the donor's	1995	2	23	18	49	8	25	18	57	2.63
	estate or heirs should be used	1996	4	26	23	35	13	30	23	48	2.72
	to encourage organ donations.	1997	1	23	18	46	11	24	18	57	2.56
3.	I am concerned that people who	1994	1	11	26	57	5	12	26	62	2.46
	choose to donate a family	1995	2	18	26	54	1	20	26	55	2.67
	member's organs end up paying	1996	4	23	31	41	2	27	31	43	2.85
	extra bills.	1997	1	15	31	48	5	16	31	53	2.60

[a]The order in which statements were read was rotated to control for order bias.
[b]SA: strongly agree, A: agree, AnD: neither agree nor disagree, D: disagree, SD: strongly disagree.
[c]Sum of percentages may not equal 100% due to rounding.
[d]Sample sizes: 1994 = 161, 1995 = 126, 1996 = 142, 1997 = 141. Scores used to compute means are based on SA = 5, A = 4, AnD = 3, D = 2, SD = 1.

.30), or sex (p. = .90). However, the samples do differ by age (p. = .01) and by income (p. = .003). These differences are addressed in a subsequent section of this paper.

Analysis of Responses. Table 2 presents information by study year on the responses to the three statements. Both the percentage responding with each response option, and trichotomized responses (strongly agree/agree, neither agree nor disagree, and strongly disagree/disagree) are presented. While this is provided for clarity and ease of discussion, the samples were actually tested for significant differences in responses with MANOVA and univariate F tests.

As shown in Table 3 (section A), multivariate significance is evident in the responses across study years (p. ranges from .001 to .033). Further, univariate F tests show that the differences across years rest with statement 3, *concern over incurring additional medical expenses* (p. = .001), rather than with the two financial incentive statements (p. = .753 and .605) (see Table 3, section C). This was anticipated from the presentation in Table 1 as there appeared to be little difference in the responses to statements 1 and 2: between 34% and 41% of the respondents strongly agreed/agreed that a contribution to funeral costs should be made, and between 24% and 32% strongly agreed/agreed that various financial incentives should be used to encourage donation. For statement 3, however, only 12% in 1994 and 20% in 1995 strongly agreed/agreed

TABLE 2. Comparison of the Demographic Composition of the Samples

Characteristic[a]	Statistical Test	Significance
Age	ANOVA	.010[b]
Education	Kruskal Wallis	.166
Income	Kruskal Wallis	.003[c]
Race	χ^2	.300
Sex	χ^2	.900

[a]Categories employed for comparisons: age: actual ages of respondents; education: high school/votech or less, some college; bachelor degree, some graduate school or degree; income: >$95K, $80K-95K, $65K-$79.9K, $50K-$64.9K, $35K-$49.9K, $20K-$34.9K, <$20K; race: black, other minority, white; sex: male, female.
[b]Mean age by sample year: 45.2 for 1994, 46.1 for 1995, 40.4 for 1996, 42.2 for 1997.
[c]Mean ranks on income are 225.38 for 1994, 235.96 for 1995, 284.40 for 1996, and 212.37 for 1997. Lower ranks correspond to lower income levels.

compared to 27% in 1996. However, in 1997 the proportion strongly agreeing/agreeing dropped to 16%.

This finding raises the question of whether the differences in expressed concern over the possibility of additional medical bills truly represent a change in sentiment or are an artifact of the demographic differences noted in the sample equivalency tests. Recall, that the groups were found to differ significantly by age (p. = .01) and by income (p. = .003).

The Effect of Age. The relationship between age and concern over incurring additional medical costs was examined with ANOVA (see Table 4). There is no significant relationship between the level of concern and the age of the respondent. Therefore, the significant change in mean age of sample by year–1994-1995, up; 1995-1996, down; 1996-1997, up–is not a concern. In any case, the significant difference in age of sample is between 1995 and 1996 and the level of concern is not significantly different in those years (see Table 3). Age can be dismissed as a factor in the changing level of concern over the course of the study.

The Effect of Income. The possibility of a relationship between income and concern over incurring additional medical costs was examined using the Kruskal Wallis test. Participants were grouped according to their trichotomized response to statement 3 and income was compared across groups. The results presented in Table 5 clearly show that income is associated with the level of "concern" (p. = .001). Individuals with lower incomes are more likely to be concerned that families of donors might incur additional medical expenses. Inasmuch as income differs significantly by sample year, 1996 > 1995 > 1994 > 1997 (refer to Table 2, note c), it appears that the increases in the level of concern over medical expenses does, in fact, represent a change in attitude, and is not due to the income differences of the samples. That is, given the trend to higher levels of income in the more recent samples and that

TABLE 3. MANOVA on Statements 1, 2, and 3 by Sample Year

A. Multivariate Tests	Test	F	Error DF	Significance
	Pillai's	2.022	1,692	.034
	Hotelling's	2.042	1,682	.032
	Wilks'	2.033	1,368	.033
	Roy's	5.527	564	.001
B. Test of Equality of Covariance Matrices	Box's M	1.463	18 (df1) 1,059,394 (df2)	.093

C. Univariate F Tests and Levene's Test of Equality of Variances

Statement	Univariate F Tests			Levene's Test of Equality of Variances			
	F	DF	Significance	F	DF1	DF2	Significance
1. A contribution should be made toward the funeral costs of an organ donor.	.753	3	.521	2.52	3	564	.860
2. Financial incentives, such as cash payments to the donor's estate or heirs, should be used to encourage organ donations.	.605	3	.612	.974	3	564	.405
3. I am concerned that people who choose to donate a family member's organs end up paying extra bills.	5.367	3	.001	1.572	3	564	.195

D. Duncans Multiple Range Test on Statement 3 Across Samples

Sample Year	Sample Means'		
	Subset 1	Subset 2	Subset 3
1994	2.46		
1997	2.60	2.60	
1995		2.67	2.67
1996			2.85
Significance:	.15	.50	.09

[a]Means within subsets do not differ significantly, $\alpha = .05$.

TABLE 4. Mean Ages by Trichotomized Responses to Statement 3: *I am concerned that people who choose to donate a family member's organs end up paying extra bills.*

Response	Mean Age	Significance[a]
Strongly Agree/Agree	43.04	.787
Neither Agree nor Disagree	43.22	
Strongly Disagree/Disagree	44.20	

[a]ANOVA.

TABLE 5. Mean Ranks of Income Level by Trichotomized Responses to Statement 3: *I am concerned that people who I choose to donate a family member's organs end up paying extra bills.*

Response	Mean Income Rank[a]	Significance[b]
Strongly Agree/Agree	189.23	.001
Neither Agree nor Disagree	244.55	
Strongly Disagree/Disagree	251.44	

[a]Lower ranks correspond to lower income levels. Income categories correspond to those presented in Table 2.
[b]Kruskal Wallis Test.

income and concern are inversely related, one would have expected the proportion of respondents expressing concern to have decreased–or, certainly, not to have increased over time.

In the most recent sample, 1997, there is a reversal of this trend, however. Income dropped and the level of concern did as well. Bear in mind that income and concern are still inversely related within each sample. All that can be concluded is that whatever forces were stoking concern have abated. See for example Cossé and Weisenberger (1998).

LIMITATIONS

The findings of this study are limited to the southeastern metro area in which study participants reside. Projecting these findings to the entire U.S. population is inappropriate. Further, as UNOS is located in this area, it is possible that area residents have greater exposure to organ donation and transplantation information and publicity than persons residing in other parts of the country. The authors have no evidence that this is the case, but the findings of this study must be considered in light of that possibility.

CONCLUSION

From a public policy perspective, this study demonstrates that there is limited support to use financial incentives to encourage organ donation. Further, the proportion of the population in favor of such incentives has not changed significantly over the course of this study. At the same time there has been increased concern that donor families may incur additional medical expenses, although this concern declined in the last year of the study. This seems to be a reasonable concern in light of the attention that health-care costs have received in recent years. However, in the U.S. organ donation process, the fact is that donor families do not incur additional medical expenses. The expenses associated with organ recovery are borne by the OPO. The implication of this is that the public must be informed of this fact.

Until the public has a more accurate understanding of the facts, it is unlikely that the level of organ donation will improve substantially. Incorrect beliefs about the process will likely be followed by a failure to become a donor or to donate a loved one's organs. This is particularly true in the lower income strata of our society that already donate at a lower rate and have a disproportionate need. These families must know that they can honor a loved one's wishes, or make that decision themselves, without incurring an undue financial burden.

REFERENCES

Altshuler, Jill S. and Michael J. Evanisko, "Financial Incentives for Organ Donation: the Perspectives of Health Care Professionals," *The Journal of the American Medical Association*, 267 (April, 1992), pp. 2037-2038.

Anonymous, "And Now a Pitch for Organ Donations," *Trustee*, 4 (April, 1996), pp. 3.

Barnett, Andrew H., Roger D. Blair, and David L. Kaserman, "Improving Organ Donation: Compensation Versus Markets,"*Inquiry*, 29 (Fall, 1992), pp. 372-378.

Churchill, Gilbert A. Jr. *Marketing Research: Methodological Foundations*, 5th ed., Hinsdale: IL: Dryden Press (1991).

Cossé, Thomas J. and Terry M. Weisenberger, "Words Versus Actions About Organ Donation: A Four Year Tracking Study of Attitudes and Self Reported Behavior," in J. Duncan Herrington and Ronald D. Taylor, eds., *Marketing Advances in Theory, Practice and Education*, Society for Marketing Advances (1998), pp. 104-105.

Davidson, M. N. and P. Devney, "Attitudinal Barriers to Organ Donation Among Black Americans," *Transplantation Proceedings*, 23 (October, 1991), pp. 2531-2532.

Farrell, Kathleen V. and Carl Greiner, "Public Attitudes, Legislation, and Ethical Components of Organ Donation," *Nebraska Medical Journal*, (October, 1993), pp. 324-330.

Fernández, M., E. Zayas, Z. A. González, L. A. Morales Otero, and E. A. Santiago-Delpin, "Factors in a Meager Organ Donation Pattern of a Hispanic Population," *Transplantation Proceedings*, 23 (April, 1991), pp. 1799-1801.

Glasson, John, Charles W. Plows, Robert M. Tenery, Jr., Oscar W. Clarke, Victoria Ruff, Drew Fuller, Craig H. Kliger, George T. Wilkins, Jr., James H. Cosgriff, Jr., David Orentlicher, Karey Harwood, and Jeff Leslie, Council on Ethical and Judicial Affairs, American Medical Association, "Strategies for Cadaveric Organ Procurement: Mandated Choice and Presumed Consent," *The Journal of the American Medical Association*, 272 (September, 1994), pp. 809-812.

Hagan, Dale W., "We Have a Kidney for You," *Saturday Evening Post*, 267 (May-June, 1995), pp. 26ff.

HHS: HHS Rule Calls for Organ Allocation Based on Medical Criteria, Not Geography. *HHS News Release*. U.S. Department of Health and Human Services (March 26, 1998a).

HHS: Improving Fairness and Effectiveness in Allocating Organs for Transplantation. *HRSA News: Fact Sheet*. U.S. Department of Health and Human Services, Health Resources and Services Administration (March 26, 1998b).

Hoffman, M. C. and M. S. Malecw, "Getting to Yes: How Nurses' Attitudes Affect Their Success in Obtaining Consent for Organ and Tissue Donations," *Dial Transplant*, 16 (1987), pp. 276-278.

Lundberg, George D., "Attitudes Toward Autopsy and Organ Donations in Sweden and the United States," *The Journal of the American Medical Association*, 271 (January, 1994), pp. 317.

McMenamin, Brigid, "Why People Die Waiting for Transplants," *Forbes*, 157 (March 11, 1996), pp. 140-148.

Novello, Antonia C., "Increasing Organ Donation–a Report from the Surgeon General's Workshop," *The Journal of the American Medical Association*, 267 (January, 1992), pp. 213.

Partnership for Organ Donation, "Hospitals Can do More to Increase Organ Donation," (March, 1996a).

Partnership for Organ Donation, "Nationwide Project to Increase Organ Donation," (December, 1996b).

Perry, Patrick, "The Greatest Gift," *Saturday Evening Post*, 267 (Jan-Feb, 1995), pp. 38-41.

Prottas, Jeffrey M., "Competition for Altruism: Bone and Organ Procurement in the United States," *The Millbank Quarterly*, 70 (Summer, 1992), p. 299.

Prottas, Jeffrey M., "Altruism, Motivation, and Allocation: Giving and Using Human Organs," *The Journal of Social Issues*, 49 (Summer, 1993), pp. 137-150.

Prottas, Jeffrey M. and H. Batten, "The Attitudes of the American Public," Unpublished Report, Health Care Financing Administration (April, 1986).

Sanner, Margareta, "Attitudes Toward Organ Donation and Transplantation: A Model for Understanding Reactions to Medical Procedures After Death," *Soc. Sci. Med.*, 38 (August, 1994a), pp. 1141-1152.

Sanner, Margareta, "A Comparison of Public Attitudes Toward Autopsy, Organ Donation, and Anatomical Dissection: a Swedish Survey," *The Journal of the American Medical Association*, 271 (January, 1994b), pp. 284-288.

Spital, Aaron, "Mandated Choice: a Plan to Increase Public Commitment to Organ Donation," *The Journal of the American Medical Association*, 273 (February, 1995), pp. 504-506.

Tamelleo, A. David, "Organ Donation: Whose Decision Is It Anyway?" *RN*, 56 (November, 1993), pp. 61-64.

The Gallup Organization, *The American Public's Attitudes Toward Organ Donation and Transplantation: A Gallup Survey for The Partnership for Organ Donation*, (February, 1993).

Tokarski, Cathy, "Tug of War," *Hospitals & Health Networks*, 68 (October 20, 1994), pp. 66-69.

UNOS, *1996 Annual Report: The U.S. Scientific Registry of Transplant Recipients and The Organ Procurement Transplantation Network*, UNOS and Health Resources & Services Administration, U.S. Department of Health & Human Services (1997).

UNOS, "Annual Report," http://www.unos.org (1998a).

UNOS, "OPTN Regulations Update," http://www.unos.org/Newsroom/archive_regs_update_102198.htm (1998b).

Wheeler, Mary S. and Alan HS Cheung (1996), "Minority Attitudes Toward Organ Donation," *Critical Care Nurse*, 16 (February, 1996), pp. 30-33.

Volunteerism Among Non-Clients as Marketing Exchange

Kimball P. Marshall

SUMMARY. Generalized exchange, one of three types of exchange proposed by Bagozzi (1975), has been neglected as an area of research. This is unfortunate because it may provide a better understanding of exchange processes involving non-client input publics (Kotler and Andreasen, 1991). This paper proposes a social marketing model in which non-client perceptions of community benefits, social responsibility, and service quality predict willingness to volunteer for public school activities. The results support a generalized exchange model which emphasizes indirect transfers of utilitarian values and fulfillment of symbolic values. *[Article copies available for a fee from The Haworth Document Delivery Service: 1-800-342-9678. E-mail address: getinfo@haworthpressinc.com <Website: http://www.haworthpressinc.com>]*

INTRODUCTION

Marketers of not-for-profit organizations may benefit from consideration of the concept of generalized exchange. Generalized exchange is one of three

Kimball P. Marshall, PhD, is affiliated with the Department of Management and Marketing, School of Business, Jackson State University, Jackson, MS 39217 (E-mail: kmarshal@netdoor.com).

The research reported in this paper was funded by a Summer Faculty Research Grant from the Mississippi Urban Research Center, Jackson State University, Jackson, MS 39217.

An earlier version of this paper was presented at the 1998 Society for Marketing Advances Annual Meeting and an abstract was published in the proceedings of that association.

[Haworth co-indexing entry note]: "Volunteerism Among Non-Clients as Marketing Exchange." Marshall, Kimball P. Co-published simultaneously in *Journal of Nonprofit & Public Sector Marketing* (The Haworth Press, Inc.) Vol. 6, No. 2/3, 1999, pp. 95-106; and: *Volunteerism Marketing: New Vistas for Nonprofit and Public Sector Management* (ed: Donald R. Self and Walter W. Wymer, Jr.) The Haworth Press, Inc., 1999, pp. 95-106. Single or multiple copies of this article are available for a fee from The Haworth Document Delivery Service [1-800-342-9678, 9:00 a.m. - 5:00 p.m. (EST). E-mail address: getinfo@haworthpressinc.com].

types of exchange situations proposed by Bagozzi in his essay "Marketing as Exchange." Generated exchange is defined by the structural relationships among the actors such that A carries out a univocal (one-way) transfer of value to B who then carries out a univocal transfer of value to C who then carried out a univocal transfer of value to A. Therefore benefits are received only indirectly. This is distinct from "restricted exchange" in which A and B transfer value directly to one another, i.e., a reciprocal exchange, and "complex exchange" in which A and B engage in restricted exchange and then B transfers the value received from A to c in a reciprocal exchange between B and C.

Restricted and complex exchanges are commonly addressed in marketing studies of commercial economic exchanges such as wholesale and retail sales situations and the management of distribution channels, but generalized exchange has generally been neglected. This is unfortunate because generalized exchange may best characterize the relationship of non-clients as an input public to a not-for-profit organization (Marshall, 1998). This study proposes a model in which willingness to engage in exchange is influenced by perceptions of community benefits, social responsibility, and the quality of service performance of the not-for-profit organization. The model is tested using data from non-clients of a public school system.

A MARKETING PERSPECTIVE OF VOLUNTEERISM IN PUBLIC EDUCATION

Marketers focus on the facilitation of exchanges between two or more parties. Typically these exchanges involve monetary transfers. However, from a social and not-for-profit marketing perspective, the medium of exchange may be something other than money and may involve symbolic values (Bagozzi 1975) and behaviors and personal time devoted to voluntary activities (Holler and Andreasen 1991). Not-for-profit organizations often depend on volunteers as key resources. Volunteers may be a source of special expertise, may supplement the formal staff, and may be a vehicle for assuring relevance to community values.

Volunteers may be drawn from both clients and non-clients of not-for-profit organizations. In the case of public school systems, parents of public school children may be a source of volunteers, but non-parents of public school children are also an important input public. In most school systems a substantial portion of the voter population does not have children in the school system (due to demographics of age and stage of family life). Therefore, public school systems may find it advantageous to involve persons who are not parents of public school students. Client volunteers, such as parents of public school children in the case of a public school system, are involved in restricted exchange relationships with the organization in regard to the direct utilitarian and symbolic benefits they receive. In contrast, non-clients–in the case of public school systems, members of the community who are not parents of public school children–are characterized by a generalized exchange relationship in regard to utilitarian benefits because they are not direct service recipients. The utilitarian benefits they receive would be transferred indirectly through improvements of quality of life in a community. However, non-client volunteers are also characterized by restricted exchange. By giving time directly to the school system, they may receive directly symbolic values such as feelings of altruism and satisfaction from fulfilling an ethic of social responsibility. Therefore, efforts to identity factors that influence volunteerism among non-clients must consider both perceptions of utilitarian values such as broad community benefits that characterize generalized exchange, and symbolic values such as fulfillment of social responsibility ethics.

Generalized and Restricted Exchange Among Volunteers

The structural situation referred to here as generalized exchange differs from restricted exchange in at least two features. First, there are more than two actors in generalized exchange. While the example in the introduction considered actors A, B and C, there may be many actors involved in the chain of indirect transfers of benefits. Bagozzi (1975) uses the example of a social welfare system. Second, the exchanges are univocal. They move in a circular direction by which eventual reciprocity is developed in the system. Without reciprocity in exchange actors would cease to voluntarily participate (Houston and Gassenheimer 1987; Marshall 1998).

While in all exchanges there is the risk that the desired reciprocal value might not be received, in generalized exchange the risk may be heightened by the indirect nature of the transfers due to the number of actors potentially involved and the time lag inherent in indirect transfers. In such a situation, perceptions of the quality of the not-for-profit organization's performance may influence willingness to engage in generalized exchange by affecting perceived risk. If the organization is not perceived as effective, the perceived risk that desired utilitarian benefits will not be received may be increased–exacerbating an uncertain situation. Perceptions of performance of the not-for-profit organization may also be expected to influence a potential volunteer's confidence that desired restricted exchange symbolic values will be received. Symbolic values of social appreciation, prestige and citizenship (Gouldner 1970) that may be desired by a volunteer may depend upon the anticipated quality of interaction with the organization. Willingness to volunteer may therefore depend on perceptions of organization performance.

Dimensions of Performance in Service Organizations

Over the past two decades marketers have devoted considerable attention to developing techniques for measuring client perceptions of service quality in for-profit organizations (Lovelock 1996). Much work has centered on two closely related approaches referred to as the SERVQUAL (Parasuraman, Zeithaml and Berry 1985, 1994; Parasuraman, Berry and Zeithaml 1991; Zeithaml, Parasuraman and Berry 1990; Zeithaml, Berry and Parasuraman 1996) and SERVPERF models (Cronin and Taylor 1992, 1994). The SERVQUAL approach involves the use of 22 items to assess clients' perceptions of the importance of specific aspects of service quality. These are then used to weight a corresponding set of 22 items that assess clients' self-reported experiences. The SERVPERF approach considers only the clients' reports of actual experiences using the same items. Although there are methodological differences, both approaches have produced highly valid and reliable indicators of service quality and both recognize five intermingled and perhaps interdependent dimensions of perceptions of service quality:

1. perceptions of *tangible aspects* of the service organization such as physical structures and physical products;
2. perceptions of *reliability of* service performance and outcome quality;
3. perceptions of *responsiveness* in specification services and the efficiency of performance;
4. perceptions of *assurance* in regard to the confidence that the customer has in the members of the organization and their job performance;
5. perceptions of *empathy* as indicated by perceptions of attention to needs of customers for personal attention and convenience.

While SERVQUAL and SERVPERF items have produced reliable and valid scales for dimensions of service quality based on customers' direct experiences in for-profit retail settings (Parasuraman, Zeithaml and Berry 1985, 1994; Parasuraman, Berry and Zeithaml 1991; Cronin and Taylor 1992, 1994), the use of such items may be problematic for assessing non-client perceptions of not-for-profit organizations since non-clients may have little or no direct contact with the organization. However, even without direct experiences, non-clients may develop perceptions of the quality of an organization's performance from the organization's own public relations efforts, from mass media reports, and from contact with other members of the community who have had contact with the organization. While such reported perceptions might not be accurate, such perceptions of the organization's service quality may influence willingness to engage in volunteer activities as a form of marketing exchange.

Propositions

This discussion leads to three propositions regarding non-clients of not-for-profit organizations:

1. The greater the perception of potential community benefits from a not-for-profit organization, the greater the willingness to volunteer for support activities;
2. The greater the belief in a social responsibility ethic regarding a not-for-profit organization, the greater the willingness to volunteer for support activities;
3. The more positive the perception of service quality of a not-for-profit organization, the greater the willingness to volunteer for support activities.

METHODOLOGY

The data used for this study were developed from a mailed questionnaire survey sent to 1,991 randomly selected registered voters in a single urban school district which had been engaged in public controversy regarding educational quality, leadership, budgets and school safety for several years. During the data collection period the new (one year) superintendent resigned. Questionnaires were returned by 298 respondents, providing a response rate of 15.0%. Of these, 124 respondents reported that they did not have school age children and were homeowners, and also provided responses to all service quality and volunteerism items used in this report. Of these, 51.6% identified themselves as men and 48.4% as women. The respondents tended to be older (to be expected since many had grown children); only 18.6% were age 50 or below, 20.3% were age 51 to 60, 35.6% were age 61 to 70, and 25.4% were over 70 years of age. Regarding education, only 4.9% did not have a high school degree, 19.5% had a high school degree only, 42.3% had only a college degree, and 33.3% had pursued graduate studies.

Because this study is focused on perceptions held by people who are not direct service recipients, it is important to document exposure and sources of information. No visits to public schools or public school offices in the past year were reported by 54.0% of these respondents, 24.2% reported only one or two visits and 10.5% reported three to five visits. Only 11.3% reported over five visits. Approximately 35.8% reported not having read any material from the school system in the past year, 26.8% reported having read material only once or twice, 15.4% reported reading school system material three to five times, and 22.0% reported more than five times. Dependence on the public media for information about the public school system is indicated by the fact that 83.1% reported having heard, read or seen public media news reports relating to the school system six or more times in the past year.

Operationalizations

The propositions presented above require operationalization of perceptions of community benefits, social responsibility, school system service quality and volunteerism. In total, 31 items were used to develop scales corresponding to these concepts. Items for community benefits and social responsibility were drawn from the literature on educational marketing (Marshall 1998). Items on aspects of public schools service quality were developed by adapting SERVQUAL-SERVPERF items (Cronin and Taylor 1992, 1994) using school system administrators as experts to assess face validity for the adapted items and their assignment to SERVQUAL-SERVPERF dimensions. Wherever possible, wording was kept as close to the SERVPERF wording used by Cronin and Taylor (1992) as possible and items were assigned in accordance with the original SERVQUAL-SERVPERF assignments. Items for the volunteerism scale (Volunteer) were developed by the researcher. School system administrators were used as experts to establish face validity of the Volunteer items.

A total of 35 items were included in the questionnaire to develop scales for the key variables used in this report. All items used in this study were scored on a 1 to 5 scale with "1" indicating "Strongly Disagree," "3" indicating "Don't Know" and "5" indicating "Strongly Agree." The assumption here is that a "Don't Know" response indicates that the respondent believes that he or she has insufficient information to make a judgement and is therefore neutral on the performance evaluation. Cronbach's Alpha (Nunnally 1978; Peterson 1994) measure of scale reliability generated by the SPSS scale reliability subroutine was applied to the set of items assigned to each scale. Items were dropped from each scale as needed to obtain the maximum reliability for that scale. Eleven items were dropped. Based on the Cronbach's Alpha results, it was determined that the Assurance performance dimension and the Responsivenes performance dimension could be combined. Only two items represented the Responsiveness dimension and only one represented the Assurance dimension. The Cronbach's Alpha for the Assurance scale was increased by combining the Responsiveness item with the two Assurance items to produce a single scale referred to here as Assurance-Responsiveness.

Table 1 reports the means and standard deviations of the 24 items that were used, and the means, standard deviations and Cronbach's Alphas for the final scales to which they were assigned. The Social Responsibility scale and the Tangibles scale exceeded Nunnally's (1978) Cronbach's Alpha criteria of .60 for exploratory research. The Community Benefits (Alpha = 73), Empa-

TABLE 1. Scale Items for Perceptions of Community Benefits, Social Responsibility, School System Service Quality Performance and Willingness to Volunteer (N = 124)

Item Number and Scale[1]	Mean	Std
Community Benefits: Cronbach's Alpha = .73	13.81	1.94
1. Good public schools can improve the lives of all people in a community.	4.78	.68
2. Good public schools increase the resale value of homes.	4.46	.92
3. Good schools attract business.	4.57	.79
Social Responsibility: Cronbach's Alpha = .66	7.19	2.38
4. People with grown children should support public schools.	4.01	1.23
5. Families whose children use private or church schools should support public schools.	3.19	1.51
Performance-Tangibles: Cronbach's Alpha = .69	5.87	1.72
6. ___ has appropriate physical facilities.	3.10	1.03
7. ___'s physical facilities are well maintained.	2.77	.94
Performance-Reliability: Cronbach's Alpha = .90	18.51	6.07
8. ___'s high schools do a good job of preparing students for college who want to go to college.	2.66	1.19
9. ___'s high schools do a good job of preparing students for jobs if they do not plan to go to college.	2.47	1.04
10. ___'s elementary and middle schools do a good job of preparing students for high school.	2.72	1.14
11. The administrators of ___ do a good job.	2.40	1.09
12. ___'s teachers do a good job.	2.90	1.20
13. ___'s employees are dependable.	2.98	.95
14. ___ manages its finances effectively.	2.38	1.05
Performance-Assurance-Responsibility: Cronbach's Alpha = .88	8.81	2.60
15. ___'s employees instill confidence (Assurance).	2.76	1.01
16. ___'s employee's are polite (Assurance).	3.02	.95
17. ___'s employee's are helpful (Responsiveness).	3.03	.93
Performance-Empathy: Cronbach's Alpha = .77	7.15	2.57
18. ___ give student's caring, personal attention.	2.78	.88
19. ___ schools are safe.	1.98	1.05
20. ___ understands what you want for public schools.	2.39	1.16
Volunteer: Cronbach's Alpha = .91	8.68	6.09
21. Serve as a tutor at study sessions.	1.98	1.28
22. Give time to supporting extracurricular activities.	2.11	1.31
23. Serve as a life skills mentor for a individual student.	2.67	1.41
24. Visit classes to read to students.	2.32	1.53

[1]All scale items scored 1 to 5 with 1 = Strongly Disagree, 3 = Don't Know and 5 = Strongly Agree.

thy (Alpha = 77), and Assurance-Responsiveness (Alpha = 88) scales exceeded Nunnally's .70 criteria for basic research. The Reliability and Volunteerism scales exceeded Nunnally's criteria of .9 for applied research.

Table 2 reports the zero-order correlations among the SERVQUAL-SERVPERF scales. Similar to Cronin and Taylor's (1994) findings, multicolinearity exists among the SERVQUAL dimensions. All correlations among the service quality dimensions were statistically significant. The highest involved the relationships of Empathy with Reliability (r = .85) and Assurance-Responsiveness (r = .67). The correlation of Reliability and Responsiveness-Assurance was also high (r = .72). In contrast, the relationships of Tangibility to Reliability (r = .31), Empathy (r = .26) and Assurance-Responsiveness (r = .19) were comparatively low although statistically significant. None of the performance quality items had a statistically significant correlation with the Perceptions of Community Benefits scale but three of the performance quality scales had statistically significant relationships with the Social Responsibility scale (Reliability = .43, Assurance-Responsiveness = .35, Empathy = .42). While multicolinearity makes tests of causal hypotheses problematic, multicolinearity among the conceptually distinct performance quality dimensions demonstrates construct validity (Churchill, 1992, pp. 387-388) for these scales as attitudes underlying the complex perception of service quality construct.

HYPOTHESES, ANALYSES AND FINDINGS

The propositions regarding the relationship of perceptions of community benefits (Community Benefits), social responsibility (Soc. Resp.) and perfor-

TABLE 2. Zero-Order Correlations Among Volunteerism and Performance, Community Benefits, Equity, and Social Responsibility Perception Scales (N = 124)

	Reli-ability	Assure.-Resp.	Empathy	Comm. Benefits	Social Resp.	Volunteer
Tangibility	.3055[1]	.1872[1]	.2599[1]	.1630	.0220	−.1838[1]
Reliability		.7168[1]	.8477[1]	.1466	.4321[1]	.1463
Assurance-Responsiveness			.6674[1]	.0639	.3465[1]	.1534
Empathy				.1488	.4245[1]	.1523
Community Benefits					.1411	.2020[1]
Social Responsibility						.3234[1]

[1]Correlation significant P < .05 (2-Tail). Null hypothesis rejected.

mance quality (Tangibility, Reliability, Assurance-Responsiveness and Empathy) as independent variables to non-client willingness to volunteer (Volunteer) as a dependent variable were tested by first assessing the zero-order correlations and then by generated multiple regression models. The statistical hypotheses corresponding to the previous theoretical propositions are that scores on the scales for Perceptions of Community Benefits, Social Responsibility and the SERVQUAL type dimensions of performance–Tangibility, Reliability, Assurance-Responsiveness and Empathy–will be positively related to scores on the scale Volunteer.

The high levels of multicolinearity noted earlier are also reflected in the low multiple regression tolerance coefficients reported in Table 3 for Reliability, Assurance-Responsiveness and Empathy. This has been observed in other studies that question the degree of independence of the SERVQUAL dimensions (Cronin and Taylor 1992, 1994). Inspection of the zero order correlations avoids the statistical issue of multicolinearity but does not allow identification of the most salient influences. Multiple regression allows identification of the influences with the greatest predictive value with all other variables in the model controlled, but, may cause a salient variable to be overlooked due to variance it shares with another independent variable. Therefore, both zero-order and multiple regression analyses were considered. Three types of multiple regression were performed. First, all variables were

TABLE 3. Multiple-Regression Full Model and Reduced Model Beta Coefficients and Explained Variation for Community Benefits, Equity Social Responsibility and Performance Perception Scales with Willingness to Volunteer (N = 124)

| | Full Model | | Reduced Model | |
	Beta	Tolerance	Beta	Tolerance
Tangibility	− .2428[1]	.8735	− .2223[1]	.9734
Reliability	.0101	.2281		
Assurance-Responsiveness	.0790	.4698		
Empathy	.0129	.2698		
Community Benefits	.1958[2]	.9472	.1958[2]	.9545
Social Responsibility	.2639[2]	.7787	.3007[2]	.9801
R-Square	.1851[3]		.1777[3]	

[1]Coefficient statistically significant (P < .05, 1-Tail) but in direction opposite from that hypothesized. Null hypothesis accepted.
[2]P < .05 (1-Tail). Null hypothesis rejected.
[3]P < .05 (2-Tail).

forced into the model to predict willingness to volunteer. These results are referred to here as the Full Model. Second, forward stepwise multiple regression was carried out. Third, backward stepwise multiple regression was carried out. Both forward and backward stepwise regression produced the same results. These results are referred to here as the Reduced Model. Since direction is specified in the hypotheses, 1-tail tests of significance of the simple-correlation and the multiple regression beta coefficients were used.

The zero-order correlations of the independent variables with Volunteer are reported in Table 2. Table 3 reports the multiple regression coefficients for the lull and the reduced models. Multiple regression produced essentially the same results as the simple correlations. Only three variables were found to have statistically significant associations with Volunteer. Tangibility produced a statistically significant but negative coefficient with Volunteer (opposite from what was predicted). Reliability and Assurance-Responsiveness did not produce significant coefficients. Therefore, we must accept the null hypothesis of no positive relationship with volunteer for the performance quality dimensions. Community Benefits and Social Responsibility produce the predicted positive significant coefficients. Therefore, we can reject these null hypotheses and recognize a positive relationship for Community Benefits and Social Responsibility with Volunteer. The Community Benefits coefficients indicate that, among this non-client population, beliefs that community quality of life types of rewards can result from good schools are positively related to willingness to contribute time to the school system Similarly, coefficients for Social Responsibility with Volunteer indicate that beliefs that support for the public school system is a broad social responsibility may enhance non-clients willingness to volunteer. Such beliefs may make non-clients responsive to symbolic rewards such as social appreciation, prestige or citizenship.

The performance quality dimension Tangibility also produced a significant correlation with Volunteer, but in the opposite direction from that predicted. The other SERVQUAL type dimensions scales–Reliability, Assurance-Responsiveness, and Empathy–did not produce statistically significant correlations. It may be that among non-clients, despite communications from the mass media, the intangible dimensions of Service Quality were not sufficiently observable to influence decision making regarding donating personal time.

The Tangible dimension scale addressed more observable factors such as the physical appearance of buildings. Although Tangibility appears to influence willingness to volunteer, more positive perceptions were associated with lower willingness to volunteer–opposite of the predicted direction. While SERVQUAL-SERVPERF research in for-profit settings has shown that perceptions of Tangibility are positively related to purchase intentions (Cronin and Taylor 1992,1994), in this non-client market of potential volunteers, positive images of the physical aspects of the school system may suggest less need for outside support. If so, this may offset the attraction quality of a positive physical environment.

IMPLICATIONS AND CONCLUSIONS

This study has demonstrated the importance of perceptions of potential community benefits of good public school systems and the importance of a Social Responsibility ethic to willingness to volunteer personal time among this population of non-parents of children in the school system. Moreover, this study has found no evidence to support the contention that dimensions of service quality found in other studies to be influential on clients' willingness to enter exchange (purchase intentions) with for-profit service businesses also positively influence non-clients willingness to volunteer time for not-for-profit service organizations. Instead, it appears that a different set of dynamics is operating. Among non-clients, the generalized exchange benefit of improved quality of community life is influential on willingness to volunteer time as may be symbolic values implied by a belief in a social responsibility ethic. Neither of these are primary characteristics of clients of for-profit service organizations or even clients of not-for-profit service organizations when direct transfers of utilitarian values dominate the exchange situation. These findings justify research into the generalized exchange concept as a used theoretical contribution to not-for-profit marketing and have practical significance for not-for-profit marketers. Non-clients represent an input public for both financial contributions and volunteer time. Appeals to non-clients that emphasize community benefits and widely shared ethics of social responsibility may enhance efforts to recruit volunteers. Further work is needed to assess the extent to which these factors also influence willingness to provide other types of input resources.

REFERENCES

Bagozzi, Richard P. (1975), "Marketing as Exchange," *Journal of Marketing*, 39 (October): 32-39.

Churchill, Gilbert (1992), *Basic Marketing Research*, Chicago: Dryden.

Cronin, J. Joseph, Jr., and Steven A. Taylor (1992), "Measuring Service Quality: A Reexamination and Extension," *Journal of Marketing*, 56 (July), 55-68.

Cronin, J. Joseph, Jr., and Steven A. Taylor (1994), "SERVPERF Versus SERV-QUAL: Reconciling Performance-Based and Perceptions-Minus-Expectations Measurement of Service Quality," *Journal of Marketing*, 58: 125-131.

Gouldner, Alvin W. (1970), *The Coming Crisis in Western Sociology*, London: Basic Books.

Houston, Franklin S. and Jule B. Gassenheimer, "Marketing and Exchange," *Journal of Marketing*, 51 (October), 3-18.

Kotler, Philip and Alan Andreasen (1991), *Strategic Marketing for Nonprofit Organizations*, Englewood Cliffs, NJ: Prentice-Hall.

Marshall, Kimball (1998), "Generalized Exchange and Public Policy: An Illustration of Support for Public Schools," *Journal of Public Policy and Marketing*, Fall, forthcoming.

Nunnally, Jum C. (1978), *Psychometric Theory*, 2nd Ed. New York, NY: McGraw-Hill.

Parasuraman A., Berry, Leonard L. and Zeithaml, Valarie A. (1991), "Refinement and Reassessment of the SERVQUAL Scale," *Journal of Retailing*, 67:420-450.

Parasuraman, A., Zeithaml, Valarie A. and Berry, Leonard L. (1985), "A Conceptual Model of Service Ouality and Its Implications for Future Research," *Journal of Marketing*, Vol. 49: 51-50.

Parasuraman, A., Zeithaml, Valarie A. and Berry, Leonard L. (1994), "Reassessment of Expectations as a Comparison Standard in Measuring Service Ouality: Implications for Further Research," *Journal of Marketing*, 58: 111-124.

Peterson, Robert A. (1994), "A Meta-analysis of Cronbach's Coefficient Alpha," *Journal of Consumer Research*, 21 (September), 381-391.

Zeithaml, Valarie A., Parasuraman, A. and Berry, Leonard L. (1990), *Delivering Quality Service: Balancing Customer Perceptions and Expectations*, New York: The Free Press.

Zeithaml, Valarie A., Berry, Leonard L. and Parasuraman, A. (1996), "The Behavioral Consequences of Service Ouality," *Journal of Marketing*, 60: 31-46.

Major Research Studies:
An Annotated Bibliography
of Marketing to Volunteers

Walter W. Wymer, Jr.
Donald R. Self

The purpose of this section is: (1) to assist marketing researchers and practitioners in assessing various areas of prior research, and (2) to assist marketing researchers and practitioners in their own literature searches as they conduct their own studies.

The selection of items in this bibliography was made by the bibliographer over a period of three years of inquiry into this field. The search for relevant works was conducted primarily through reading works and selecting references for further reading. Indexes were searched across disciplines. The Payton Philanthropic Studies Library (http://www-lib.iupui.edu/special/ppsl.html) was an excellent source for dissertations dealing with volunteerism.

The criteria for selection was primarily based on a judgment that the work would have an interest to a marketing scholar interested in both nonprofit marketing and marketing to volunteers. Individual works represent scholarly journal articles, books, edited volumes, conference proceedings, and dissertations. (In one case, a trade journal article was accepted). In virtually all instances, the annotated bibliographies were written from the original documents, not from abstracts. 131 abstracts are included below.

Walter W. Wymer, Jr., DBA, is Assistant Professor of Marketing, Christopher Newport University, Newport News, VA 23606 (E-mail: wwymer@cnu.edu).

Donald R. Self, DBA, is affiliated with the Marketing Department, Auburn University Montgomery, Montgomery, AL 36124 (E-mail: dself@monk.aum.edu).

[Haworth co-indexing entry note]: "Major Research Studies: An Annotated Bibliography of Marketing to Volunteers." Wymer, Walter W., Jr. and Donald R. Self. Co-published simultaneously in *Journal of Nonprofit & Public Sector Marketing* (The Haworth Press, Inc.) Vol. 6, No. 2/3, 1999, pp. 107-164; and: *Volunteerism Marketing: New Vistas for Nonprofit and Public Sector Management* (ed: Donald R. Self and Walter W. Wymer, Jr.) The Haworth Press, Inc., 1999, pp. 107-164. Single or multiple copies of this article are available for a fee from The Haworth Document Delivery Service [1-800-342-9678, 9:00 a.m. - 5:00 p.m. (EST). E-mail address: getinfo@haworthpressinc.com].

SUBJECT HEADINGS

The subject headings selected for this section were developed in an effort to remain consistent with the American Marketing Association (AMA) typology, and to allow for the future development of additional important nonprofit marketing topics. The specific sub-sections of marketing to volunteers was developed in an effort to categorize an array of cross-disciplinary work into a meaningful, parsimonious framework for marketing scholars.

Marketing to Volunteers	Number of Articles
1. Recruitment	38
2. Retention	17
3. Reactivation of former volunteers to service	0
4. Segmentation	10
5. Descriptive studies	43
6. Other	19

1. RECRUITMENT

Anderson, John C. and Larry F. Moore (1978), "The Motivation to Volunteer," *Journal of Voluntary Action Research,* **7, 51-60.**

The purpose of the study is to examine the frequencies of reported motives for volunteering and to compare personal background variables of volunteers with reasons given for volunteering. Questionnaires were sent to 198 Canadian volunteer agencies, resulting in 1,062 usable responses. The authors found that most people volunteer to help others and to feel needed. One-third of the sample reported volunteering was motivated by a desire to occupy spare time. Few people volunteer to make friends. The study also examines how motives for volunteering vary with demographic variables (gender, age, social class, education, employment).

Bendapudi, Neeli, Surendra N. and Venkat Bendapudi (1996), "Enhancing Helping Behavior: An Integrative Framework for Promotion Planning," *Journal of Marketing,* **60 (July), 33-49.**

Using prior cross-disciplinary research, the authors develop a conceptual model of factors leading to financial contributions to charitable organizations. This model could easily be extended to volunteer recruitment. Although a very broad model, it discusses possible antecedents and moderators affecting one's decision to contribute as well as possible donor responses and consequences to various groups. An emphasis is given to the type of message delivered to prospective contributors. Propositions are offered.

Burnett, John J. (1981), "Psychographic and Demographic Characteristics of Blood Donors," *Journal of Consumer Research*, **8 (June), 62-66.**

The purpose of this study is to differentiate blood donors from non-donors using demographic and psychographic variables. The sample is derived from the blood bank's list of donors and from the local telephone directory (N = 577). The analysis used stepwise multiple discriminant analysis. Results show that " . . . donors tend to be male, married with children, have rare blood types and low self-esteem, to be low risk takers, very concerned with health, better educated, religious and quite conservative."

Chang, Cyril F. (1994), "The Influence of Church and Synagogue Attendance on the Probability of Giving and Volunteering," *Journal of Nonprofit & Public Sector Marketing*, **2 (4), 15-25.**

In a re-analysis of a 1990 Gallup national survey of volunteering and giving in the U.S., Chang examines the correlation between church/synagogue attendance frequency and donation (time and money) behavior. Using logistic regression analysis, Chang finds that the more frequently one attends a religious service, the more likely one is to volunteer or contribute to the organization. Other findings: (1) religious service attendance loses its association with volunteering and contributing below a threshold of one attendance/week, and (2) church/synagogue membership is not as good a predictor as service attendance.

Clark, Margaret S. (1991), *Prosocial Behavior, Vol 12, Review of Personality and Social Psychology.* **Newbury Park, CA: Sage Publications.**

This edited volume provides 12 chapters presenting various theoretical perspectives on helping behavior. Helping behavior is categorized as emergency helping behavior and non-emergency helping behavior (volunteerism). The volume presents important theoretical perspectives from the psychology discipline. The volume also contains literature reviews. A must-read for researchers interested in theory building in volunteerism. Sociological-based theories on volunteerism are not represented in this volume.

Clary, E. Gil, Mark Snyder, John T. Copeland, and Simone A. French (1994), Promoting Volunteerism: An Empirical Examination of the Appeal of Persuasive Messages," *Nonprofit and Voluntary Sector Quarterly*, **23 (3), 265-280.**

Using student subjects, this study examines the utility of different persuasive messages. Abstract/concrete appeal efficacy is examined as is using reasons for volunteering versus using counter-arguments for not volunteering. Study 1; 40 male/42 female undergraduate students. Study 2; 11 male/29 female students who are active volunteers.

Findings. When using the strategy of emphasizing reasons for volunteering, concrete messages are more effective than abstract messages. When using the strategy of countering objections to volunteering, abstract messages were more persuasive. Implications for retention of volunteers–countering abstract reasons for quitting is more persuasive than emphasizing concrete reasons for remaining a volunteer.

Clary, E. Gil, Mark Snyder, and Arthur A. Stukas (1996), "Volunteers' Motivations: Findings From a National Survey," *Nonprofit and Voluntary Sector Quarterly*, **25 (4), 485-505.**

In a re-analysis of 1992 Gallup survey data of volunteering and giving in the U.S., the authors examined motives for volunteering using their instrument, the Volunteer Function Inventory. The findings provide support for the authors' model. The authors use a six-factor motivational model to differentiate volunteers from non-volunteers, volunteers by type of volunteer activity, and volunteers by demographic variables (gender, age, race, income).

Cnaan, Ram A. and Roben S. Goldberg-Glen (1991), "Measuring Motivation to Volunteer in Human Services," *Journal of Applied Behavioral Sciences*, **27 (3), 269-284.**

In this study, 258 human service volunteers and 104 non-volunteers rank the importance of 28 motives (identified in previous research) for volunteering. The study examines the dimensionality of people's motivation to volunteer. The findings indicate that when all 28 motives were subjected to various types of factor analysis, most items were grouped together on one factor. A unidimensional scale was obtained. The authors propose that volunteer motivation may be a unitary composition of multiple motives. The composite motive might be thought of as "a rewarding experience." Volunteers do not act on either altruistic or egoistic motives, but on both.

Dovidio, John F., Jane A. Piliavin, Samuel L Gaertner, David A. Schroeder, and Russell D. Clark III (1991), "The Arousal: Cost-Reward Model and the Process of Intervention," in *Review of Personality and Social Psychology*, **vol. 12, M.S. Clark, ed. Newbury Park, CA: Sage, 86-118.**

This chapter describes a cost-reward model of helping behavior. The model is primarily developed for emergency helping behavior, but some ideas are useful for researchers interested in non-emergency helping behavior (e.g., volunteering) as well.

The model proposes that there are two major factors related to emergency helping intervention: emotion and cognition. When someone sees a person in dire need, that person's plight arouses unpleasant emotions which the potential helper is motivated to reduce. However, the potential helper considers the costs/benefits of helping. The chapter goes into detail about variables influencing emergency helping and the authors provide a literature review of emergency helping behavior.

Dunn, Terrence Herbert (1988), "Volunteers and Predictable Motivations," Ph.D. dissertation, Colorado State University.

The author sampled 525 volunteer youth group leaders via a mail survey. Respondents provided information related to what factors affected their volunteer experience. The author also collected demographic data. The typical volunteer was a white female, middle class, with young children.

The study tested three motivation theories (needs theory, expectancy, and exchange theory). Needs theory performed best. The study also examined changes in volunteer motivation over time. Needs theory, with Maslow's hierarchy of needs, explained the changes in needs over time as volunteers' lower level needs were satisfied, moving them to satisfy higher level needs.

Edwards, John N. and Randall White (1980), "Predictors of Social Participation: Apparent or Real," *Journal of Voluntary Action Research*, 9, 60-73.

The authors test 11 variables, found significant in prior research, using bivariate analyses, in a multivariate framework, to test the variables' predictive utility. The variables are family size, age, education, gender, marital status, head of household education and occupation, years in residence, health, income, and community size. The focus is on six levels of social participation. One level is volunteering.

Methods. Telephone interviews using a census enumeration district quota sample of women (174), men (233), ages 45 and over. Analysis: multiple regression.

Findings. The significant variables in the regression on voluntary associations are family size, education, head of household education and occupation, and income. The authors conclude that variables used in prior research, while significant, account for only a small proportion of the variance. More needs to be known.

Ellis, Susan J. (1993), "Building a Circle of Resources," *The Nonprofit Times***, 7 (Sept), 14.**

In this commentary, Ellis recommends that recruiters look to those near the organization's location. Since they are neighbors (businesses, residents, etc.), there is a natural ease with which to develop social bonds. Developing social bonds a priori facilitates volunteer recruitment.

Farrar, Robert B. (1985), "Factors Affecting Volunteerism in Church Related Activities," doctoral dissertation, University of Houston.

This dissertation explores why people choose or don't choose to volunteer in their churches. Members of four Protestant churches (different denominations) returned 265 questionnaires. Good source of information on church volunteers. Gives recruitment tips on p. 21. Placing volunteers, p. 22. The primary reason people give for ending their church volunteer service is that they feel their work did not make a meaningful contribution to the church. Number one reason for never volunteering is not being asked. Motives for church volunteering: (1) put faith into action, (2) being part of the church community and to help the church meets its needs. These two were very close together in importance.

Gora, Jo Ann and Gloria Nemerowicz (1991), "Volunteers: Initial and Sustaining Motivations in Service to the Community," *Research in the Sociology of Health Care***, 9, 233-246.**

The authors examine the initial and sustaining motivations of 514 rescue squad volunteers. The sample came from 21 New Jersey rescue squads. Volunteers' initial motives for volunteering were: wanting to contribute to the community, help others, and get medical training for future job. The actual job routine doesn't support altruistic motives. Initial motivations are changed into motives to support the squad (the social support group) in time. Family support was considered important in sustaining volunteer commitment over time.

Heshka, Stanley (1983), "Situational Variables Affecting Participation in Voluntary Associations," in *International Perspectives on Voluntary Action Research***, D. H. Smith and J. V. Til, eds. Washington, D.C.: University Press of America, 138-147.**

While most research on volunteering focuses on aspects of the individual, this work examines influences of situational variables on recruitment and participation in voluntary associations. The data was collected using interviews of 142 recent recruit volunteers from four Canadian agencies. The author categorizes situational variables into three categories. Analysis: cross tabulations and cluster analysis.

The most frequent situational pattern consisted of a person who becomes a volunteer after seeing a notice in the newspaper or on a poster. This person lives with one or two other persons, and has little social linkage to voluntary associations. This person also reported having a reduced workload which facilitated volunteering.

The second most frequent situational pattern involved a person who lives with more than two other people, some of whom are members of voluntary associations. This situational pattern demonstrates a social linkage to a voluntary association. Information is obtained from personal contact.

The next most frequent situational pattern was derived from volunteer recruits who were bored with their lifestyles. They volunteer to add activity to their routines even though the voluntary association may not be conveniently located to them.

Other results. Female volunteers tended to be less fully employed and sought out volunteer work to reduce boredom. Home owners are more likely to be volunteers, to be recruited, and to spend little time deliberating over the decision to volunteer.

Jackson, Elton F., Mark D. Bachmeier, James R. Wood, and Elizabeth A. Craft (1995), "Volunteering and Charitable Giving: Do Religious and Associational Ties Promote Helping Behavior?" *Nonprofit and Voluntary Sector Quarterly*, 24 (1), 59-78.

Central question: Do religious or voluntary association ties promote secular volunteering and charitable giving?

This study looks at social determinants of volunteering. The authors find that belonging to associations and being active in a church group were social determinants of volunteering.

This paper discusses the Swartz and Howard model. The model attempts to account for a person's decision to volunteer for an organization. Values are placed in the motivation portion of the model, on an equal level with nonmoral costs and benefits and social costs and benefits. The process model implies that people go through a complex systematic cost/benefit analysis after first deciding that a need exists, that the need can be responded to, and that they are capable of responding to the need. It is unclear how the model assigns costs and benefit weights in the moral element of the motivation cell. The model proposes that if benefits exceed costs, participation occurs, if benefits and costs are roughly equal, then a person goes into denial, looking for defenses for not participating. The model does a good job explaining the decision making process of proving helping behavior. It is unlikely the model can be properly tested.

The main conclusion of the study is that religious participation increases secular helping when one is active in a group within a church. Church attendance is not important, but being part of a church group is. The authors give the reason that being part of a church group fosters value-based norms for helping behavior.

King, Rosalie Rosso and Jacquelyn Fluke (1989), *Volunteers: America's Hidden Resource.* **Lanham, MD: University Press of America.**

This book is authored by a university arts professor and a practitioner. They give summary demographic and motivational data from a study they performed, but give no methodological information regarding the study itself.

Number one reason for volunteering (both genders) in the arts is a belief in the arts as a national resource. Women's other reasons: second is ability to meet people, third desire to help others. Men's other reasons for volunteering in the arts: second is need to perform a patriotic and civic duty within their community, third psychological rewards.

More women hold committee chair positions. More men hold board positions. Women donate slightly more time per month than men. The majority of people donate 10-20 hours per month. Arts volunteers tend to be well educated. Roughly 75 percent hold college degrees. Age: largest group, 31-35 years. Smallest category, over 65 years.

The book is well written and an easy read. This book is targeted for volunteer administrators in the arts, and this is where it is of greatest value.

Mahoney, John and Constance M. Pechura (1980), "Values and Volunteers: Axiology of Altruism in a Crisis Center," *Psychological Reports,* **47 (3, pt. 1), 1007-1012.**

Compares the values (using Rokeach Value Survey) of 42 hotline telephone service volunteers with a matched control group. Twelve values discriminate between volunteer and control groups. Two values differentiate volunteers who completed their training from volunteers who dropped-out during training. "It appears that appeals for solicitation of volunteers should focus on altruistic and experiential aspects of volunteering, since these dimensions appear to be most compatible with values of volunteers" (p. 1011).

Manzer, Leslie Lee (1974), "Charitable Health Organization Donor Behavior: An Empirical Study of Value and Attitude Structure," Ph.D. dissertation, Oklahoma State University.

The purpose of this dissertation is to determine if donation levels are a function of a person's value system and organization-specific attitudes. Variables: donation levels (heavy, light, and non-donor), values (Rokeach Value Survey), and attitudes regarding the Oklahoma Lung Association (target organization). Data collected from organization files (donation levels) and a mail survey. Analysis: multiple regression, factor analysis, and canonical analysis. Probability sample: 162 heavy donors, 200 light donors (donors from organization files), 154 non-donors (from phone directory).

Findings. Of the values, Freedom, Happiness, Pleasure, and Salvation were significant. Level of donation is a function of values and attitudes. Attitudes explain donor behavior better than values. Specific values are related to specific attitudes. Donation behavior is influenced by situational experiences and perceptions.

McClintock, Charles G. and Scott T. Allison (1989), "Social Value Orientation and Helping Behavior," *Journal of Applied Social Psychology,* **19 (4), 353-362.**

This study examines the relationship between social values and helping behavior. Individuals are categorized by their social values into three groups: cooperators, individualists, or competitors.

The authors predict that subjects identified as cooperators would donate more of their time to the cause than subjects identified as competitors and individualists.

Student subjects (208 male, 436 female) were tested on social values. Two weeks later they were mailed a request to volunteer from 0 to 10 hours of their time to the university.

"The data from the present study clearly demonstrate that students who were identified as cooperative in social value orientation were more generous in their helping responses than were students identified as individualists or students identified as competitors. The differences, moreover, were strong. Cooperators donated approximately twice as many hours of their time to the subject pool than did non-cooperators" (p. 359).

Miller, Lynn E. (1985), "Understanding the Motivation of Volunteers: An Examination of Personality Differences and Characteristics of Volunteers' Paid Employment," *Journal of Voluntary Action Research,* **14 (2-3), 112-122.**

Questionnaires: 90 respondents who are volunteers from three different volunteer organizations. No control group. The central question: do some people volunteer in order to satisfy needs that are not satisfied through other activities? The findings indicate that those volunteers whose regular employment fails to satisfy their needs for psychological growth tend to be involved and satisfied with volunteering to the extent that they (a) felt personally in control of their lives, and (b) wanted and expected that volunteering would satisfy their growth needs. Volunteers whose regular employment does provide opportunities for psychological growth were more motivated by other potential rewards of volunteering.

Mitchell, Mark Andrew and Susan Lee Taylor (1997), "Adapting Internal Marketing to a Volunteer System," *Journal of Nonprofit & Public Sector Marketing*, 5 (2), 29-42.

In this conceptual work the authors describe the utility of an internal marketing approach to volunteer recruitment and retention. Volunteer recruitment is viewed as the successful match between a potential volunteer's values and the organization's culture. Volunteer retention is enhanced by positive relationships between paid staff and volunteers, characterized by an atmosphere of trust.

Internal marketing is viewed as the manipulation of an organization's culture (its shared beliefs, values, and norms) to produce desired outcomes. Recruitment is accomplished by first determining what benefits current volunteers are deriving from their service, then finding a target market of potential volunteers which desires those benefits the organization provides. The authors discuss several issues relating to internal marketing. They also include an action plan for managers of volunteers.

Noble, Elizabeth Brooke (1992), "Differences in Empathy Levels as a Function of Volunteerism and Motivation to Volunteer," Ph.D. dissertation (no. 903), Northeast Missouri State University.

Purpose: to determine if empathy can account for volunteering and amount of time volunteered. Empathy is viewed as having four dimensions: perspective taking, fantasy, empathic concern, and personal distress. There were 215 college student subjects, 156 of whom had volunteered. Volunteers were grouped into two categories (low and high), by mean number of hours volunteered (mean, high = 51; mean, low = 7). Used Interpersonal Reactivity Index and Student Community Service Involvement Survey to measure empathy. Two-factor ANOVAs were used in the data analysis.

Findings. Of the student volunteers, 112 were motivated by altruism, 30, egoism, and 14, social obligation. One significant finding: "levels of empathic concern were significantly higher when motives were based in altruism rather than egoism" (p. 37). The author proposes that college student service learning may help to promote empathy and a community orientation (rather than a self-orientation).

O'Connor, Robert J. and Rebecca S. Johnson (1989), "Volunteer Demographics and Future Prospects for Volunteering," in *The Future of the Nonprofit Sector: Challenges, Changes, and Policy Considerations*, V. A. Hodgkinson, R. W. Lyman, eds. San Francisco: Jossey-Bass, 403-415.

This paper looks at previous surveys and U.S. census data to project the prospects for volunteers during the next 5 to 12 years.

The time donated just to charitable organizations was worth $86 billion (in 1986). Fifty-two percent of volunteers are involved in fund-raising. Volunteers are more likely than non-volunteers to donate money to the organization.

The " . . . volunteer tends to be a person of above-average income and education who is middle-aged or slightly younger and domestically settled with a spouse and child" (p. 406). The proportion of women in the workforce is projected to increase. Nonprofit organizations will have to alter their traditional approach to recruiting volunteers. Volunteer satisfaction is becoming more important. Managers must begin to think of volunteers as customers and attend to their needs.

Okun, Morris A. (1994), "The Relation Between Motives for Organizational Volunteering and the Frequency of Volunteering by Elders," *The Journal of Applied Gerontology*, 13 (2), 115-126.

Purpose: to examine the influence of motives for volunteering on frequency of volunteering by elders. The study consisted of a re-analysis of a Marriott Senior Living study of senior volunteers. Top 3 reasons for volunteering were (1) help others, (2) feel useful or productive, and (3) fulfill a moral responsibility. The strongest correlate of frequency of volunteering was the motive, to feel useful or productive. Other significant variables: education, work status (full time employment decreased frequency of volunteering), being a Democrat (increased frequency). The paper makes a point to note that motivation for volunteering is multi-faceted.

Okun, Morris A. and Nancy Eisenberg (1992), "Motives and Intent to Continue Organizational Volunteering among Residents of a Retirement Community Area," *Journal of Community Psychology*, 20 (3), 183-187.

Using a sample of 252 senior volunteers, this study looks at the effect of motivation on intent to continue volunteering. The study finds that, rather

than relying on separate motivation variables, the interaction of three motivation variables was the most significant predictor. Aggregating motivation
variables in a multidimensional format is more predictive.

Since volunteers have multiple motives for volunteering, motive scores
are better predictors of intent to continue when the multidimensional approach to aggregation is used.

Volunteer motives are measured using 13 items adapted from prior research. Motives contain 3 factors: (1) knowledge, (2) value-expressive, and
(3) social-adjustive. Intent to continue is one item: "During the next 6
months, do you intend to do volunteer work for ___ ?"

As its theoretical base, the authors use Snyder's functional approach, from
Katz's functional approach to attitudes. Therefore, the authors use a 13 item
scale to factor analyze onto 3 functions: value-expressive, social-adjustive,
and knowledge.

**Smith, David H. (1966), "A Psychological Model of Individual Participa-
tion in Formal Voluntary Organizations: Application to Some Chilean
Data,"** *The American Journal of Sociology,* **72 (3), 249-266.**

Smith uses two samples of individuals from Chile (first, N = 171; second,
N = 122). Findings show that volunteers from formal voluntary organizations
(fvo) are discriminated from non-volunteers by general attitudes about volunteering as well as specific attitudes regarding a target fvo. Active volunteers
are discriminated from less active volunteers by personality traits. Individuals will volunteer to the extinct that they have proximity to the fvo, communicate with fvo volunteers, have similar social backgrounds with fvo volunteers, and share similar interests with fvo volunteers.

**Thippayanuruksakul, Nittaya (1989), "Motivations and Benefits of Vol-
unteering as Perceived by University Students," Ph.D. dissertation,
Oklahoma State University.**

This study's purpose was to identify motivations of student volunteers and
their perceived benefits of volunteering. The sample was derived from a
questionnaire administered to students in four home economics classes (N =
276, 73% female). The questionnaires contained four sections. The first
section, demographic variables (gender, age, major, student classification,
enrollment status, marital status, membership in organizations). The second
section, motivations for volunteering (a list of possible motivations consistent with Herzberg's motivation-hygiene theory). Third section, perceived
benefits of volunteering (list of descriptive sentences). Final section, volunteer work environment (possible hygiene factors). Analysis consisted of factor analysis, student t-distribution t-tests, and one-way ANOVAs.

Findings. The most important motives for volunteering, in order, were: help other people, skill development for career, help build resume, work with interesting people, do a task that student can do well. Strength of volunteer motivators were: (1) achievement, (2) job/career development, (3) community service, and (4) new experiences. Females tended to show higher levels of motivations for volunteer work than males.

Watts, Ann DeWitt and Patricia Klobus Edwards (1983), "Recruiting and Retaining Human Service Volunteers: An Empirical Analysis," *Journal of Voluntary Action Research*, **12 (3), 9-22.**

The purpose of this study: to investigate the association of four organizational variables with recruitment and retention strategies. The four organizational variables are agency function, size, proportion of female volunteers, and volunteer turnover rate. The recruitment strategies are word of mouth, newspaper appeals, contacts with relatives of clients, and radio/television appeals. The retention strategies are reimbursement for volunteer expenses, volunteer training sessions, potential for volunteer to be promoted to paid staff, scheduling flexibility, potential for increased responsibilities.

The sample was taken via mail questionnaires from administrators of 124 volunteer agencies in five Virginia cities. Analysis: Chi-square test for independent samples.

Findings. Ninety-four percent of agencies use word-of-mouth recruiting; 56 percent use mass media. Administrators reported both methods were effective in recruiting volunteers. For retention strategies, 80 percent reported using traditional methods (training, flexible scheduling, and increasing responsibility), while 42 percent reported using non-traditional strategies (reimbursement, transfer to paid employment). No relationship was found between retention strategies used and retention rate. Agency administrators reported that their retention methods were much less effective than their recruiting methods. The traditional retention strategies were considered to be twice as effective as non-traditional strategies. Readers should note that actual retention and recruitment rates were not measured, just administrators' perceptions.

Widmer, Candace (1985), "Why Board Members Participate," *Journal of Voluntary Action Research*, **14 (4), 9-23.**

An exploratory study into motivations of board member volunteering. Used interviews, questionnaires, and observations to collect data from 98 board members in 10 human service agencies. The theoretical domain the author used for volunteering is the incentive approach (i.e., people volunteer in order to receive desirable benefits).

A large number of board members, 43%, reported that they talked first with a friend on the board (10).

Twenty-two board members gave social reasons for joining the board (12).

Two ideologically motivated board members saw this as a chance to practice their ideology (14).

Rated highly in the survey are: (1 and 2 tie) (1) I want to contribute to the important work this agency does in our community, (2) I want to support the goals of this agency, (3) I feel that this is a job I can do that uses the skills, training, or experience that I have, (4) I want to help provide service for those less fortunate than I, and (5) I consider it my civic duty to participate in community work.

Wiehe, Vernon R. and Lenora Isenhour (1977), "Motivation of Volunteers," *Journal of Social Welfare*, 4 (2-3), 73-79.

The purpose of the study is to determine the motivation of people calling a volunteer referral center. Participants calling the center were mailed a 16-item questionnaire. Participants (N = 249), in effect, were ranking the importance of four predetermined motives: personal satisfaction, self-improvement, altruism, and demands from outside.

Altruism and personal satisfaction were ranked the most important. Self-improvement and demands from outside were ranked least important. Definitions and analyses by age categories are included.

Williams, Robert F. (1987), "Receptivity to Persons with Mental Retardation: A Study of Volunteer Interest," *American Journal of Mental Retardation*, 92 (3), 299-303.

Subjects (Ss) were 39 male, 39 female undergraduate students from an anthropology class. Ss completed questionnaires measuring values, perceptions of mentally retarded persons, attitudes and beliefs concerning volunteer work with mentally retarded persons, and demographic variables.

Results show that the best predictors of student volunteers with mentally retarded persons are (1) the importance they place on certain values, and (2) their attitudes toward the volunteer activity for which they are being recruited. The author discusses the usefulness of values versus attitudes in predicting volunteer behavior, concluding that values are superior (probably because values have a stronger motivational component compared to attitudes).

Wymer, Walter W., Jr. (1997), "A Religious Motivation to Volunteer? Exploring the Linkage Between Volunteering and Religious Values," *Journal of Nonprofit & Public Sector Marketing,* **5 (3), 3-18.**

In prior literature, there has been some controversy regarding the influence internalized religious beliefs have on rates of volunteering. While there was a growing consensus among sociologists that the correlation between church membership/attendance and volunteerism is related to social influences, not religious beliefs, Wymer examines this issue by using a methodology allowing for a closer investigation of the linkage between religious beliefs/values and volunteering.

Using a mail survey approach (N = 1,058), the findings indicate that social influences do discriminate volunteers, in general, from people who do not volunteer. However, when looking at the type of volunteer activity, whether serving in a religious or a secular organization, volunteers in religious organizations are differentiated by being strongly motivated to volunteer by their religious beliefs.

Wymer, Walter, Glen Riecken, and Ugur Yavas (1996), "Determinants of Volunteerism: A Cross-Disciplinary Review and Research Agenda," *Journal of Nonprofit & Voluntary Sector Marketing,* **4 (4), 3-26.**

The authors integrate prior literature on volunteerism from several disciplines into a framework which represents factors which influence a person's decision to volunteer. The emphasis is on social and psychological factors rather than demographic correlates of volunteering. The framework includes person-related variables (personality, values, attitudes), social interactions (previous, current, anticipated), efficacy (skill utilization, skill development), and contextual variables (time, money, and psychological). The article provides a comprehensive review of prior research and provides a useful framework for future research. Good bibliographic source of prior work.

Yavas, Ugur and Glen Riecken (1981), "Volunteer Recruitment: A Marketing Approach," *The Changing Marketing Environment: New Theories and Applications: 1981 Marketing Educators' Conference Proceedings.* **Chicago: American Marketing Association, 77-80.**

This is among the first empirical works in the marketing field to focus specifically on volunteerism. The sample is composed of 329 non-volunteering males in a Midwestern city via a telephone survey. The emphasis is on respondents attitudes about volunteering in general and the local Big Brothers organization in particular. The non-volunteers reported positive attitudes regarding volunteering. However, they felt constrained by family, job, etc.

Respondents most likely to volunteer are white collar types, married, over 35, with above average incomes. Those most likely to volunteer also held more accurate perceptions about Big Brothers. Those most likely to volunteer believe that they were more similar to volunteers than respondents unlikely to volunteer.

Yavas, Ugur and Glen Riecken (1985), "Can Volunteers be Targeted?" *Journal of the Academy of Marketing Science*, **13 (2), 218-228.**

This article supports the topic of volunteer segmenting/targeting into marketing as a legitimate topic for marketing scholars. Marketing activities in nonprofit organizations are described as contributing to a resource attraction function. They write, " . . . identification of prospective donors, and determination of the appropriate appeals to reach them, are prerequisites to the success of resource attraction efforts of nonprofit agencies. The purpose of this study was to investigate the usefulness of demographic and attitudinal variables in profiling time donors and nondonors" (p. 224).

Telephone survey. Muncie, IN. 329 respondents. Dependent variable–"Do you volunteer your time to any organizations?" Thirty percent said yes. Independent variable–(1) Attitudes [series of statements], (2) demographics.

"Demographics alone, and a combination of demographics and attitudes, were able to discriminate the donor and nondonor groups" (p. 221). The authors use stepwise discriminant analysis of the data.

" . . . attitudinal variables do compliment demographic variables and contribute to a better separation of donor/nondonor groups" (224).

Results show that volunteers: (1) felt less influenced by family/job demands on their time, (2) are 35 and over, (3) have at least attended college, (4) hold white-collar jobs, (5) feel that volunteering will benefit the community, (6) seek individual benefits, and (7) are high in willingness to make time.

Yavas, Ugur, Glen Riecken, and Emin Babakus (1993), "Efficacy of Perceived Risk as a Correlate of Reported Donation Behavior: An Empirical Analysis," *Journal of the Academy of Marketing Science*, **21 (1), 65-70.**

Sample of 349 via telephone interviews. The perceived risk volunteers and contributors have of wasting their time or money was significantly different from non-participants in some cases. The ability of the variable, perceived risk, to predict volunteer/contributor membership was weak. However, the model markedly improved by including demographic variables (education, gender, age, income).

Zalusky, Sharon (1988), "Social Responsibility and Empathy in Adolescent Volunteers," Ph.D. dissertation, California School of Professional Psychology, Los Angeles.

Is empathy a precondition or correlate to helping behavior (volunteering)? Empathy has a motivational component, as well as an affective and cognitive component. The author uses Emotional Empathy Scale (EES) to measure empathy. Empathy is defined as heightened responsiveness to another's emotional experience. There is a good literature review of how empathy is related to prosocial behaviors.

Subjects (N = 84) were between ages of 13 and 19 years old; volunteer (N = 58) and non-volunteer (n = 26) groupings. Empathy as a differentiator is partially supported (p = 0.056). Empathy is significantly related to social concern and social responsibility.

2. RETENTION

Applebaum, Seymore (1992), "Recruiting and Retaining Volunteers from Minority Communities: A Case Study," Ed.D. dissertation, University of Toronto.

The purpose of this dissertation was to examine an organization known for successful minority volunteer recruitment and retention in order to better understand what organizational characteristics are needed. The author examined the Children's Aid Society of Metropolitan Toronto. This case study used document review, participant observation, and staff/volunteer interviews.

Much of the dissertation provides the reader with information from interviews. Fifteen volunteers were interviewed and their comments are relayed to the reader by the author. For the practitioner, there is a listing of recruiting and retaining tactics. Very little is specific recommendations are provided to assist the recruitment/retention of minority volunteers (the purpose of the dissertation). The author recommends (as general advice) that organizations wishing to increase their volunteer minority representation ought to make the recruitment of minority volunteers a priority and well as combating any existing racism in the organization.

Babchuk, Nicolas and Alan Booth (1969), "Voluntary Association Membership: A Longitudinal Analysis," *American Sociological Review*, 34 (1), 31-45.

Purpose: (1) to obtain longitudinal information on the extent of voluntary affiliation, (2) to find situational variables and correlates of membership,

(3) to learn more about the types of associations people join, and (4) to examine the stability and change of voluntary membership.

A probability sample was drawn from Nebraska adults. Data was collected twice, at the beginning and end of the study, four years later. There were 402 subjects who participated in personal interviews.

Findings: (1) 80 percent of people were affiliated with one or more associations, (2) almost half of respondents were members of 3 or more groups, (3) being married and male were positively correlated with affiliation, (4) length of residence in a community was directly correlated with affiliation, (5) education and occupational status were positively associated with affiliation, (6) there was a curvilinear relationship with affiliation–40 to 59 year range had the greatest affiliation, and (7) there are further discussions on affiliation by organization type.

Main points: (1) a large proportion of the population joins associations, (2) people change their associations, (3) parents participate in organizations while their children are involved, and (4) men tend to be more involved in job-related associations.

Brown, Eleanor P. and Jan Zahrly (1989), "Nonmonetary Rewards for Skilled Volunteer Labor," *Nonprofit and Voluntary Sector Quarterly*, 18 (2), 167-177.

The study examines the utility of three theories of volunteer reward (leisure, investment, and a perceived association between volunteering and desirable outcomes) in explaining volunteering. Data was collected from 28 crises intervention volunteers using questionnaires (response rate = 50%). Sample: mean age = 29, white, college-educated, working an average 26 monthly hours for primary volunteer organization, and working an additional average 19 hours to 2.3 other volunteer activities.

Findings. About half of the volunteers seek human capital accumulation; the other half derive psychic benefits from volunteering. Age (−) and locus of control (+) were significant when regressed on the proportion of the volunteer's total monthly volunteer time spent on organizational activities. Managers should place volunteers seeking psychic benefits in organizational activities generally. Managers should place volunteers desiring to increase their skills in activities where this would most likely occur.

Clary, E. Gil (1987), "Social Support as a Unifying Concept in Voluntary Action," *Journal of Voluntary Action Research*, 16 (4), 58-68.

This conceptual paper brings the concept of social support into the domain of voluntary action research. The first part of the paper is spent describing and defining social support as a construct. Social support is defined as "relationships with other people that are marked by emotional attachment and the giving of support." The concept has two dimensions, emotional support and task-oriented support. The author continues on to discuss relevant research on social support and its linkage to voluntary action.

Cnaan, Ram A. and Toni C. Goodfriend (1998), "The Performance Dilemma: Issues in Management of Volunteers in Human Service Organizations," *Journal of Social Service Research*, **forthcoming.**

This paper examines volunteer performance. Realizing that volunteers cannot be managed as paid employees, the authors examine the effectiveness of various management practices on the performance of a sample of 510 volunteers from 105 human service organizations. Sample: mean age = 50.6 years, 71 percent female, 82 percent white, and 40 percent married. Data was collected via personal interviews from trained graduate students. Regression analysis.

Volunteer performance was measured in three dimensions: volunteer satisfaction, longevity of service, and average monthly hours volunteered. An interesting finding is that demographic variables do not predict volunteer commitment even though demographic variables are highly correlated with recruitment.

Using careful recruitment of volunteers and acts of recognition improves volunteer satisfaction, average monthly hours volunteered, and length of service (retention).

Dailey, Robert C. (1986), "Understanding Organizational Commitment for Volunteers: Empirical and Managerial Implications," *Journal of Voluntary Action Research*, **15 (1), 19-31.**

This study examines the antecedents of volunteer commitment. The author proposes a model of organizational commitment. Personal characteristics and job characteristics influence job involvement and job satisfaction, which in turn influence organizational commitment.

A sample was taken from political campaign workers (N = 138) using a questionnaire. Measures were taken for organizational commitment, job characteristics (job involvement, job satisfaction), and personal characteristics (need for achievement and affiliation). Analysis: stepwise regression.

Findings. Job satisfaction, work autonomy, job involvement, and feedback from the work were strong predictors of organizational commitment. Personal characteristics were not significant predictors of organizational commitment.

Implications. Characteristics of the tasks or jobs volunteers perform are very important. Task characteristics influence job satisfaction which influences organizational commitment. Managers need to give thought in designing jobs. Researchers should include tasks characteristics into their research.

Fischer, Lucy Rose and Kay Banister Schaffer (1993), *Older Volunteers: A Guide to Research and Practice.* **Newbury Park, CA: Sage.**

In their review of previous research, demographic profiles show that as education, income, and occupational status increase so does the likelihood of volunteering. Poor health was a significant negative predictor of volunteering. Active church members who attend at least once a week are more likely to volunteer. Married people are more likely to volunteer. Why do these demographic factors relate to volunteering? These authors suggest these demographic factors are indicators of perceived personal resources. "These various resources affect both the costs and the opportunities for volunteering in a variety of ways" (24).

On page 44, the book provides a useful table reviewing prior research on volunteer motivations. More people believe they should volunteer than actually do volunteer. Most people report multiple motives for volunteering. Motives may be additive. Trying to understand motivations may be futile. It may be better to understand what types of people under what types of social situations are more likely to volunteer.

Some points: people who are more likely to volunteer have a sense of empathy. They have an altruistic identity. People who feel good about themselves and are in a good mood are more likely to help others. Research shows that church members are more likely to volunteer.

Gidron, Benjamin (1983), "Sources of Job Satisfaction Among Service Volunteers," *Journal of Voluntary Action Research*, **12, 20-35.**

Gidron looks at how 12 indices relating to the volunteer job context and content influence volunteer satisfaction. Analyses: factor analysis and stepwise multiple regression. Volunteers from different volunteer centers (type and number of volunteers not given) were sampled using a questionnaire approach.

Findings. Overall job satisfaction of volunteers was related to two facets of job content (work itself and achievement) and two facets of job context (convenience and absence of job stress factors). Volunteers want their work to be challenging and interesting, and make use of their skills and interests. Aspects of the job task seemed to have a stronger effect on overall job satisfaction than social benefits of the volunteer experience. Volunteers need a task which allows for self-expression, which is challenging, and where achievements can be recognized.

Hobson, Charles J., Anna Rominger, Kathryn Malec, Colleen L. Hobson, and Kathy Evans (1996), "Volunteer-Friendliness of Nonprofit Agencies: Definition, Conceptual Model, and Applications," *Journal of Nonprofit & Public Sector Marketing*, 4 (4), 27-42.

This conceptual paper defines volunteer-friendliness as "the extent to which a nonprofit agency's staff, policies, and programs provide a positive, pleasant, and rewarding experience for volunteers and prospective volunteers." The authors argue that a volunteer-friendly environment should produce many positive benefits.

A model of volunteer-friendliness is presented. The model consists of four components: (1) volunteer attraction and recruitment, (2) initial interaction with agency staff, (3) volunteer utilization and assignment, and (4) post-volunteering follow-up. Important factors which make up each component are discussed in the article. The authors suggest practical steps for organizations to become more volunteer-friendly. A research agenda is proposed.

Lafer, Barbara Helene (1989), "Predicting Satisfactoriness and Persistence in Hospice Volunteers," Ph.D. dissertation, Seton Hall University.

Using 75 prospective female hospice volunteers from 10 hospice programs, this research investigated performance (satisfactory/persistent, unsatisfactory/persistent, dropout) using personality variables. Results show some predictive ability when personality variables relate to job performance.

Discriminant function analysis was used to determine predictability of variables. Classification analysis was then used to test the adequacy of the discriminant functions extracted.

Hospice volunteers were similar to other volunteers in terms of age, marital status, education, work status and prior volunteer involvement.

This study could be extended into other areas. A future study could look at volunteer characteristics in terms predicting tenure and satisfactory performance.

Okun, Morris A. and Nancy Eisenberg (1992), "Motives and Intent to Continue Organizational Volunteering Among Residents of a Retirement Community Area," *Journal of Community Psychology*, 20 (3), 183-187.

Using a sample of 252 senior volunteers, this study looks at the affect of motivation on intent to continue volunteering. Volunteer motives are 13 items adapted from prior research. Motives contained 3 factors: (1) knowledge, (2) value-expressive, and (3) social-adjustive.

The study finds that, rather than relying on separate motivation variables, the interaction of the three motivation factors is the most significant predictor. Aggregating motivation variables in a multidimensional format is more predictive.

Since volunteers have multiple motives for volunteering, motive scores are better predictors of intent to continue volunteering when the multidimensional approach to aggregation is used.

Omoto, Allen M. and Mark Snyder (1995), "Sustained Helping Without Obligation: Motivation, Longevity of Service, and Perceived Attitude Change Among Aids Volunteers," *Journal of Personality and Social Psychology*, 68 (4), 671-686.

Using a sample of 116 AIDS volunteers (demographics of sample differ markedly from other research of human service volunteers) the authors test their three stage model of AIDS volunteering. The stages are (1) antecedents of AIDS volunteering, (2) experiences as an AIDS volunteer, and (3) consequences of AIDS volunteering. The authors have developed a five factor, 25-item measure of attitudinal functions served by volunteering. The five factors are (1) values, (2) understanding, (3) personal development, (4) community concern, and (5) esteem enhancement. Analysis: regressions and structural equation analysis (LISREL).

Findings. Greater motivation for volunteering predicts longevity of service. The greater a volunteer's social support, the less time the volunteer remains active. A volunteer's helping disposition is related to satisfaction and social integration into the organization. Greater satisfaction is related to longer length of service.

Puffer, Sheila M. and James R. Meindl (1992), "The Congruence of Motives and Incentives in a Voluntary Organization," *Journal of Organizational Behavior*, 13, 425-434.

This study measures three types of volunteer motives and incentives (benefits they receive from their volunteer work). The categories of motives/incentives are normative, rational, and affiliative. When the same volunteer incentives are provided to the volunteer as motives the volunteer has for volunteering, then the motives and incentives are said to be matched. The study looks at the relationship between matched and unmatched motives/incentives on volunteer attitudes and performance.

Methods. Two questionnaires, one for supervisors and one for volunteers. The sample was derived from supervisors and volunteers at the United Way in Buffalo, New York; N = 201. Regression analysis.

Findings. Matched motives/incentives had a positive impact on attitudes. Unmatched motives/incentives had a positive impact on performance. It is important to provide incentives which reflect the organization's values, while considering volunteer motives. Managers may have to reach a compromise between keeping volunteers happy and stimulating high performance.

Rubin, Allen and Irene M. Thorelli (1984), "Egoistic Motives and Longevity of Participation by Social Service Volunteers," *The Journal of Applied Behavioral Science*, 20 (3), 223-235.

The research question: Does a person, motivated to volunteer by the expectation of egoistic benefits, quit when those benefits are not realized from the actual volunteer experience? The conclusion: generally, yes.

The authors state " . . . in a setting in which service volunteers are likely to experience meager egoistic benefits their longevity of participation is inversely related to the extent to which they feel motivated to volunteer by the need for–or expectation of–egoistic benefits" (p. 223).

The sample was composed of 90 former Big Brothers/Big Sisters volunteers from an Austin, Texas, agency whom had quit during a nine-month period. Multiple regression analysis. The data came from case worker reports and questionnaires.

Many human service organizations face a situation in which the client feels a sense of humiliation. This humiliation prevents positive expressions of reinforcing behaviors for volunteers. If volunteers came into the situation with excessive needs/expectations of self-gratifying benefits from their volunteer experience, then their expectations/needs will not be met. These volunteers then are likely to quit.

People with high levels of egoistic expectations/needs may be easy targets as potential volunteers. However, they may turnover quickly also. This problem has created a steady need for volunteers in volunteers agencies.

This study was theoretically based on social exchange theory and ephemeral roles.

Sundeen, Richard A. (1992), "Differences in Personal Goals and Attitudes Among Volunteers," *Nonprofit and Voluntary Action Research*, 21 (3), 271-291.

This study is a re-analysis of data from an Independent Sector survey from 1988. The purpose was to determine if " . . . personal values regarding religion, charity, and politics, as well as attitudes toward the roles and responsibilities of government, individuals, and charitable institutions, distinguish between volunteers and non-volunteers, and between volunteers to various kinds of organizations and for various kinds of activities" (274). The analysis used a logistic regression procedure. The sample size of the national survey was 2,775.

Findings. Volunteering and giving are more important to volunteers than to non-volunteers. Volunteers believe that it is important to help others. Volunteers place less confidence in non-charitable institutions than do non-volunteers. There is no difference in attitudes regarding the roles and responsibilities of government between volunteers and non-volunteers. Motivational and attitudinal structure of volunteering is multidimensional, not unidimensional. Other results not discussed here; see article. The author concludes that attitudes and values help to predict volunteer behavior.

Williams, Dennis E. and Kenneth O. Gangel (1993), *Volunteers for Today's Church: How to Recruit and Retain Workers*. Grand Rapids, MI: Baker Books.

This book is written for practitioners. It discusses the importance to churches of church volunteers. The authors discuss sound recruiting practices. Some major points on recruiting are: (1) the right person must be selected, and (2) the recruit must be told in specific terms the duties of the task and its responsibilities. In terms of volunteer performance, the major point is to make sure that people are given a thorough orientation because volunteers perform at the level at which they are recruited. In terms of volunteer retention, a major point is to give volunteers the recognition they deserve as well as to make sure to communicate to volunteers the importance of their work to the church.

Wright, Newell D., Val Larson, and Roger Higgs (1995), "Marketing of Voluntarism: The Case of Appalachian Mountain Housing," *Journal of Consumer Satisfaction, Dissatisfaction, and Complaining Behavior*, 8, 188-197.

This is an ethnographic study of a charity which builds homes for the poor. The authors conclude that volunteers are the most important constituency (because poor people needing housing are plentiful whereas volunteers are not). Therefore, nonprofit organizations must be concerned with volunteer satisfaction.

There were two volunteer functions: building and fund raising. The building function was looked after closely. A lot of preplanning went in to make sure volunteers were having fun and were not idle at the work site. Volunteer leaders even anticipated the negative experiences of volunteers (sore muscles the day after building) by telling volunteers that the soreness they would feel was a good feeling, meaning that they had done some good. Volunteers enjoyed building.

Conversely, volunteers disliked the fund raising aspect very much. It caused turnover as well. The authors suggested that the managers needed to put as much thought and preplanning for fund raising as they did for building. The authors also recommended that volunteers with marketing/fund raising expertise should be recruiting volunteers for the fund raising function.

3. REACTIVATION OF FORMER VOLUNTEERS TO SERVICE

No scholarly works dealing with this topic were identified.

4. SEGMENTATION

Adams, David S. (1980), "Elite and Lower Volunteers in a Voluntary Association: A Study of an American Red Cross Chapter," *Journal of Voluntary Action Research,* **9, 95-108.**

The purpose of this case study (participant observation and interviews) is to better understand differences between elite (board members, N = 38) and lower (other volunteers, N = 35) volunteers regarding how they became volunteers, their perceptions regarding the Red Cross, and their involvement with its activities.

Among the elite volunteers, women tend to be promoted upward. Men tend to be recruited based on their occupational status. Lower volunteers tend to be recruited by friends and family or from associates from other organizations to which they belonged. Lower volunteers reported being motivated by wanting to help others and by the rewards of being a volunteer. Other information regarding elite and lower volunteer activities is discussed.

Clary, E. Gil, Mark Snyder et al. (1998), "Understanding and Assessing the Motivations of Volunteers: A Functional Approach," *Journal of Personality & Social Psychology,* **74 (6), p. 1516-1530.**

Presents a study which applied functionalist theory to the question of the motivations underlying volunteerism. Application of the functional approach to motivation; functions served by volunteerism; motivational foundations of volunteerism; implications for the practice of volunteerism.

Heidrich, Katheryn Wiedman (1988), "Lifestyles of Volunteers: A Market Segmentation Study," Ph.D. dissertation, University of Illinois at Urbana-Champaign.

If distinct lifestyle segments exist within the volunteer market and if these can be identified, voluntary organizations may be able to improve their recruitment and retention strategies.

H1: Each type of voluntary organization has a unique type of volunteer, characterized by particular lifestyles.

H2: Types of roles within voluntary organizations are preferred by people with distinct lifestyles.

Three types of volunteer organizations are investigated: Business/Professional, Expressive, and Service. Four types of roles are studied: Direct Service, Leadership, General Support, and Member-at-large.

Variables. Socioeconomic-demographic measures, personal values, volunteering type, personality style, and leisure activity style.

Mail survey, 443 members of 15 volunteer organizations. Discriminant Analysis to test hypotheses. Classification Analysis is used to test the ability of the discriminant functions to correctly classify "new" cases.

The author concludes that the volunteer market may be meaningfully segmented and that volunteers' differing lifestyles may lead to effective targeting of particular groups.

Killeen, Johanne and Michael McCarrey (1986), "Relations of Altruistic Versus Competitive Values, Course of Study, and Behavioral Intentions to Help or Compete," *Psychological Reports,* **59 (2), 895-898.**

The purpose of this study is to determine if people would incur significant personal costs in order to choose activities which help them to behave in ways consistent with value priorities.

Variables. Three altruistic and three competitive instrumental values from Rokeach Value Survey. Subjects were asked to volunteer for either an altruistic or a competitive task.

Methods. Undergraduate nursing (N = 83) and business (N = 170) students. Subjects were asked to rank six values. They were told that university organizations would be calling to see if they would volunteer 10-20 hours. Fisher's exact test was used in the analysis.

Findings. Business students tend to have competitive value orientations. Nursing students tend to have altruistic value orientations. Business students tend to volunteer for the competitive organization. Nursing students tend to volunteer for the altruistic organization. Conclusion: people tend to behave, at some cost, in ways that correspond to their personal value orientations.

Rohs, Frederick Richard (1986), "Social Background, Personality, and Attitudinal Factors Influencing the Decision to Volunteer and Level of Involvement Among Adult 4-H Leaders," *Journal of Voluntary Action Research,* **15 (1), 87-99.**

The purpose of this study is to determine if certain social background, personality, and attitudinal variables could account for a 4-H volunteer's decision to volunteer and length of service. Social background variables are age, gender, marital status, income, education, occupational status, length of residence in community, number and ages of children, previous 4-H member-ship, and interpersonal roles. The personality variable is "flexibility." Attitu-dinal factors are value of 4-H organization, attractiveness of 4-H, influential role of significant others. Dependent variables are continuing as a 4-H volun-teer, number of years of service, level of involvement.

Path analysis is used to analyze the data. Sample: 300 4-H leaders from Ohio, mean age is 39 years, 70 percent female, over 60 percent had been in 4-H as a youth, 84 percent are married, 88 percent have children.

Findings. Age, years as 4-H member, children in 4-H, and attractiveness of 4-H have positive influence on volunteer's length of service. Occupational status has a negative influence on volunteer's length of service.

Schlegelmilch, Bodo B. and Carolyn Tynan (1989), "Who Volunteers?: An Investigation into the Characteristics of Charity Volunteers," *Journal of Marketing Management*, 5 (2), 133-151.

The authors segment volunteers based on demographics, activities/life-styles, and psychographics. Volunteers are classified by the type of volunteer work they did (1) Occasional fund raising events. (2) Sponsored events sought for an activity. (3) Helping with street collections. (4) working for a charity on a volunteer basis). Volunteers were also classified according to the amount of time they gave.

Results. Chi-square contingency tables and one factor analysis. Sample, 494 questionnaires from mail survey and personal interviews in the UK (72 percent of donors were female). The segmentation was largely successful. A number of significant results are available.

"The managerial relevance of this type of information lies in the improved scope for targeting likely volunteers" (143).

Future research section gives some good ideas. For example, we need a better understanding of why people volunteer. Also need research for a closer analysis of the heavy volunteers.

Tschirhart, Mary (1998). "Understanding the Older Stipended Volun-teer: Age-related Differences among AmeriCorps Members," *Public Productivity & Management Review*, 22 (1), 35-48.

Age-related differences in interests, perceptions of work, retention, and public service motivation of AmeriCorps members are reported. Individuals aged 50 and over demonstrate a greater service development than their youn-ger colleagues. Mixed support was found for the role substitution theory for shy seniors seek work. Hypotheses and a survey were distributed about 1 year later to members of the original sample. Knowing what encourages older adults to join, to be successful, and to stay in an organization is useful for the development of recruitment, training, work assignment, and retention strategies.

Wymer, Walter W., Jr. (1997). "Segmenting Volunteers Using Values, Self-Esteem, Empathy, and Facilitation as Determinant Variables," *Nonprofit & Public Sector Marketing,* **5 (2), 3-28.**

Responding to prior research from a sociological and psychological perspective which tended to portray volunteers as a homogeneous population, the author set out to determine if volunteers could be effectively segmented into subgroups using selected variables. Demographic variables, which were overused in prior research, are not used in this study to determine the efficacy of the variables self-esteem, empathy, personal values, and facilitation in differentiating sub-groups of volunteers. Volunteers were categorized by volunteer role and by organization type. Sample size: 944 volunteers (72% female), 114 non-volunteers from over 37 organizations in two Midwestern cities.

Findings. The variables are useful in differentiating volunteers who work in five of six types of volunteer organizations. The variables are also useful in differentiating subgroups of volunteers serving in four types of volunteer roles. The author presents results from each analysis and interprets results in the paper. The study demonstrates that the population of volunteers is diverse. However, homogeneous subgroups of volunteers can be segmented for target marketing purposes. The variables chosen in this study are useful in segmenting volunteer subgroups, particularly values. Values show potential motivational components of volunteering which can be used to construct marketing communications in recruitment appeals.

Yavas, Ugur and Glen Riecken (1993), "Socioeconomic and Behavioral Correlates of Donor Segments: An Application to United Way," *Journal of Nonprofit & Public Sector Marketing,* **1(1), 71-83.**

The purpose of this article is to determine if non-donors, sporadic donors, and heavy donors can be differentiated using risk (money, social, ego) and demographic variables (education, marital status, gender, occupation, type of housing, home ownership, age, and income). The United Way was the target organization.

Phone survey; 194 non-donors, 46 sporadic donors, and 115 consistent donors. Chi-square analysis.

Findings. Marital status differentiates all three groups (consistent donors, 71 percent married). "These findings suggest that middle aged people who are married, college educated and upscale in occupation and income are the consistent donors to the United Way" (77). In terms of risk, consistent donors perceive the least risk of giving money. Sporadic donors perceive the most risk.

Yavas, Ugur, Glen Riecken, and Ravi Parameswaran (1981), "Personality, Organization-Specific Attitude, and Socioeconomic Correlates of Charity Giving Behavior," *Journal of the Academy of Marketing Science,* **9 (1), 52-65.**

The purpose of the study is to determine if the variables identified in the title could differentiate United Way donors from non-donors. Personality, measured using CAD (personality inventory). Organization-specific attitudes, measured using a series of statements measured with Likert scales. Socioeconomic variables: education, marital status, sex, occupation, type of housing, home ownership, age, children at home, income, membership in various organizations.

Questionnaires produced 217 respondents (155 donors, 62 non-donors). Discriminant analysis.

Findings. Socioeconomic variables are the best predictors of donor membership, followed by attitudes. Personalty variables actually reduce the predictive ability of the model when added. "Variables which differentiate donors and nondonors are home ownership, having children, membership in various organizations, and respondents' specific disposition towards United Way" (61).

5. DESCRIPTIVE STUDIES

Allen, Natalie J. and J. Philippe Rushton (1983), "Personality Characteristics of Community Mental Health Volunteers: A Review," *Journal of Voluntary Action Research,* **12 (1), 36-49.**

Purpose and method. By examining prior literature (19 studies), the authors investigate if findings from altruism studies can be applied to mental health workers. In other words, can mental health workers be identified as altruistic personalities?

Findings. Community volunteers are more empathetic than non-volunteers. In terms of internalized moral standards, volunteers demonstrate more concern with societal and religious beliefs than with economic values. Volunteers also have higher moral standards. Volunteers have habitually more positive moods, and are more accepting of others. Volunteers report feeling in greater control of their lives and greater independence. Volunteers have greater emotional stability, and feel more satisfied with their lives than non-volunteers.

Auslander, Gail K. and Howard Litwin (1988), "Sociability and Patterns of Participation Implications for Social Service Policy," *Journal of Voluntary Action Research,* **17(2), 25-37.**

This article examines the effect of sociability and demographic variables on the variety of voluntary associations in which a person participates (dependent variable).

Social networks have two dimensions: (1) informal interpersonal relationships (personal ties) with friends and relatives, and (2) formal voluntary associations which provide other sources of social support.

Using a secondary analysis of telephone survey data (2,751 respondents) the authors report, "In regard to employment status, persons who are occupied out of the household–either employed or studying–had above average variety of participation rates, while all others had below average rates. Ranking lowest were persons who were laid off/on strike, averaging only 0.61 kinds of groups, and the disabled, 0.65 kinds of groups" (33).

The two most useful variables are education followed by income. "Findings suggest that persons with a greater number of close personal ties will also participate in more voluntary organizations" (25). "Persons with fewer close personal ties will tend to participate in fewer kinds of voluntary associations, and those with greater number of close personal ties, in more kinds of voluntary associations" (35).

One point to be made in this study is that the dependent variable is variety of organizations, not time spent volunteering.

Berger, Gabriel (1991), "Factors Explaining Volunteering for Organizations in General and for Social Welfare Organizations in Particular," doctoral dissertation, Heller School of Social Welfare, Brandeis University.

This dissertation uses a secondary analysis of 1990 Independent Sector national survey data. It uses LISREL (structural equation modeling software) to estimate models. The author sought to obtain a multivariate model of volunteerism.

Berger reports, " . . . altruistic helping behavior is rooted in deeply held prescriptive norms of justice, fairness, and social responsibility which have been incorporated in some individuals' value systems" (79). There seem to be two reasons for getting involved: (1) expressing a concern for the community, (2) to protect personal interests.

Caldwell, Jackie and Jean Pearson Scott (1994), "Effective Hospice Volunteers: Demographic and Personality Characteristics," *The American Journal of Hospice and Palliative Care*, March/April, 40-45.

The purpose of this study is to examine the characteristics of highly effective hospice volunteers. Thirty-two (of 50) Texas hospice programs participated in this study. Directors were asked to identify their most dependable and effective volunteers, and to distribute questionnaires to them. Of the 244 questionnaires which were distributed, 156 were returned (response rate of 64%). Measures were taken for demographic variables, a measure of religious activity, community volunteer involvement, and previous death experiences. The Myers-Briggs Type Indicator was used to assess four personality indices: extroversion-introversion, sensing-intuitive, thinking-feeling, and judgment-perception.

Findings. The sample was typically middle aged (mean age = 56 years), female (87%), white (95%), and married (73%). The mean monthly number of hours volunteered was 19. The mean length of service was 3.4 years. The majority of volunteers were involved in direct patient care. "The largest proportion of female volunteers were extroverted, sensing, feeling, judging personality types, whereas, for male volunteers, the largest proportion were introverted, sensing, thinking, judging personality types." The authors discuss the implications of these findings for recruitment and training.

Chambre, Susan M. (1993), "Volunteerism by Elders: Past Trends and Future Prospects," *The Gerontologist,* **33 (2), 221-228.**

Surveys of volunteerism show that senior citizen volunteerism has increased over the past 25 years. This article discusses cultural, demographic, and programmatic factors contributing to this increase. Cultural factors: the former negative stereotype of seniors is changing. Seniors are more active and living longer. Demographic factors: seniors are better educated, more affluent, and more likely to be native born. Seniors are filling volunteer roles once filled by traditional female home-makers. Programmatic factors: government-sponsored programs to increase senior volunteering are increasing (e.g., SCORE, ACTION, RSVP, SERVE, VITA). There is also an increasing number of private initiatives to stimulate senior volunteering.

Chevrier, Fiona, Roxanne Steuer, and Jackie MacKenzie (1994), "Factors Affecting Satisfaction Among Community-Based Hospice Volunteer Visitors," *The American Journal of Hospice & Palliative Care,* **July/August, 30-37.**

Working under the assumption that satisfied hospice volunteers remain with the hospice organization longer, the authors sought to better understand correlates of hospice volunteer satisfaction. The literature review section points out some prior work regarding turnover of hospice volunteers. The most important factor, for example, in one study appears to be an under-use of volunteers, leaving volunteers feeling demoralized.

One hundred hospice volunteers, selected randomly from an organizational population of 143, from a Canadian hospice organization, were surveyed by telephone. The sample was 77% women, and 46% of the sample were between the ages of 40 and 59 years. The authors measured satisfaction using the Work scale of the Cornell Job Description Index.

Overall, hospice volunteers are very satisfied with their work. Satisfaction is not significantly related to volunteer tenure, volunteer activity, satisfaction with training, or the newsletter. Satisfaction is significantly associated with volunteers' perceptions of organizational support, of being a valuable team member, of having their skills fully used, of satisfaction with client matches, of having their expectations met, and of role clarity. Volunteer satisfaction was also related to feelings that the volunteer work was needed, and feelings of being helpful in improving clients' quality of life. The authors reported some differences by age and gender. Managerial implications of the findings were discussed.

Cnaan, Ram A. and Laura Amrofell (1994), "Mapping Volunteer Activity," *Nonprofit and Voluntary Sector Quarterly*, 23 (4), 335-351.

This conceptual paper aims to clarify the domain of volunteerism and its typology. The classification of volunteer activity is conducted by using a sentence mapping sequence methodology. The authors describe the divergent facets of volunteerism by using combinations of ten factors: who is the volunteer, what is being volunteered, the level of formality of the volunteer work, the frequency of volunteering, the amount of time allocated per volunteer episode, relatedness of beneficiaries, characteristics of beneficiaries, who manages volunteers, management activities, and volunteers' rewards. One main contribution of this article is that it highlights the diversity of samples in prior research on volunteerism. Caution should be exercised before applying findings from one study to another.

Cnaan, Ram A., Amy Kasternakis, and Robert J. Wineburg (1993), "Religious People, Religious Congregations, and Volunteerism in Human Services: Is There a Link?" *Nonprofit and Voluntary Sector Quarterly*, 22 (1), 33-51.

Purpose. To explore the link between religious beliefs and volunteerism and to shed light on the impact of religious observance on volunteering.

Method and Sample. Tri-city interviews by graduate students resulted in data from 466 volunteers and 405 non-volunteers. Sample frame of volunteers came from participating nonprofit organizations. Non-volunteer group participants were selected by friends of volunteer respondents. 72% female. Used a 10-item measure for internal religious beliefs. Also collected data to measure demographic variables, social-psychological variables, and a variable representing "motivation to volunteer."

Findings. Volunteers do not have higher levels of intrinsic religious motivation. "The findings for the entire sample indicated that three main factors were significant: education (those with college or a higher level of education scored lowest on intrinsic religious motivation), age (older people scored higher on intrinsic religious motivation), and religion (Catholics and Protestants score higher than Jews and others)" (44).

Note: the comparison group of non-volunteers was selected by the sample group of volunteers because they were friends. The two groups, therefore, may share common values, beliefs, and interests.

Curtis, James E. (1971), "Voluntary Association Joining: A Cross-National Comparative Note," *American Sociological Review,* **36 (5), 872-880.**

Using the variables social class, sex, age level, and marital status, the author proposes that Americans are not really more intensive association joiners than citizens of Canada, Great Britain, Germany, Italy, and Mexico. The data came from a Canadian national survey (Canada's data) and from a 1963 five country study. Findings indicate that U.S. citizens and Canadians are more likely to be members of voluntary associations (about 50% of population) than citizens of the other countries (about 33% of population are joiners). The difference between rates of participation in America and Canada and that of other countries appears to be related to the relatively lower rates of participation of women in the other countries.

Americans and Canadians are more likely to be members of multiple organizations (36%) compared to citizens of the other countries (18%). In terms of demographic correlates, social class, education, income, and occupational status are directly associated with joining in all countries. The inverted U-shaped curve for age was present in all countries; that is, as age increases, so does participation–to a point, then participation declines as a person gets older.

The author concludes that voluntary participation in the five countries is similar with the exception of participation by women. Women participate in associations less in Germany, Mexico, Italy, and Great Britain, Curtis argues, because women are more emancipated in the U.S. and in Canada.

Curtis, James E., Edward G. Grabb, and Douglas E. Baer (1992), "Voluntary Association Membership in Fifteen Countries: A Comparative Analysis," *American Sociological Review,* **57 (April), 139-152.**

The purpose of this study is to determine the degree to which Americans are more likely to join voluntary associations than people from other countries. The authors perform a secondary analysis from a multi-national World Values Survey (1981-1983). U.S. participants are compared to participants from 14 other industrialized Western nations.

The results show that Americans are unsurpassed as joiners of voluntary associations (73% of population are voluntary association members). The comparison countries differ widely in the proportion of their populations which report voluntary association membership (range is from 26% in Spain to 67% in Northern Ireland). When controlling for church membership, American participation declines and is surpassed by Great Britain, the Netherlands, and Australia. When controlling for labor union memberships, the U.S. is not significantly different from Canada, Great Britain, and Northern Ireland. Results also show that education, employment status, and age are directly correlated with higher levels of participation. When church membership is excluded, age has an inverted U relationship with participation.

Cutler, Stephen J. (1976), "Age Differences in Voluntary Association Memberships," *Social Forces,* **55 (1), 43-58.**

In prior research, voluntary association membership with respect to age has been found to have a curvilinear relationship. As people get older, they participate in organizations more, until about age 45 or so, when participation declines as age increases. The author suspects that the relationship between age and voluntary association membership is mediated by education and income. He proposes that older people are less educated than their younger counterparts and that older people have lower income levels. The author uses secondary data taken from two previous national surveys (total N ~ 4,000).

Using multiple classification analysis, the author finds the typical decline in participation with age. However, after controlling for education and income, the findings indicate that participation does not decline with age. The author concludes that differences in participation rates by age is a function of other demographic characteristics, not age.

Dempsey, Norah Peters (1988), "Women and Volunteerism: An Examination of the Changing Patterns, Types and Motivations," Ph.D. dissertation, Bryn Mawr College.

The author examines changes in women's volunteering activities after more women have entered the paid work force. The author approaches the phenomena from a sociological perspective.

The author surveyed women college alumni and uses regression data analysis. She finds several significant variables. Significant variables include: (1) volunteers have more children than non-volunteers, (2) they have more hobbies, (3) they report higher income levels, (4) they are more likely to be married, (5) and their husbands are more likely to serve on boards of the volunteer agency.

Edwards, Gary and Jon Hughes (1998), *Gallup Poll,* **58 (20), p. 1-2.**

Presents findings from a survey conducted by Gallup Poll on volunteerism in Canada. Percentage of Canadian adults who donated to charitable organizations during 1997; statistical information from the survey; methodology of the survey.

Fahey, Maureen (1986), "Lay Volunteers Within an American Catholic Parish: Personality and Social Factors," Ph.D. dissertation, University of San Francisco.

The purpose of this dissertation is to determine if personality and social variables can be used to differentiate between volunteers and non-volunteers. The author measures personality differences between volunteers and non-volunteers using the Personality Orientation Inventory (POI). Volunteers in the study are adults serving in one of 12 ministries in the parish. There were a total number of 214 participants in the study: 75 volunteer leaders, 84 regular volunteers, and 55 non-volunteers.

The author reports that volunteers are guided significantly more by internalized principles and motivations than are non-volunteers who are more susceptible to peer pressure. Volunteer leaders are significantly more sensitive to their own needs and feelings than regular volunteers and non-volunteers. Volunteer leaders feel significantly freer to be spontaneous.

Fitch, Robert T. (1987), "A Comparative Study of the Interpersonal Values of Community Service Volunteers, Extracurricular Activity Volunteers and Non-Volunteers on the College Campus," Ph.D. dissertation, University of Georgia.

Used Survey of Interpersonal Values on 285 undergraduate students. Students involved in service activities were significantly higher on scales of Conformity and Benevolence, and lower on Independence than comparison groups.

Florin, Paul, Eric Jones, and Abraham Wandersman (1986), "Black Participation in Voluntary Associations," *Journal of Voluntary Action Research,* **15 (1), 65-86.**

Purpose. To better understand black volunteerism by using cognitive social learning variables, and to compare the significant variables to those found in prior research.

Method. Personal interviews (45 to 60 minutes) of 470 black adult residents of a suburb of Nashville, Tennessee (63% female, ave age = 44 years). Measures are taken for two sets of variables: traditional demographic variables, and items operationalizing cognitive social learning variables (CSLV). The authors use discriminant function data analysis, followed by classification analysis.

Findings. The CSLV variables significantly differentiate black volunteers by high/low levels of volunteering (28% variance accounted for). The classification analysis correctly classified 78% of group members. The set of traditional demographic variables is about equal in variance accounted for, cases correctly classified, and unique variance to the smaller set of CSLV variables. Significant traditional variables are: home ownership, self-esteem, intended length of residence, age, length of residence, occupation, internal locus of control, marital status, and education.

Implications. CSLV variables are preferable to traditional variables because they are fewer in number and are theoretically driven. The more middle class and educated a person is, the more likely s/he is likely to volunteer. Higher self-esteem and internal locus of control are associated with higher level of volunteerism. Higher participation is also related to having requisite skill sets, valuing the community, and feeling a sense of duty.

Frisch, Michael B. and Meg Gerrard (1981), "Natural Helping Systems: A Survey of Red Cross Volunteers," *American Journal of Community Psychology,* 9 (5), 567-579.

Purpose. To examine the characteristics and motives of Red Cross volunteers. To examine the relationship between youth service on later adult volunteer service and financial support.

Method. Mailed 13-item questionnaire. One hundred, ninety-five Red Cross chapters were randomly selected. Three questionnaires were sent to each chapter. Sixty-seven percent response rate. Best response came from larger cities. Sample: 60% female, 94% white, average age = 49, average education = 15.5 years, average Red Cross service = 12 years.

Findings. Found distinction between self-serving and altruistic motives. Highest altruistic motives: to help the less fortunate, to practice ideals and convictions, and to be a good neighbor. Highest self-serving motives: career exploration, develop contacts, and learn how to better relate to people. Altruistic motives are more emphasized among volunteers. Youth volunteers are more likely to report more self-serving motives. Seventy-eight percent of adult volunteers report being a Red Cross volunteer when a youth. Predictors of adult Red Cross volunteerism are age, receiving Red Cross services, and Red Cross youth volunteering.

Implications. "Volunteerism may be encouraged by being cognizant of the existence of two distinct kinds of rewards for participation in voluntary organizations, and by framing requests for volunteer help with the value systems of specific target populations in mind" (575). Volunteers are predominantly female (males predominate in leadership roles). Youth involvement is important in stimulating later adult volunteer service.

Gerard, David (1985), "What Makes a Volunteer?" *New Society*, 74 (Nov. 8), 236-238.

Data from the 1981 European Values Study undertaken by Gallup using a nationally representative British sample (N = 1,231) is examined to identify factors influencing volunteerism and the characteristics of volunteers.

Factors that were measured and number of items measuring each factor include: (1) attitudes towards others-4 items, (2) religious commitment-5 items, (3) political activism-1 item, (4) indicators of reflectiveness-3 items, and (5) attitudes to material factors-4 items.

"Recently, most explanations of volunteering have been in terms of the psychological concepts of social exchange and reciprocal benefit. There is an inherent ambiguity in the motives for voluntary action. The idea of reciprocal benefit-i.e., each side gives something to the other-is clearly relevant to the relationship between volunteers and their beneficiaries. But it cannot explain everything about volunteering. Nor does the theory of social exchange-i.e., each side gets something out of it-do justice to the richness and variety of human motives. It emphasizes self-interest and the role of calculation in social relations. Obligations are contingent upon expected benefits. Discussion of motives needs to be broadened to include, at very least, beneficence and solidarity" (237).

"Among the most striking results is the enduring importance of religious motivation. Over 70 percent of all volunteers described themselves as 'a religious person,' and over 50 percent attend church at least monthly. About a third report having had a profound religious experience, compared to less than one fifth of the remaining population" (238).

Beneficence and religious orientation help predict charity volunteerism. Activists, however, reject charity, and tend to be well-educated and young. Solidarity predicts them. They stress rights, protests, and moral autonomy, and the necessity for structural change. They have more permissive attitudes to social behavior.

"The religious orientation of volunteers is reflected in their social attitudes and values" (238).

"The voluntary workers studied reported better health, found greater meaning in life, and expressed a greater preference for active pursuits. The interviewers assess them as self-assured" (238).

Gibboney, Robyn (1996), "Service Learning and Commitment to Community: Exploring the Implications of Honors Students' Perceptions of the Process 2 Years Later," *Nonprofit and Voluntary Sector Quarterly*, **25 (4), 506-524.**

The author taught a course (13 students) whose students were required to volunteer in one of three types of volunteer activities: (1) altruism, (2) philanthropy, and (3) public service. Students were required to keep journals of their course experience, part of which was to "volunteer" 3 to 5 hours/week during the semester. Two years later, the author interviewed the students. The purpose of the study is to learn what effect their service learning had on subsequent activities, goals, and values. (It should be noted that these students were enrolled in a philanthropic studies curriculum.)

Findings. The students said that the course broadened their perceptions of service and philanthropy. The majority of students indicated a desire to be involved in their communities.

Gillespie, David F. and Anthony E. O. King I (1985), "Demographic Understanding of Volunteerism," *Journal of Sociology and Social Welfare*, **12 (4), 798-816.**

Purpose. The authors are interested in identifying demographic correlates of the reasons people give for volunteering.

Method and Sample. Mail survey of American Red Cross volunteers of a large Midwestern city. The survey resulted in 1,346 usable questionnaires (response rate = 27%). Demographic characteristics of sample are similar to other studies. Gender: female/male = 80%/20%, whereas other studies report a ratio of female/male of 70 to 30 %.

Findings. The top 10 reasons for volunteering are: to help others, to contribute to the community, to obtain training and skills, enrich personal life, had some time available, to be needed, to make new friends, reputation of Red Cross, career exploration, to be around others. As the age of the volunteer increased, the reason for volunteering increased toward "to help others" and away from "to obtain training and skills." Males were more likely to volunteer to obtain training and job skills. In terms of marital status, widowed and single people (who tended to be older) were more likely to volunteer to help others.

Hettman, Dennis W. and Elizabeth Jenkins (1990), "Volunteerism and Social Interest," *Individual Psychology*, **46 (3), 298-303.**

The purpose of this study is to examine social interest as a possible motivator of volunteer work. Do volunteers score higher on the Social Interest

Scale (SIS) than non-volunteers? Is social interest a better predictor of volunteering than available leisure time? Do volunteer sub-groups differ in their SIS ratings?

Method. Subjects are 120 individuals in the San Francisco Bay area. Sixty are volunteers in one of three different agencies; 60 are residents (non-volunteers) from neighborhoods near the volunteer agencies. Volunteers' surveys are left for them to complete at the volunteer agencies. Non-volunteers' surveys are distributed door-to-door.

Findings. Volunteers are younger, better educated, and report lower incomes than non-volunteers. Volunteers score higher on the SIS. The activity levels between the two groups is very similar except that volunteers watch more television or listen to music. Legal advocacy volunteers score higher on the SIS than health care or youth volunteers.

Hobfoll, Stevan E. (1980), "Personal Characteristics of the College Volunteer," *American Journal of Community Psychology,* **8 (4), 503-506.**

Sixty-one female undergraduate students participated as subjects. Volunteers, as compared to non-volunteers, were found to score higher only on social responsibility. They also expressed more positive evaluations of the client population than non-volunteers. There were five personality scales measuring self-acceptance, empathy, dogmatism, tolerance, and social responsibility.

Hougland, James G., Jr. and James A. Christenson (1982), "Voluntary Organizations and Dominant American Values," *Journal of Voluntary Action Research,* **11 (4), 6-26.**

Purpose. To investigate the question of whether adherence to dominant American values is linked to social participation.

Method. Randomly selected mail survey of North Carolina residents (response rate = 70%) resulted in 3,115 usable surveys. Respondents were asked to rate their level of participation (volunteerism) from a list of 9 types of voluntary organizations. Values were assessed using two types. There were 7 social values and 7 personal values. The sample was partitioned into three groups: non-volunteers, token volunteers, and active volunteers.

Findings. The ability of the values used in this study to differentiate the three sample sub-groups is weak, but values are significant if demographic variables are controlled for. Values do not differentiate volunteers into a homogenous group. Rather, volunteers differ in value orientation by organization type.

Hougland, James G., Jr. and James R. Wood (1980), "Correlates of Participation in Local Churches," *Sociological Focus*, 13 (4), 343-358.

Purpose. The purpose of this study is to determine if background variables can predict church participation. Also, the authors' examine the effects of organizational characteristics, interpersonal influence, orientation toward the church, and activity in other organizations on church participation.

Methods. The data came from a random, stratified sample of church members from 58 Protestant churches. Respondents had to have attended church or made a contribution at least once in the prior two years. Two follow-up mailings, N = 2,165, response rate = 54%.

Measures. Degree of participation (attendance, small group involvement, number of conversations with pastor, communication with other members). Contributions, size of congregation, pastor's tenure, interpersonal influence, activity in other organizations, individual background characteristics, identification, attitudinal measures, and more. Correlation and regression analysis.

Findings. Number of friends in church is highly correlated with active participation and proportion of income donated. Tables showing correlations is available. Reactions to church explains 47 percent of variance of active participation. Reactions to church and interpersonal influence are most powerful predictors of active participation. Individual background characteristics are most important predictors of proportion of income donated.

Implications. Researchers should use more than one measure of participation (e.g., background variables). Participation may be multidimensional. For example, in this study, passive participation is viewed as donating money to the church, whereas active participation is viewed as more behavioral involvement in church groups and activities.

Huss, Jean Mary (1988), "A Descriptive Study of Older Persons Performing Volunteer Work and the Relationship to Life Satisfaction, Purpose in Life, and Social Support," Ph.D. dissertation, University of Iowa.

This study seeks to determine the relationship of volunteer work to life satisfaction, meaning of life, and social support of older persons. Pretest/posttest design (6 months between tests). Sample (age > 60 years): pretest sample size, volunteers = 33 non-volunteers = 32; posttest sample size, volunteers = 31, non-volunteers = 30. Volunteers came from 20 RSVP programs in Iowa. Participants were solicited by phone, then large print questionnaires were mailed. Five parts to questionnaire: (1) demographic, (2) description of volunteer work, (3) life satisfaction index, (4) purpose of life test, and (5) social provisions scale.

Findings. Average age = 69, 80% female. Volunteering improves seniors' score on life satisfaction index (regardless of type of volunteer work), purpose of life test, but not on social provisions scale. Motivations for senior volunteer work are: to help others, to be with people, to keep active and involved, and to be useful and productive. Volunteers expect to receive psychological benefits from their volunteer work.

Lafer, Barbara and Stephen S. Craig (1993), "The Evaluation of Hospice Home Care Volunteers," *The Hospice Journal*, 9 (1), 13-20.

The purpose of this project was to create a measure for evaluating hospice home care volunteers. Using 27 performance criteria from Lafer's dissertation study to compose an evaluation instrument, the authors surveyed, via mail, hospice volunteer coordinators. They received responses from 111 of 212 coordinators (52%). Information from the survey was used to modify and extend the original 27 criteria. A second mailing of the modified instrument was sent to 50 coordinators (33 replied). Then a third iteration of the instrument was mailed to a national sample of 241 coordinators (139 responded).

From these iterations, the authors refined, added, and dropped individual performance criterion measures in their instrument. The face validity of the instrument, due to their rigorous use of feedback from coordinators appears to be very strong. The reliability and remaining validities were not assessed.

Lemon, Mona, Bartolomeo J. Palisi, and Perry E. Jacobson, Jr. (1972), "Dominant Statuses and Involvement in Formal Voluntary Associations," *Journal of Voluntary Action Research*, 1(2), 30-42.

The purpose of this article is to propose the idea that social participation (includes volunteerism) is explained by looking at the dominant statuses in a society. A dominant status is a social characteristic (e.g., gender, income, education) which is most valued by a society. The general proposition is that individuals who are characterized by relatively more dominant status dimensions are more likely to participate in social institutions. "Statuses are relative not only to societies, but to specific groups within society" (34).

Method and Findings. Mail survey to college students. N = 500, response rate = 63%. Five of eight tests of significance are in the predicted direction (gender, age, marital status, college class, and subject major). Three tests are not in the predicted direction (social class, being Protestant, and grade point average).

Conclusion. The findings generally support the claim that dominant status characteristics are related to social participation. Individual social characteristics are less effective predictors of participation than total number of dominant status characteristics.

Luloff, A.E., W.H. Chittenden, E. Kriss, S. Weeks, and L. Brushett (1984), "Local Volunteerism in New Hampshire: Who, Why, and at What Benefit," *Journal of the Community Development Society,* **15 (2), 17-30.**

This report focuses on a study of volunteerism in an eight-town area in New Hampshire, conducted during late 1978 and early 1979. The survey results indicate that the typical volunteer is male, 51 years old, married, owns a single family home, has resided in his current town for about fifteen years, and serves on an average of three committees during his tenure in the community. Respondents volunteer for two main reasons: to enhance their local prestige, or to serve the community.

Sample is comprised of volunteers for local governments. The most important reason for serving is a sense of public duty.

"Cuts in federal funds and grants have necessitated the elimination of many services, thus stimulating an increase in the use of free labor and monetary contributions from private sources" (8).

"There is extensive agreement that one's social class (as indicated by personal income, education, and occupation) and age are strongly related to holding membership in voluntary associations. Those with higher incomes, higher levels of formal education, and employment in higher status occupations are generally found to volunteer most frequently. At the same time, middle-aged individuals (40-59) tend to have higher levels of volunteerism than those younger or older. Other characteristics found to influence voluntary affiliation include gender, marital status, tenure in community, home and/or business ownership, and church attendance. Interestingly, size of local community has not been found to significantly affect the rate of voluntary affiliation" (19).

Marriott Senior Living Services (1991), *Marriott's Seniors Volunteerism Study.* **Washington, DC: author.**

In a national survey, 962 telephone interviews were conducted with respondents over 60 years of age. Using a 95% level of confidence, the findings are:

1. 41% (15.5 million) of 37.7 million Americans over 60 did some kind of volunteer work during the previous year.
2. 14 million (37.4 %) are potential volunteers who are or may be willing to volunteer if asked.
3. 4 million current volunteers would volunteer more time if asked.
4. Seniors volunteer an estimated 992 million days generating 3.6 billion hours of volunteer service during the past year. On average, seniors

volunteer more than one day/week or 64 days/yr. Average time volunteered is 3.6 hours/day.

5. 83% volunteer to help others. 65% volunteer to feel useful or productive. 52% volunteer to fulfill a moral responsibility. 1/3 said volunteering is a social obligation. 1/4 wanted companionship. 5% volunteer to alleviate feelings of guilt.
6. 45.5% men, 35.5% women.
7. 57% volunteer for churches or religious organizations, 32% volunteer for social service organizations, 25% for civic or cultural organizations, 22% for schools or educational institutions, and 16% for health-related organizations.
8. Over 66% of seniors with college degrees perform volunteer service while only 37.5 percent of those with only high school diplomas provide services.

Penner, Louis A. and Maria A. Finkelstein (1998), *Journal of Personality & Social Psychology,* **74 (2), p. 525-537.**

Presents a panel survey which examined the dispositional and structural determinants of volunteerism. Percentage of adults who spend time as unpaid volunteers for service organizations in the United States; reference to prosocial personality orientation; information on the role identity model of volunteerism; further information.

Perkins, Kenneth B. (1989), "Volunteer Firefighters in the United States: A Descriptive Study," *Nonprofit & Voluntary Sector Quarterly,* **18 (5), 269-277.**

Purpose. To better understand the human capital of this group of volunteers. To better understand how to recruit and retain them.

Method and Findings. A questionnaire was administered at 250 volunteer fire departments in five states during their monthly meetings (N = 3,188). Ave. age, 36; 96%, male; 96%, white; 10%, college degrees. 73% of respondents were not members of other volunteer organizations. Volunteers report being firmly committed to their volunteer organizations and roles (average tenure was 10 years). Respondents report that half or more of their friends are also fire fighters.

Implications. While the supply of volunteer fire fighters appears to be stable, minorities and women are not being adequately tapped. The major obstacle is that these volunteer groups are fraternal and don't easily assimilate persons who differ. In recruitment appeals, the message could emphasize the excitement and benefits of being a fire fighter as well as being part of a team.

Perry, William H. (1982), "A Study of Older Volunteers in Leon County, Florida," doctoral dissertation, Florida State University.

A comparison of 75 volunteers with 56 non-volunteers reveals that volunteers have higher levels of self-esteem and peer relations than non-volunteers.

Schram, Vicki R. and Marilyn M. Dunsing (1981), "Influences on Married Women's Volunteer Work Participation," *Journal of Consumer Research*, 7 (March), 372-379.

Purpose. Using a economic framework (cost/return approach to volunteer work based on human capital theory), the authors examine determinants of volunteer work for married women and factors influencing the level of volunteer work.

Method. A sample of married female homemakers in Champaign-Urbana, Illinois, were interviewed (N = 231). The dependent variables are participation in volunteer work and average weekly hours volunteered. The independent variables are demographic in nature. The are a couple of questions assessing the interviewee's plans to (re)enter the paid workforce. Multiple regression analysis.

Findings and Conclusion. The more highly educated and the more negative the husband feels about his wife working outside the home, the more likely the woman is to volunteer. "A homemaker was more likely to volunteer a lot if she (1) was more highly educated, (2) was younger, (3) had lived in her present home a longer period of time, (4) was more satisfied with her marriage, (5) had worked some or most of the time since marriage, and (6) had not lived in the community all her life" (378). Human capital theory is generally not supported in this study. Future research was recommended that would be multidisciplinary in nature.

Schultz, Gail L. (1975), "The Use of the Sixteen Personality Factor Questionnaire to Profile Personality Characteristics of Suicide Prevention Volunteers," M.A. thesis, San Francisco State University.

This study sought to differentiate the personalities of hotline volunteers from the general population (demographic data are included). Over nine months, 77 hotline volunteers (34, with 2 or more years of experience, were senior volunteers; 43, junior) were given a personality inventory. Analysis: t tests of means.

Findings. Volunteers tend to be female (86%) and about 41 years old. About half of the volunteers are unemployed or retired. About 75 percent of volunteers report prior volunteer experience (concentrated in human services). Most volunteers are married with children. About 83 percent of volunteers report a history of depression, 42 percent rating their depression moderate to severe (36 percent had consulted a professional for their depression). Three-fourths of volunteers report experience with a suicidal other. The primary motivation for volunteering is to help others. "Volunteers, compared to non-volunteers, tended to be less conforming, more tender-minded, imaginative, forthright and radical." "Senior volunteers, compared to junior volunteers, were more surgent and less tender-minded" (p. iii).

Shure, Richard S. (1988), "The Identification of Those Most Likely to Volunteer: Characteristics of Male Volunteers in the Big Brothers/Big Sisters Program," doctoral dissertation, University of Illinois at Chicago.

The author examines demographic and motivational variables of male Big Brother volunteers in three cities. Survey research. Different theories are briefly described in the literature review. The author proposes that the best theoretical approach for studying volunteers is exchange theory.

There are two types of individual goals within the exchange theory concept: instrumental and expressive. "Instrumental goals are directed outside the individual. They are goals to be achieved for some segment of the community, the community as a whole, or the larger society. The activity is the means to an end. Expressive goals are for the immediate gratification of the individuals involved. They, not a third party, reap the rewards as part of the process" (p. 117).

Demographic results. Volunteers are more likely to: have initiated volunteer work while at an age between 20 and 29, be white, have had parents who volunteered, have come from homes with fathers present, report being in excellent or good health, and be single.

Motivational results. Volunteers believe in the purpose of organization. They report that the work filled a personal need. They believe what they do as a volunteer is respected in their community.

Smith, David Horton and Burt R. Baldwin (1974), "Parental Socialization, Socioeconomic Status, and Volunteer Organization Participation," *Journal of Voluntary Action Research*, 3, 59-66.

Purpose. Examine correlates of parental volunteerism and demographic variables on volunteer participation.

Method and Findings. Sample came from interviews (n = 304) and mail questionnaires (n = 45), response rate = 63%, from 8 Massachusetts towns and cities. Higher parental socio-economic status (SES) is correlated with greater numbers of voluntary organizational memberships. Parents' SES influence on child's adult volunteerism is mediated by child's adult SES. Parental attitudes and volunteer work influence child's subsequent adult volunteer service.

Implications. "Parental behavior and attitudes and attitudes influence the later, adult behavior of their children" (64). Volunteerism is influenced by one's SES, and one's parents' attitudes and behavior toward volunteer work.

Sundeen, Richard A, and Sally A. Raskoff (1994), "Volunteering Among Teenagers in the United States," *Nonprofit and Voluntary Sector Quarterly,* 23 (4), 383-403.

The authors use data from a 1992 Independent Sector national survey to examine characteristics of teenage volunteers. Using logistic regression analysis, the authors report that teenage volunteers, compared to non-volunteers, are more likely to come from families with higher occupational status, are more likely to be employed on a part-time basis, and are more likely to have higher grade point averages. Teenage volunteers are not differentiated by gender or age. (Note that this sample was stratified to match U.S. population demographic profile.)

Teenage volunteers are more likely to come from smaller cities than larger cities. Teenagers whose parents volunteer are much more likely to volunteer than teenagers without the parental role model. Teenage volunteering is inversely related to the number of children in the family. Living in a single parent family is not related to teenage volunteering.

The frequency of church attendance and church membership is associated with higher rates of teenage volunteering. Teenagers in schools encouraging volunteering are more likely to volunteer. Female teenagers are more likely to volunteer in health activities (e.g, hospital candy stripers).

In terms of number of hours volunteered, age and grade point average are associated with greater numbers of hours volunteered, while being Catholic is associated with fewer hours volunteered.

Vaillancourt, François and Micheline Payette (1986), "The Supply of Volunteer Work: The Case of Canada," *Journal of Voluntary Action Research,* 15 (4), 45-56.

Purpose. To determine if the costs and benefits of volunteer work as represented by demographic variables explain the decision of whether or not to volunteer. The framework views volunteerism in utilitarian terms using a human capital model.

Method. Mail surveys included as a supplement to a Canadian government national labor force survey (N = 43,000). The dependent variable was whether or not one volunteered during the past year. Independent variables are age, education, marital status, sex, occupation, work status, and hours worked. Probit data analysis.

Findings. Volunteer activity is highest in the most heterogeneous regions of Canada and lowest in the most homogeneous regions. The association between age and volunteer activity is the typical inverted U shape found in prior research. As age increases, volunteerism increases until middle age, then decreases as the individual gets older. Volunteer activity is highest in the 35-44 year age group, and declines as age increases. Volunteer activity increases with education. Married individuals do more volunteer work than singles. Women do more volunteer work than men. In terms of occupation, higher level white collar workers and sales representatives are most likely to volunteer. In terms of the association between hours worked and volunteer activity, men who work longer hours are more likely to volunteer; the opposite is true for women.

Conclusion. While the authors conclude that their findings support the use of an economic model (i.e., human capital theory) to describe volunteerism, this conclusion should be accepted with caution. For example, the authors predict that higher levels of education are related to higher rates of volunteerism because more educated individuals see volunteering as helping them financially (career-wise). The authors are making a causal inference from a correlation, education and volunteer activity. The human capital model fails to account for civic duty or altruism.

Warburton, Jeni, Robyne Le Brocque et al. (1998), *"Older People-The Reserve Army of Volunteers?: An Analysis of Volunteerism Among Older Australians," International Journal of Aging & Human Development,* **46 (3), p. 229-245.**

Examines volunteer behavior among elderly Australians. Description of the research population; overview of labor trends and economic restructuring in Australia; details on volunteering; research methodology employed in this examination; analysis of statistical data on measurement used in logistic regression analysis.

Wilson, John and Thomas Janoski (1995), "The Contribution of Religion to Volunteer Work," *Sociology of Religion,* **56 (2), 137-152.**

The authors investigate the influence of religion on volunteerism. They predict that (1) religious parents will raise children who volunteer, (2) members of more liberal denominations will be more likely to volunteer, (3) more active church members will be more likely to volunteer, and (4) active members in liberal churches will be more likely to volunteer than active members in more conservative churches.

Using a re-analysis of secondary data from a three panel national survey, the authors find that " . . . only among conservative Protestants does parental religiosity have any impact on young adults' volunteering" (148). Church activism was related to volunteering, but only for Catholics. Conservative Protestant churches are most likely to encourage member volunteering, but for church activities, not community activities. Conservative Protestants who attend church are much more likely to volunteer than conservative Protestants who do not attend church.

Wineburg, Robert J. (1994), "A Longitudinal Case Study of Religious Congregations in Local Human Services," *Nonprofit and Voluntary Sector Quarterly*, **23 (2), 159-169.**

Wineburg proposes that churches are increasingly involving themselves in social services and civic activities. His purpose in this paper was to place a meaning on this trend and to better understand what churches are doing. Wineburg's information comes from his involvement with several congregations in his local area. The author finds that churches get involved outside of their church in an effort to have a moral influence outside their church walls. However, in involving themselves in community areas where social services/ improvements are needed, churches find political/governmental barriers to actually getting something positive accomplished. This experience then develops an interest in civic activism. Therefore, churches find themselves in two areas: social welfare and political activism. The author suggests that the policies of the 1980s had was a stimulus for churches involving themselves in social welfare. The interest of churches in welfare policy is expected to increase.

Wuthnow, Robert (1991), *Acts of Compassion: Caring for Others and Helping Ourselves.* **Princeton, NJ: Princeton University Press.**

Wuthnow is arguably the most influential sociologist in the field of voluntary participation. This book, his most well-known, explores some important issues related to volunteerism (e.g., American individualism and altruism). Wuthnow is especially insightful in the area where volunteerism and religion intersect. This book is heavily influenced by a survey Wuthnow conducted. However, the book could be more forthcoming on methods.

Some Conclusions. The growing sense of American individualism has dampened helping the needy as an important activity. Religious motives for helping the needy are activated when people are part of a religious social community. The erosion of religious institutions will negatively impact organized helping activities. Religion supports altruism (helping others) as an important societal value. Our culture supports the idea that there must be limits or boundaries to our caring of others. Americans have created social institutions to take care of the needy, relieving themselves of individual responsibility for helping. We, as a society, need to teach people to be compassionate. We do this by showing them that being compassionate toward others benefits themselves and that being compassionate is not at odds with individualism.

Yavas, Ugur and Glen Riecken (1997), *"Images of Volunteer Organizations: A Positioning Approach,"* **Journal of Nonprofit & Public Sector Marketing, 5 (1), p. 81-98.**

The purpose of this study is to assess the images of ten volunteer organizations among people in a Southeastern community. Correspondence analysis is used as the analytical tool. Results of the study were helpful in determining relative positioning of attributes, volunteer organizations and the interrelationship among them. The implications of the results are discussed.

6. OTHER TYPES OF STUDIES

Capon, Noel and Elizabeth Cooper-Martin (1990), "Public and Nonprofit Marketing: A Review and Directions for Future Research," *Review of Marketing 1990,* **volume 4, Valarie Zeithaml (ed.). Chicago: American Marketing Association, 481-536.**

"During the past 20 years, public and nonprofit (PNP) marketing has emerged as an important subfield within the marketing discipline. PNP marketing focuses on the use of marketing concepts and strategies by charitable, scientific, educational, recreational, social, cultural, political, civic, government, trade or professional and religious organizations" (481).

It's time to stop discussing nonprofit marketing in its entirety and to be more targeted in our research objectives. Nonprofit marketing is too broad a field to comprise meaningful research objectives. This review highlights areas that have been researched and where more research needs to be conducted.

Researchers should avoid simply applying for-profit concepts to non-profit marketing. Instead, they should focus on the differences of non-profit marketing and make the research need clear. The authors favor an increase in hypothesis testing and theory building, as well as methodologies for non-profit research.

Areas for future research are:

1. Mission development and modification. We know little about these processes and about the roles played by professional staff, trustees and other publics in decisions regarding mission.

2. How non-profits plan and the variables that affect the ways they plan.
3. We need more research on all four marketing mix elements and to generalize these across multiple non-profit types.
4. Volunteers need research since control is often difficult and ideology may be pitted against sound management practice. Also, volunteers may affect the offering directly by enacting preferences or indirectly in their roles as service providers. There were no volunteer segmentation studies identified in this review.

Future review articles should focus on specific areas within non-profit marketing. They should have a broader sweep in literature searches than conventional marketing journals.

Chambre, Susan Maizel (1987), *Good Deeds in Old Age: Volunteering by the New Leisure Class.* Lexington, MA: Lexington Books.

The purpose of the book is to explore social characteristics that influence whether or not an elderly person volunteers. Older volunteers are more active individuals, generally. They have stronger family ties and are more involved in their religious institutions. Older volunteers are more affluent, better education, and have developed job-related skills.

The data the book is based upon is derived from a National Council on the Aging study. The author examines volunteering as a role substitute and the elderly transition from former roles (widowhood, retirement). Socio-economic variables are also examined (higher education is strongly associated with elderly volunteering). The possibility that older volunteers are more active and are social "joiners" is proposed. The author also looks at the association between volunteering and life satisfaction. The typical elderly volunteer is portrayed as a semi-retired person, satisfied with life, and in an economic position and having desirable skills conducive to volunteering. A path model of elderly volunteerism is presented. The end of the book contains a descriptive summary as well as good ideas on recruiting and retaining older volunteers.

Clary, E. Gil (1987), "Social Support as a Unifying Concept in Voluntary Action," *Journal of Voluntary Action Research*, 16 (4), 58-68.

In this conceptual article, Clary examines the relationship between social support and voluntary participation in organizations. Clary discusses the concept of social support. Clary defines social support as a two dimensional construct: (1) emotional support, and (2) task-oriented support.

Clary discusses the relationship between social support and the health of individuals. Individuals who are characterized as receiving social support appear to be healthier and live longer.

Clary argues that managers need to ensure that volunteers are receiving effective social support. Social support of volunteers will have beneficial effects, either on the relationships among volunteers, clients and staff or on the task performance of volunteers, or both.

Ellis, Susan J. (1985), "Research on Volunteerism: What Needs to be Done," *Journal of Voluntary Action Research*, 14 (2-3), 11-14.

Ellis discusses problems with the state of research on volunteerism. First, she says that there needs to be a common typology and indexing of research so that researchers are using a common set of constructs and have access to all prior work. Ellis says that we need to learn how volunteer subgroups differ instead of grouping all volunteers into a common population. She suggests all groups of volunteers should be investigated.

In terms of motivational issues, Ellis feels that we need to better understand how motives change over time. What is the link between receiving service from the organization and subsequent feelings of gratitude that motivate volunteering?

We need to learn more about volunteerism in other countries, about the history of volunteering, and about volunteer leaders. We need to know more about how to screen out inappropriate volunteers, about legal risk issues, about volunteers' recognition preferences, and more.

Moe, Terry M. (1980), "A Calculus of Group Membership," *American Journal of Political Science*, 24 (4), 593-632.

This conceptual article discusses interest group membership by relying on an incentive approach to understanding behavior.

"*Material incentives* are tangible costs and benefits. *Solidary incentives* are intangible costs and benefits of a social nature deriving, for example, from friendship, camaraderie, recreational activity, status, social pressure, or a sense of belonging. *Purposive incentives* are intangible costs and benefits ultimately grounded on values of a suprapersonal nature, e.g., notions of right and wrong, moral or religious principles, political ideology, and notions of fairness and justice" (615).

This economic model of interest group membership reduces all determinants of membership to cost or benefits. The author presents a person's satisfaction from expressing a value through his or her membership in an organization as a benefit. This model portrays the three incentive types as motivators for becoming group members. The three incentives are mediated by an efficacy requirement.

Murnighan, J. Keith, Jae Wook Kim, and A. Richard Metzger (1993), "The Volunteer Dilemma," *Administrative Science Quarterly,* **38 (4), 515-538.**

The authors examine when and why people volunteer. They also examine the role altruism plays in volunteerism.

There were a series of four experiments using University of Illinois management students to role play in dilemmas in which students reported an intention to volunteer in an isolated (i.e., no social influences) environment. There were three dilemmas: (1) not enough people volunteered and one more will not help, (2) one more volunteer will lead to group success, and (3) enough people have already volunteered. Categorical data modeling was used in the analysis.

The authors find that fewer people volunteer when group size increases; increasing volunteers' payoffs increases volunteering; and the number of volunteers increase with need, but at a decreasing rate as group size increases. The authors conclude that volunteerism increases as rewards increase, that volunteerism decreases as the work it requires increases, and that pure altruism does not exist.

Omoto, Allen M. and Mark Snyder (1990), "Basic Research in Action: Volunteerism and Society's Response to AIDS," *Personality and Social Psychology Bulletin,* **16 (1), 152-165.**

The authors share conclusions from their previously-reported study of AIDS volunteers. The article discusses the antecedents of AIDS volunteerism, experiences of the volunteers and the people with whom they work, and the consequences for the volunteers and for society.

The authors' theoretical basis for understanding AIDS volunteers is Katz's (1960) functional approach to attitudes. This theory " . . . suggest[s] that people may hold the same attitudes or engage in similar behaviors for different motivational reasons and to serve different psychological functions" (155). The psychological functions can be social adjustive functions, value expressive functions, or ego defensive functions.

This functional approach originates from the search for functional underpinnings of people's attitudes. People hold attitudes to serve functions. If you can identify the functions, you can better understand behavior.

Results from the authors' study of AIDS volunteers shows that volunteers are strongly motivated by their personal values. For example, this study found that the value-expressive function was much more prominent among volunteers. The authors write, " . . . value-expressive considerations figure prominently in most volunteers' decisions to volunteer; they indicate that they became involved because AIDS volunteer work afforded them the opportunity to act on their personal values, convictions, and beliefs or to 'do something about issues that are important to me'" (160).

Omoto, Allen M., Mark Snyder, and James P. Berghuis (1993), "The Psychology of Volunteerism: A Conceptual Analysis and a Program of Action Research," in *The Social Psychology of HIV Infection*, John B. Pryor and Glen D. Reeder (eds). Hillsdale, NJ: Lawrence Erlbaum.

The chief contribution of this work is the conceptual model of the volunteer process the authors' propose. There are three stages of their volunteer process model. The three stages are antecedents of volunteering, the volunteer experience itself, and the consequences of volunteering. These three stages are discussed at three levels of analysis: the organization, the individual volunteer, and the volunteer's society.

The authors' theoretical perspective is derived from the functional approach to attitudes, where volunteers' attitudes are related to four psychological functions: social adjustive, value-expressive, knowledge, and ego defense.

Sager, Wilfred Gus (1973), "A Study of Changes in Attitudes, Values, and Self Concepts of Senior High Youth While Working as Full-time Volunteers with Institutionalized Mentally Retarded People," Ph.D. dissertation, University of South Dakota.

The author investigates changes in young people as a result of an intensive volunteer experience. Subjects are 17 women and 5 men from Youth Service Corps working in a nine week summer program.

The author reports significant positive changes in subjects' self-esteem (using Tenn Self Concept Scale), self-satisfaction, and social self.

"After such an intense summer's experience, youth's self-esteem increases; they like themselves more, feel more valuable and worthwhile, and have greater self-confidence. Also, they feel more self-satisfied and self-accepting" (p. vi).

Schindler-Rainman, Eva and Ronald Lippitt (1977), *The Volunteer Community: Creative Use of Human Resources*, 2nd ed., La Jolla, CA: University Associates.

Although this book is of greatest benefit to the practitioner, it is also a must-read for the researcher new to volunteer marketing and an interesting read to the experienced researcher. Taking a social-psychological approach, the volunteer is viewed from Kurt Lewin's perspective. Volunteering is the result of various forces (personal, interpersonal, and situational) acting on the individual. Recruitment is the control of these forces.

The practitioner is given good ideas on how to foster volunteer commitment. For example, avoid creating unrealistic expectations for the new volunteer, watch out for devaluation of volunteer commitment by family/group members, maintain general morale, and help the volunteer understand that he/she does make a difference. One major contribution is a good bibliography of pre-1977 research/work on volunteerism.

Schweitzer, Carole (1998), "Corporate Assets," *Association Management*, 50 (1), 30-37.

A report from the Points of Light Foundation entitled "Corporate Volunteer Programs: Benefits to Business" outlines some indicators of corporate involvement in nonprofit leadership and speaks to the positive connection between volunteerism and corporate profitability. Phyllis Campbell, president of U.S. Bank, Washington, past chair of the Greater Seattle Chamber of Commerce, and newly-appointed campaign chair of United Way, King County, feels one reason that volunteerism is growing more exponentially than incrementally is that social problems are increasing dramatically due to cutbacks in funding and other factors.

Shapiro, Benson P. (1974), "Marketing in Nonprofit Organizations," *Journal of Voluntary Action Research*, 3 (3/4), 1-16.

This is a "must read" article for nonprofit marketing researchers. It describes the beginning of interest in nonprofit marketing among marketing research scholars. The article also provides a framework in which to understand marketing functions related to nonprofit organizations.

Some history of how nonprofit marketing started.

> *1st event*-(Kotler and Levy 1969), "Broadening the Concept of Marketing."

> *2nd event*-August 1970 when the Fall Conference of the American Marketing Association presented a program based on the theme "Broadening the Concept of Marketing."

> *3rd event*-July, 1971, the *Journal of Marketing* published an issue primarily devoted to nonprofit marketing.

These three events are important because they established nonprofit marketing as an important area of inquiry within the larger marketing domain.

In regards to volunteer issues, Shapiro wrote, " . . . for the nonprofit organization, attracting volunteer workers (who work without normal pay) is part of the resource attraction process" (5).

"Generating volunteer labor is an important form of resource attraction" (7).

"Because there are great potential benefits to applying marketing thinking to nonprofit situations, the application should continue. The benefits include the improvement of both marketing thought and the operations of nonprofit organizations" (12).

"Another possible approach to the study of marketing in nonprofit organizations is to focus on a specific element of the marketing mix in a specific marketing function (e.g., resource attraction). Such studies will almost certainly produce useful generalities but will be most difficult because of the dispersion of the literature and experts" (13).

Sinisi, Christina S. (1993), "The Origin of Volunteerism: Socialization Antecedents and Personal Variables," Ph.D. dissertation, Kansas State University.

This dissertation assesses the ability of various parenting and personality variables to predict volunteering behavior. While researchers in the past have assessed the influence of socialization variables on volunteerism, individual studies have (a) confounded different parenting variables and (b) overlooked possible personality correlates of volunteering.

Two studies were conducted. In Study 1, 105 volunteers (69 females) for the Red Cross and United Way and 50 non-volunteers (28 females) returned questionnaires concerning volunteering, empathy, religiosity, parents' behavior, and perceptions of volunteers' motives for helping. Discriminant analysis revealed that volunteers rated their mothers as having presented a stronger model of volunteering behavior, both behaviorally and verbally, than did non-volunteers. Volunteers also rated their mothers as more lenient, and their fathers as stricter disciplinarians, than did non-volunteers. Individuals who had volunteered perceived volunteers in general as being motivated more by a concern for others, and less by a need to avoid guilt or shame, than did non-volunteers.

Study 2 consisted of two separate sessions. In the first session, the above questionnaires were administered to high school students. Two weeks later, another experimenter, posing as a recruiter, asked the students to volunteer for the local United Way and/or Red Cross organizations. Of the 120 high school students (68) females who participated, 32 expressed a desire to volunteer. Discriminant analysis revealed that high school students willing to volunteer were more likely to rate their mothers as having presented a strong behavioral model of volunteering and to perceive volunteers as being motivated by a concern for others than those unwilling to volunteer.

Smith, David Horton (1981), "Altruism, Volunteers, and Volunteerism," *Journal of Voluntary Action Research*, 10 (1), 21-36.

In this conceptual paper, Smith argues that there is *no* altruism. Rather, he argues that all volunteering is motivated by an expectation of psychic benefits.

"No matter how altruistic an act appears, there is invariably, so far as is known, some important degree of psychic reward or intrinsic satisfaction derived for one's self from the performance or anticipated performance of the act. Altruism makes one, at least those who practice it, 'feel good'–receive psychic rewards for their selves, contribute to a positive self-image, induce ego enhancement, etc." (23).

"For various reasons, whether as a result of personal vanity and pride or socioculturally induced constructions of reality, some people who perform altruistic acts as defined above refuse to admit the actual or probable presence of some self-satisfying (and hence selfish) psychic rewards directly resulting from altruistic action. This is understandable, but hardly changes the psychological facts of the matter" (24).

Smith, David Horton (1983), "Synanthrometrics: On Progress in the Development of a General Theory of Voluntary Action and Citizen Participation," in *International Perspectives on Voluntary Action Research*, David H. Smith and Jon Van Til, eds. Washington, D.C.: University Press of America, 80-94.

Smith notes that the study of voluntary action is necessarily conducted across academic disciplines. Disciplines have paradigms which create barriers to synthesize cross-disciplinary research on a common area. Smith makes this point and provides an outline for his general theory of voluntary action. The outline consists of 30 "adaptive propositions" and 14 "methodological-interpretive propositions." Although the general theory is too general to be of great use to marketing researchers, it may stimulate some productive ideas.

Smith, David Horton (1994), "Determinants of Voluntary Association Participation and Volunteering: A Literature Review," *Nonprofit and Voluntary Sector Quarterly*, 23 (3), 243-264.

Smith reviews American literature on voluntary participation in programs and associations for the period 1975-1992. He concludes that studies are too narrow in the kinds of variables they use and that the explanatory power is reduced as a result.

Participation is greater for certain kinds of variables: contextual (e.g., community size), social background (e.g., education and gender), personality (e.g., extroversion and assertiveness), attitudes (liking volunteer work or the organization), and the situation (e.g., being asked to join the organization). Smith reports that using more variables from these different variable categories will increase the explained variance in future studies.

Stubblefield, Harold W. and Leroy Miles (1986), "Administration of Volunteer Programs as a Career: What Role for Higher Education?" *Journal of Voluntary Action Research*, **15 (4), 4-12.**

This study sought to better understand the characteristics of volunteer administrators (VAs) and the nature of administration of volunteer programs as a career. A 16 page mail survey was sent to 1,042 volunteer administrators; 463 usable surveys were returned.

Volunteer administrators were typically female (89%) and white (96%) and college educated (67%). VAs viewed themselves as professionals and felt loyal to their organization. Most VA's believed that VA's should be college educated.

The authors cautioned universities against offering programs for VAs: (1) 1/4 of the sample felt a high school diploma was an appropriate degree, (2) VAs don't feel loyal to their profession, (3) faculty lack knowledge in the field, (4) VA professional associations have not endorsed certification requirements, and (5) society has yet to recognize that a VA requires extensive training and education. The authors suggests that as the first generation of VAs have worked to achieve social acceptance, the future may be more receptive to higher education programs and the professionalism of VAs.

Tanenbaum, Robert Lee (1981), "The Influence of Widowhood and Divorce, Self-esteem, and Locus of Dependence on Volunteering Help," Ph.D. dissertation, Northern Illinois University.

The author describes psychological theories that provide the rationale for why self-esteem and volunteering are related. The author concludes: "Thus, self-theory (e.g., Rogers), psychoanalytic theory (e.g., Freud), ego psychology (e.g, Erickson), and equity theory (e.g., Adams) predict that in comparison to the high self-esteem individual, the person with low self-esteem would be less likely to volunteer help" (12).

The subjects are 48 women who are current members of six regional chapters of parents without partners, and divorced or widowed within a two year period. The author finds a significant main effect for self-esteem. Subjects with high self-esteem volunteer more.

Van Till, Jon (1987), "The Three Sectors: Voluntarism in a Changing Political Economy," *The Journal of Voluntary Action Research*, **16 (1/2), 50-63.**

This conceptual article is concerned with how to place the third sector into the whole political economy.

"The third sector, called 'voluntary' or 'independent' or 'nonprofit,' amounts in size to the remaining 6% of the national economy. It accounts for 9% of total national employment" (50).

"Federal dollars, which amount to some 40% of the income of nonprofit organizations, have been greatly cut since 1982. Charitable contributions have stayed below 2% of total income as a series of tax changes have reduced philanthropic incentives, particularly for persons in the highest income brackets" (59).

Van Till argues that all philosophy of science orientations are useful for studying voluntary action and nonprofit organizations.

Index

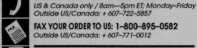

TO ORDER: CALL: 1-800-HAWORTH / FAX: 1-800-895-0582 (Outside US/Canada: + 607-771-0012) / E-MAIL: getinfo@haworthpressinc.com

☐ **YES**, please send me **Using Public Relations Strategies to Promote Your Nonprofit Organization**

_____ in hard at $49.95 ISBN: 0-7890-0257-4. (Outside US/Canada/Mexico: $60.00)

- Individual orders outside US, Canada, and Mexico must be prepaid by check or credit card.
- Discounts are not available on 5+ text prices and not available in conjunction with any other discount.
- Discount not applicable on books priced under $15.00.
- 5+ text prices are not available for jobbers and wholesalers.
- Postage & handling: in US: $4.00 for first book; $1.50 for each additional book.
  Outside US: $5.00 for first book; $2.00 for each additional book.
- NY, MN, and OH residents: please add appropriate sales tax after postage & handling.
- Canadian residents: please add appropriate sales tax after postage & handling, then add 7% GST after postage & handling.
- Payment in UNESCO coupons welcome.
- If paying in Canadian dollars, use current exchange rate to convert to US dollars.
- Please allow 3-4 weeks for delivery after publication.
- Prices and discounts subject to change without notice.

Signature_____

☐ **BILL ME LATER** ($5 service charge will be added).
(Not available for individuals outside US/Canada/Mexico. Service charge is waived for/jobbers/wholesalers/booksellers.)
☐ Check here if billing address is different from shipping address and attach purchase order and billing address information.

☐ **PAYMENT ENCLOSED $**_____
(Payment must be in US or Canadian dollars by check or money order drawn on a US or Canadian bank.)

☐ **PLEASE BILL MY CREDIT CARD:**

☐ AmEx ☐ Diners Club ☐ Discover ☐ Eurocard ☐ Master Card ☐ Visa

Account Number_____

Expiration Date_____

Signature_____

THE HAWORTH PRESS, INC., 10 Alice Street, Binghamton, NY 13904-1580 USA

FAX

Please complete the information below or tape your business card in this area.

NAME_____

INSTITUTION_____

ADDRESS_____

CITY_____

STATE_____ ZIP_____

COUNTRY_____

COUNTY (NY residents only)_____

E-MAIL_____
May we use your e-mail address for confirmations and other types of information?
( ) Yes ( ) No. We appreciate receiving your e-mail address and fax number. Haworth would like to e-mail or fax special discount offers to you, as a preferred customer. We will never share, rent, or exchange your e-mail address or fax number. We regard such actions as an invasion of your privacy.

☐ **YES**, please send me **Using Public Relations Strategies to Promote Your Nonprofit Organization** (ISBN: 0-7890-0257-4) to consider on a 60-day examination basis.
I understand that I will receive an invoice payable within 60 days, or that if I decide to **adopt the book, my invoice will be cancelled.** I understand that I will be billed at the lowest price. (Offer available only to teaching faculty in US, Canada, and Mexico.)

Signature_____

Course Title(s)_____

Current Text(s)_____

Enrollment_____

Semester_____

Office Tel_____ Hours_____

Decision Date_____

May we open a confidential credit card account for you for possible future purchases? ( ) Yes ( ) No

(33) (18) 10/99 BIC99